Beyond Racial Capitalism

Beyond Racial Capitalism

Co-operatives in the African Diaspora

Edited by

CAROLINE SHENAZ HOSSEIN
SHARON D. WRIGHT AUSTIN
KEVIN EDMONDS

OXFORD
UNIVERSITY PRESS

OXFORD
UNIVERSITY PRESS

Great Clarendon Street, Oxford, OX2 6DP,
United Kingdom

Oxford University Press is a department of the University of Oxford.
It furthers the University's objective of excellence in research, scholarship,
and education by publishing worldwide. Oxford is a registered trade mark of
Oxford University Press in the UK and in certain other countries

Published in the United States of America by Oxford University Press
198 Madison Avenue, New York, NY 10016, United States of America

British Library Cataloguing in Publication Data
Data available

Library of Congress Control Number: 2022935474

ISBN 978–0–19–286833–6

DOI: 10.1093/oso/9780192868336.001.0001

Printed and bound by
CPI Group (UK) Ltd, Croydon, CR0 4YY

To the people who braved the COVID-19 pandemic to stand up and speak out against anti-Black racism while wearing their masks during the summer of 2020. This was a collective movement where people who cared about ending anti-Black racism came together to make sure their voices were heard. The global co-operative sector should be taking notes on how to culturally diversify and to start seeing informal Black co-operative systems of all kinds as part of the co-operative identity and sector.

Foreword

Tiffany Willoughby-Herard

Beyond Racial Capitalism: Co-operatives in the African Diaspora, edited by Caroline Shenaz Hossein, Sharon D. Wright Austin, and Kevin Edmonds for Oxford University Press, brings together Black and racialized scholars who explore political theorist Cedric Robinson's conceptualization of "racial capitalism" in order to bring it into studies of the Black social economy as lived and created throughout the African diaspora. Contributors place the "Black radical tradition", simply described as "the refusal to accept life in captivity" and the force that wills us to create maroonage spaces in conversation, with writings by exemplary feminist political economists including Nina Banks, Caroline Shenaz Hossein, Jessica Gordon-Nembhard, and H. L. T. Quan to demonstrate that the Black social economy is essential to the Black radical tradition historically and conceptually. Contributors explain that fugitivity itself has relied on dimensions of Black co-operative economics.

Co-operative thinking and practice enabled Black people to sabotage the coercive nature of slavery itself and to weaken the market economy that followed in its "afterlife" and "second" life (Tomich 2003; Hartman 2007). Such cooperative thinking prioritized affirming the self-determination and inherent humanity of those deemed natural and inherent slaves. In the economic order of the Black social economy, cooperation performed an alchemy of social reality: turning bondspeople into free people, turning plantations into sustainable small-scale food-independent communities, and turning predatory credit and lending markets into member-owned financial unions. White-led social, legal, juridical, electoral, educational, and economic institutions engaged in legally protected conspiracies to extract and accumulate wealth and to demand the tribute of relentless and agonizing forms of humiliation from generations of enslaved and colonized persons and their descendants.

In the face of this onslaught, Black social economies used cooperation of a different and higher ethical order to restore and recapture the human and economic value that was being siphoned off from Black people—for the benefit of those very people. Cooperative economics then used the socially constructed rules and regimens around exchange, trade, and value to concretize Black rights and to establish boundaries around what could be stolen from Black people. Rather than focus on Black belonging in the civic sphere, Black social economies invited Black people to affirm their worth through the things that could belong to Black people. Economic independence defined as owning land and growing food and cooperating was an essential part of the toolkit for surviving and resisting the white will to make Black people into the chattel property of others. The principles that guide cooperation in the Black social economy have been relevant from slavery to the present because this decision to do violence to Black value animates the only constant in the white libidinal economy.

Exclusion and Erasure

The contributors are concerned about the deliberate exclusion of Black and other racialized people from histories of the cooperative movement (solidarity clubs, rotating savings and credit associations, mutual aid societies, informal groups well known around the world in dozens of languages) *and* from formal financial, micro-credit, and lending institutions. Both forms of exclusion—from knowledge production and institutions— contribute to a mythology of whiteness and Europeanness as inherently entrepreneurial, thrift-oriented, and focused on economic advancement and individual wealth accumulation. Such fictitious "forger[ies] of memory," to turn to another Robinson (2007) concept used to define the porous and iterative nature of racial regimes, is the cornerstone of grave injuries faced by Black and racialized communities in North America. These injuries result in new forms of criminalization of racialized newcomers that repeat the forms of criminalization that are the institutional and ideological backbone of generations of slavery, post-slavery era genocide, and land theft from Black and Indigenous farmers in the Old and New World colonies—Ireland, Canada, the United States, the Caribbean, and Central America.

Mapping cooperatives among racialized and colonized people is important because enslaved persons and contemporary Black and racialized migrants are from places where these social economic organizations are widespread and recognizable as cornerstones of genuine (albeit marginalized and even criminalized) democracy-sustaining economic transformation. Moreover, such documentation disabuses the notion of "White Canada" which Canadian feminist cultural geographer Katherine McKittrick (2006) has so carefully excavated. McKittrick's Black Radical Tradition historiography uses the demolition and erasure of Black place and space in Canada as yet another example of the manufacture of white settler colonies which are alleged to be destined for economic prosperity because they are populated by demographics whitened by being allowed to do heinous and murderous genocide to Indigenous, African descendant, and racialized populations. McKittrick (2006) illustrates exactly the fashion through which these white settler colonies only become possible as democratic nations through disappearing Black and racialized persons who are building and sustaining survival-focused social economies.

As explained in the Preface to this book, such white nationalist ideologies exist through repressing historical accounts of the "risks that Black people take [and have taken] to humanize [the] economy" while being stigmatized as agents of economic undevelopment and financial failure. Further, these erasures create a mythological white cooperative culture that results in caricatures of Black people as economically insignificant, incapable, and backward. Using Robinson's method of a long historical account of the economic life of the enslaved and their descendants from the Americas *and* their descendants from postcolonial Africa, the Caribbean, Latin America, and Southeast Asia marks yet another way in which super-development in the Global North has been dependent on the people and ideas of the Global South.

Antique Legacies and Cultural Resources

Having framed the problem, the authors offer carefully rendered case studies that demonstrate not just entrepreneurship but also a system of dynamic cultural values around what wealth is, what it is for, and how African-descended communities define money and finance as collaborative social projects that "can produce resistant and transformative approaches to society." In Chapter 4, contributors Patricia Campos Medina, Erika Nava, and Sol Aramendi reveal that Black and Indigenous social economies exist to create a sense of community that allows racialized migrants to develop collective and pluri-vocal vocabularies for identifying the forms of economic exclusion that they face, create alternative financial pathways, and make meaning with the next generations so that they can create a base for challenging the extant conditions.

Readers learn that "cooperative economic development for Black liberation is not a new concept" (see Preface). As Robinson explains, Africans subjected to the barracoons and Middle Passage were not "empty cargoes." African and other racialized people in the past and the present brought pro-social definitions of economic life such as mutualism and collectivity with them. Braided into the semiotics of greetings, gestures, naming practices, rites of passage, and ways of responding to catastrophic environmental and public health disasters like imperialism in the past and COVID-19 in the present were prophetic visions that resulted in distinctive belief systems. According to Hossein, Edmonds, and Austin in the Introduction, these belief systems include "being in community is essential to one's life" and values such as "trust, reciprocity, and self-help". Such principles enabled making "conscientious decision[s] to opt for humane cooperative systems despite the hardships they encounter[ed]" and required practical commitments to "decolonize economic institutions and sites of organizations" (see Introduction).

The editors trace cultural resources to African antiquity and to notions of exchange and trade as enriching participants in interactions instead of using usury, trickery, or fraud to hoard value while reducing other people's labor, skills, insights, beliefs, or products to less than nothing. This produces "equitable work in the economy" and a social economy that is distinctive, that is resilient to global world crisis, and that strives for ethical and moral high ground through disavowing dispossession, theft, enslavement, exploitation, extortion, and stealing the livelihoods of the poor to benefit the rich and protected (see Preface). So while hostile readers may recoil at the identitarian descriptions of these strategically deployed collective cultural resources as "instinctive" and "ancestral" and "hereditary" the authors are using culture to describe definitions of economic well-being that are durable and long-lasting and which constitute ways of being and what Oyèrónké Oyěwùmí (2001) called "worldsense."

Beyond Racial Capitalism draws readers into the lived experiences of the founders and sustainers of collectivist economic sociality and toward dynamic economic relations whose aim is the development of all instead of the protection and insulation of those who benefit most from unregulated "invisible" anthropomorphized market relations. In order to make such claims about alternative visions for what an economy exists for, authors must detail the myriad ways in which actual racialized people have built such economic social relations in the face of erasure and enclosure. Each case turns toward premodern, precolonial, and eighteenth- and nineteenth-century macroeconomic questions about the nature of slavery, captivity, forced migration, and the related mismanagement and manipulation of common global resources that today still create extraordinary wealth for some and grinding poverty for others.

Secrecy is Survival

Readers who are seeking liberatory potential and radical resistance in every social phenomenon will make the mistake of attempting to generalize the promises of survival in the Black social economy to the rest of the world. I will admit to genuinely wanting to see this text as a handbook for reconsidering the commons and breaking racial capitalism full stop. Amina Mama and Adotey Bing-Pappoe's Chapter 5, however, cautions against my own desire as a reader to generalize the Black social economy. Mama and Bing-Pappoe describe how the social visions that animate the Black social economy may not be transferable to people whose racialization history has not been made by becoming the chattel human commodities of enslavement, colonialism, and genocide.

Rather the Black social economy has contended against the universalizing tendencies of racial capitalism through building purposefully internal and small communities of people who know and trust each other and who can exert social influence on each other through their many shared roles and relationships. Thus, the contributors are "going beyond" racial capitalism by visioning and practicing a different way to organize economic and social life outside of and in antagonism to the racial capitalism that recreates slavery, second slavery, exclusion, marginalization, and devaluing Black and racialized persons and communities in order to extract wealth and accumulate value. The signature example of the necessity of trust and secrecy is the Underground Railroad as an informal community of people most often unknown to each other who engaged in criminalized civil disobedience.

By recognizing the sovereignty of fugitives determined to escape the monetary-juridical regime of slavery, abolitionists among the free and enslaved (documented and undocumented) "committed to democracy and share[d] decision-making. Building consensus and practicing collective governance buil[t] cohesion" among the contraband whose secrecy was a critical part of survival (Hossein et al., Introduction). The risks they took together to escape were yet another Middle Passage, albeit one in which the social economy that they built was not reliant on schemes that simply produced, farmed, and financed debt. These origins of a social economy require inheriting practices of resistance and the will to retell stories of the origins of commercial power in [the] theft of African people without guarantees that such testimony or memory would guarantee freedom from new forms of violence, restitution, reparation, or mainstream truth-telling about the racist routes of capitalist economic exchange.

Though accused of being secretive, stigmatized as covers for illicit forms of criminalized exchange, and disregarded for being grounded in African cultural retentions an oppressed people seek refuge and mobilize together because of their mutual understanding of the hazards in society and the history of white sabotage. Secrecy, maroonage, and fugitivity become the impetus for forms of survival and definitions of selfhood/development/and group transformation that are: (1) steeped in Ubuntu, (2) categorically antithetical to Eurocentric definitions of self/economic development/and group transformation, and (3) not wedded to debt farming to mediate the catastrophic effects of dislocation.

Building Futures in the Present

When participants in the Black social economy acknowledge and respond to enslavement, land theft, and the global racial wealth divide with obligations to lift and improve the conditions of entire peoples, we are witnessing a will to collectivize on their own terms. Even the construction of this text that thinks racialized and Indigenous migrants in the same frame as descendants of enslaved persons points to collectivizing on their own terms—again following a distinctively Robinsonian approach to political economy. Racialized migrants craft communal economic strategies to survive oppressive economic conditions that are structured to incorporate them into the most dangerous, poorly remunerated, legally unprotected, exploitative and extraction-prone, and unhealthy parts of the essential workforce of the wealthy parts of any society. Employers, neighbors, and civil sphere state functionaries often implement institutionalized racialized immigration bias, linguistic racism, and petty gendered xenophobia regardless of the employment status, education level, or personal history of migrants.

The normative experience of racialized migrants is being subjected to discriminatory financial and lending systems while also being baited about their responsibility to integrate despite the many racial barriers. Nigerian immigrants turn to the age-old Ajo system as a solution. Through Ajo, Nigerian immigrants gain access to bulk finances to invest in different avenues—such as financial instruments, businesses, and down payments for houses—that aid their incorporation (taken from Olawoye-Mann's Chapter 2).

Such baiting is not inconsequential as it forms the actual path to a broken and damaged belonging evidenced in the long history of those African and Indigenous people who have witnessed their citizenship rights in the Americas be paradigmatically described in Dr. Martin Luther King's (1963) heartbroken words as "a bad check." In Tatiana Benjamin and Sharon D. Wright Austin's Chapter 3, they note: "Even as Black women advance economically and socially, they are still facing inadequate services that do not account for racial and gender disparities." Further, Benjamin and Austin find government and other state agencies have been created to rectify histories of biased lending and prohibition of Black commercial enterprise have taken up a color-blind ideology that props up and revises pre-Civil Rights Era justifications for harming Black and racialized communities. This has resulted in the discontinuation of policies to improve conditions for African Americans in favor of the same meager economic interventions being spread across the many profound needs by all racialized peoples.

Thus, agencies gather data that streamlines "efforts" that do not actually pull up the roots of racial capitalism. Ultimately, the conditions that make defrauding Black and racialized people through racial capitalism enable racial liberal progress instead of fundamental change. The contributors are demanding a move "beyond racial capitalism," not simply accommodation with or minimal legal regulation of racial capitalism. Rather than transforming the rules of the game, Benjamin and Austin identify an institutionalized constraint that gaslights non-migrant people of color. If these communities do not define their belonging solely and primarily through championing the economic needs of racialized migrants, the domestic forms of discriminatory and ultimately morally bankrupt lending and finance (for racialized people) simply get extended to racialized migrants—whose migration was compelled through the international variant of the same forms of blatantly discriminatory global currency manipulation and financial speculation.

Among the many things that I find compelling about these contributions is that they have carefully been curated to avoid the more obvious divide-and-conquer rhetorics necessary to prop up white minority rule in the racially, ethnically, and culturally diverse societies of the Americas and the Old World Colonies. Indeed, by linking the histories of economic problem-solving and cooperative building in *migrant and non-migrant* racialized communities, the contributors and editors have stepped away from competing ethnic interests and the individualism that underwrite those short-term political solutions, in favor of a nuanced and sophisticated account of forms of anti-capitalist ethics. *Beyond Racial Capitalism* draws on the resources of heritage including economic relations to build sustainable social ties toward a social vision of economic and financial fugitivity for Indigenous, migrant, racialized, and Black people.

Irvine, California
12 December 2022

Works Cited

Atkins, K. 1993. *The Moon is Dead! Give Us Our Money! The Cultural Origins of an African Work Ethic, Natal, South Africa, 1843–1900.* London: Heinemann.

Benjamin, T. and Austin, S. D. W. Chapter 3, "The Black Social Economy: Black American Women Using Susu and Co-operatives as Resistance."

Bing-Pappoe, A. and A. Mama. Chapter 5, "Routes out of Racial Capitalism: Black Co-operatives in the United States."

Campos Medina, P., E. Nava, and S. Aramendi. Chapter 4, "Tandas and Co-operativas: Understanding the Social Economy of Indigenous Mexican Immigrants Settled in Perth Amboy, New Jersey and Staten Island, New York, U.S.A."

Gordon Nembhard, J. 2014. *Collective Courage: A History of African American Co-operative Economic Thought.* University Park: Pennsylvania State University Press.

Hartman, S. 2007. *Lose Your Mother: A Journey Along the Atlantic Slave Route.* New York: Farrar, Strauss & Giroux.

Hossein, C. S. Chapter 1, "Black Canadian Co-operators and Countering Anti-Black Racism."

Kelley, R. 1992. *Freedom Dreams: The Black Radical Imagination.* Boston: Beacon Press.

King Jr., M. L. 1963. "I have a dream" speech. Washington, DC, August 28.

McKittrick, K. 2006. *Demonic Grounds: Black Women and the Cartographies of Struggle.* Minneapolis: University of Minnesota Press.

Olawoye-Mann, S. Chapter 2, "Beyond Coping: The Use of Ajo Culture among Nigerian Immigrants to Counter Racial Capitalism in North America."

Oyěwùmí, O. 2001. "Translation of Cultures: Engendering Yoruba Language, Orature and World Sense," in Elizabeth Castelli (ed.), *Women, Gender and Religion: A Reader.* New York: Palgrave.

Robinson, C. J. 2007. *Forgeries of Memory and Meaning: Blacks and the Regimes of Race in American Theater and Film Before World War II.* Raleigh: University of North Carolina Press.

Robinson, C. J. 2021 [1983]. *Black Marxism: The Making of the Black Radical Tradition,* 3rd edn. Raleigh: University of North Carolina Press.

Tomich, D. 2003. "The 'Second Slavery': Bonded Labor and the Transformation of the Nineteenth-Century World Economy," in *Through the Prism of Slavery: Labor, Capital, and World Economy,* 56–71. Lanham: Rowman & Littlefield.

Preface

Economic cooperation lies at the root of community building. Since March 2020, people around the world have been grappling with the devastation of COVID-19 and they want to find new economies and ways of living. The pandemic has taken the lives of millions of people and wreaked havoc on many businesses and livelihoods, especially those of Black and racialized people. Through grassroots collectives and cooperatives, Black people have kept their communities alive. While the rest of the world professes a "rebirth of mutual aid," cooperatives are not a new concept for the African diaspora. Black and racialized citizens, especially newcomers, have always been the targets of economic exclusion. As a result, cooperatives, of all types, have been an effective way to counter racism in both business and the larger society.

Cooperative development for Black liberation is not a new concept. As long as Black people have been exploited and oppressed in the global capitalist order, they have had to figure out ways to bond and tap into an active form of social capital to get things done. It is clear that cooperative development has always been an integral part of the Black freedom movement. Some examples include the Haitian Revolution, the Underground Railroad and Maroon communities, and the proliferation of Black cooperatives during the Great Depression, the Freedom Farm and other 1960s cooperatives led by vanguard organizations like the Black Panthers. In *Development as Freedom*, the Nobel prize winning economist Amartya Sen (2000) explained that what people can achieve is deeply affected by the kinds of economic opportunities, political liberties, and social powers that exist. It is with this knowledge that Black people living in the periphery chose to collaborate, come together, and build economies out of sight. Thus, it is evident that cooperatives have always been used by Black folks as a tool for liberation and collective determination.

In *Beyond Racial Capitalism: Cooperatives in the African Diaspora,* the authors are mainly from African backgrounds, as well as Latin American and Indigenous backgrounds. Each chapter examines the ways in which economic cooperation is used to pursue equitable development. The book is inspired by principles outlined in W. E. B. Du Bois' text *Economic Co-operation among Negro Americans* (1907). In this ground-breaking book, Du Bois discussed the importance of economic cooperation for people of African descent. As our chapters will explain, the cooperatives that Black and Indigenous people design and organize demonstrate the need for community residents to know and trust each other.

In present day, the Black Lives Matter (BLM) movement is a site of contestation. Many individuals are aware of its role as an activist, civil, human, and political rights movement. Yet, BLM is also an example of economic and social cooperation where people are cooperating for their very survival. Throughout the world, it encourages people to further causes of concern to them by mutual aid, giving circles, and supporting each other. In Canada, BLM started a mutual aid fund to support Black-led community groups to advance their causes. Moreover, as of 2021, BLM has explicitly supported cooperative development as part of its policy platform. Many cooperative initiatives have emerged in recent years as a result of BLM organizing, including the Black Church Food Security Network in Baltimore, Maryland, the Village Financial Co-operative in Minneapolis, Minnesota, and the Black Lives Matter Housing Team in Louisville, Kentucky.

The cooperative institutions of social and community capital often reside in alternative community economies, out of sight from the white, mainstream gaze. Their informal nature is often demonized and viewed as illegal and inferior. Yet the informal domain is precisely where oppressed groups must seek refuge and mobilize together to contest power. We remember the slaves who left the plantations for the hills and later cooperated in informal spaces to flee from terror and bondage. Today, we still see the vestiges of Maroons in the Quilombolas of Brazil, the Susus of Trinidad, and the Kombits and Grwoupmans of Haiti. As W. E. B. Du Bois pointed out in his 1907 book, Black people defined the Underground Railroad as a cooperative. It also was hidden because it was too dangerous to publicly move Black people out of slavery. Economist Jessica Gordon Nembhard (2014) uncovered the explanation of why Black farming cooperatives were often hidden from view, and it was because they were viewed as subversive and threatening to the dominant white powers.

This hidden cooperative history is one reason why the stories of the Black social economy are a treasure trove of Black political economy strategies rooted in cultural resources. Each of the editors of this book, Caroline Shenaz Hossein, Sharon D. Wright Austin, and Kevin Edmonds, grew up in Black diasporic communities in Canada, the United States, and the Caribbean. Each one of them also has observed that formal co-op organizing is one way that people resist the oppressions they endure and they do it together. Oliver C. Cox (1959), a Caribbean sociologist who worked for most of his life at Lincoln University in Missouri, was the first scholar to tie the world system to a racist endeavour. His work was sidelined for a very long time because his ideas were too "radical" to be accepted, and he argued that "neutral" development theories were racist because they subjugate people based on their racial identity.

This book proposes a counter to that form of development. We examine Black co-op organizers who intend to meet their own needs and also generally enhance Black economic independence. As Robin D. G. Kelley (2002, 195) clarifies in *Freedom Dreams*, "Black folks in the diaspora are surviving and creating in the 'liberated zones' of North America's ghettos a co-operative world without wages or money." Indeed, the Black social economy is a way to envision, organize, and implement these Black freedom dreams. Moreover, it is more than a practical immediate strategy, but is also a revolutionary process to replace the contradictions of our current everyday reality with our wildest collective dreams of Black liberation.

Most mainstream political economy theories do not acknowledge the risks Black people take trying to humanize the economy and society through cooperatives. Because European Marxist theory was not internationalized (Johnson and Lubin 2017), it could not account for experiences on the African continent. Cedric Robinson (1983) made it clear that white Marxists have not been able to adequately explain the total impact of racism and racial regimes. Erica Edwards (2017, 252) argues that "Cedric People" have continued his legacy of critiquing Western civilization and articulating the "other world-building that is necessary for the survival of Black thought and Black being." In this edited book, each author is one of the "Cedric People". In this role, they explain the manner in which Black people are working together for their collective well-being.

Black citizens, living outside Africa, have had to rethink mainstream economics—as well as the accepted alternatives—in ways to protect and uplift their own communities. Leanne Betasamosake Simpson (2020) has shown in her work *As We Have Always Done* that capitalism and its extraction has been vested in individualism and competition that run contrary to the community well-being, unity and cooperation of the Nishnaabeg people. Political scientist Tiffany Willoughby-Herard (2015), also one of the "Cedric People," explains that major foundations pay for the knowledge informing what we understand Black suffering to be, and that sharing alternatives countering this controlled understanding is actively suppressed. She calls this the project of global whiteness.[1] This book explains Black people's investment in economic cooperation despite global whiteness and the hegemonic culture of capitalism. Black organizing requires the thoughtful sharing and pooling of resources to ensure people can achieve their goals. It also values collective well-being over individualism, and directly challenges a capitalist ideology. Therefore, the Black organizing efforts that we discuss in each chapter allow racially marginalized people to build their community with agency and collective determination below the radar.

We utilize the Black social economy framework in our analyses because it is about collective and politicized action for people of African descent. Rooted in Black feminist theory, it draws on the plethora of work on the political economy written by Black scholars who understand the double bind of being Black and female when it comes to organizing for liberation. Intersectionality is a term that characterizes the dual oppression Black women encounter because of their race and gender. Each author discusses Black life and struggle, lived experience, and capitalist economies in a specific cultural context. The Black social economy provides a better understanding of how cooperatives take hold in environments of racial capitalism. It is rooted in intersectionality and lived experience because Black women lead the collaborative efforts in many of these communities. Most have been persecuted because of the race, gender, and class. However, as we will explain, they persevere because of their quest for better lives for themselves, their families, and their communities. Telling

[1] See Erica Edward's chapter "Cedric People" in Johnson and Lubin (2017).

these stories is often risky for scholars because those in power prefer that these cases of knowledge-making languish in obscurity.

1. These nine cases argue that Black people in the diaspora have developed various economic alternatives in communities plagued by racial capitalism. The cases explain various Black social economy efforts in eleven countries that are in the Black diaspora, but are outside Africa, including the United States, Canada, St. Vincent, Haiti, Grenada, Trinidad, Jamaica, Guyana, St. Lucia, Ireland, and Brazil. The cooperatives, and especially those in the informal arenas, all emphasize commoning of goods, mutual aid, and self-help.
2. By collectively organizing their community members, these activists prove that alternatives do exist and always have. Black cooperatives allow individuals who are excluded from the mainstream to lead their own economic systems. This is why these stories need to be acknowledged. Otherwise, we miss the chance to draw on the experience of groups doing this kind of equitable work within economies. Black people and especially women were engaging in cooperatives long before the terms of "access," "inclusion," and "equity" became a focus in some societies. These cases mentioned in each chapter provide additional information about Black cooperativism and about the many contributions of marginalized people in the African diaspora.

This collective work is about "rethinking racial capitalism" and shows that in the dehumanization of Black people through an extreme variant of the capitalist system, some people will create their own systems that make them free and happy (Bhattacharyya 2018). While many books on cooperatives exist, they exclude the Black diaspora cooperative experience. The International Co-operative Alliance defines cooperatives as voluntary and member-owned institutions where people decide democratically how to run business. The cooperative sector is guided by a set of principles similar to those used by Black folks who choose solidarity economies and are fighting for equity. However, the formal cooperative alliance has no dedicated seat of representation for the African diaspora.

Pivoting to Black resistance and resilience in the form of cooperation to Black social economy is how Black people live in places with business exclusion, wealth disparities, and anti-Black violence. We can only infer that this exclusion is designed to ignore the way that deeply traumatized groups use cooperatives to transform social and economic systems. By drawing on Robinson's (1983) contributions in *Black Marxism* and on the Black social economy framework, we seek to fundamentally upend the white normative narrative of cooperatives, situate Black cooperative practice within the Black radical tradition, and focus on the praxis of Black cooperators. We hope that in this work of transgressing against those who want to secure authority that we are liberating the minds of those who want to imagine a new world (Spivak 2000; hooks 2003). We want to arrive at a place of togetherness where we can finally "see" each other.

Black people in the African diaspora have imagined and sought to model various alternatives to the development programs that racial capitalism underwrites. The data and narratives of Black social economy are a counter distinction, if not the negation, of racial capitalism. In conclusion, this book emphasizes Black resistance, resilience, and empowerment. Community residents use the Black social economy as the antidote for living in the midst of extreme wealth inequalities and anti-Black violence. In the Black social economy, policitized actions occur in order to bring about equity and inclusion. The cooperators in each chapter are willing to come together because of their common interests in transforming their economies and fighting for social change.

Caroline Shenaz Hossein, University of Toronto Scarborough, Canada
Sharon D. Wright Austin, University of Florida, U.S.
Kevin Edmonds, University of Toronto, Canada

Works Cited

Betasamosake Simpson, L. 2020. *As We Have Always Done: Indigenous Freedom through Radical Resistance.* Minneapolis, MN: University of Minnesota Press.

Bhattacharyya, G. 2018. *Rethinking Racial Capitalism: Questions of Reproduction and Survival.* London: Rowman & Littlefield.

Cox, O. C. 1959. *The Foundations of Capitalism.* New York: Philosophical Library Inc.

Du Bois, W. E. B. 1907. *Economic Co-operation among Negro Americans.* Altanta, GA: Atlanta University Press.

Edwards, E. 2017. "Cedric People," In Gaye Theresa Johnson and Alex Lubin (eds.), *Futures of Black Radicalism*, 251–254. Brooklyn: Verso.

Gordon Nembhard, J. 2014. *Collective Courage: A History of African American Cooperative Economic Thought and Practice.* University Park: Pennsylvania University Press.

hooks, b. 2003. *Teaching Community: A Pedagogy of Hope.* New York: Routledge.

Johnson, G. T. and A. Lubin. 2017. *Futures of Black Radicalism.* Brooklyn: Verso.

Kelley, R. D. G. 2002. *Freedom Dreams: The Black Radical Imagination.* Boston: Beacon Press.

Robinson, C. J. 1983. *Black Marxism: The Making of the Black Radical Tradition*, 2nd edn. London: Zed Press.

Robinson, C. J. 2019. *Cedric Robinson: On Racial Capitalism, Black Internationalism, and Cultures of Resistance*, edited by H. L. T. Quan. London: Pluto Books.

Sen, A. 2000. *Development as Freedom.* New York: Anchor Books.

Spivak, G. C. 1988. "Can the Subaltern Speak?" in C. Nelson and L. Grossberg (eds.), *Marxism and the Interpretation of Culture.* Basingstoke: Macmillan.

Willoughby-Herard, T. 2015. *Waste of a White Skin: The Carnegie Corporation and the Racial Logic of White Vulnerability.* Oakland: University of California.

Acknowledgments

We are humbled by the work of the African diaspora to build cooperative systems despite the immense hardships they endure. We thank each contributor in this book for daring to write a case about the Black and racialized experience in cooperative economics when we know that it is not easy work to do. And for sticking through this project during a difficult period. We all weathered a global pandemic, and this project has been delayed many times as a result of it. In this period of lockdown, we took the time to rewrite the cases in light of new times.

We thank our loved ones for all the time they have given us to write with the hope that this work will become a part of the canon in the field of political economy. We would like to thank the research assistants: Megan Pearson, Jane Lumumba, Semhar Berhe, and Katherine Earnshaw at York University; James Patriquin from Carleton University's Department of Political Science in Ottawa; and Rachel Rosen, Rodney Womack, and Miryam Elshaer from the University of Florida Political Science Department's Junior Fellows Program for their dedication related to the Black Social Economy project.

We would like to thank the following scholars for their support in the intellectual shaping of this work—Professors Faye V. Harrison, Fantu Cheru, Jessica Gordon Nembhard, Curtis Haynes Jr., Beverley Mullings, Lisa Aubrey, and John Rapley—as well as the pioneers of Black politics—James Jennings, Mack Jones, Minion K. C. Morrison, Jewel Limar Prestage, Dianne Pinderhughes, William E. Nelson Jr., Wilbur Rich, and Hanes Walton Jr. A special note of gratitude to Professor Christabell PJ of Kerala University and head of the DISE Collective in Kerala, who made extensive comments on this book because she believes in this project. We are humbled by the vote of confidence from our colleagues in the National Conference of Black Political Scientists (NCOBPS) and the Black Research Network (BRN) at University of Toronto.

The funds from the Canada Research Chair and Government of Ontario's Early Researcher Award supported this project, with the hiring of RAs, book cover, attending conferences, and editing costs. The University of Toronto also covered some of the editing expenses. We are grateful for the feedback on our chapters and points made on racial capitalism by Joshua Myers at Howard University. Rene Hatcher at the Marshall Law School also provided many useful edits on an early draft of this manuscript. Artist Chelsea Heard captured the meaning of this book in a beautiful cover. We are thankful to Colette Stoeber for giving her time to proofread this manuscript.

Our editor Adam Swallow believed in this book when many others did not. We admire his dedication to making transparent the processes that help to diversify what knowledge gets produced at Oxford University Press. We are grateful for the guidance of Ryan Morris, our editor, who assisted us well and Sandhiya Babu who carried us through the production process. A big thank you goes to Charles Lauder for your careful copy editing. We will never know the delegates, many editing assistants, and the two anonymous reviewers whose suggestions improved this project. We are humbled by all of the work you do. Blessings.

Contents

PART II REFLECTIONS: ON COOPERATION IN THE AFRICAN DIASPORA

List of Figures

List of Tables

List of Acronyms

AAUW	American Association of University Women
ACORN	Association of Community Organizations for Reform Now
BLM	Black Lives Matter
BYP100	Black Youth Project 100
CAM	Caribbean Airmail
CBA	Brazilian Aluminum Company/Companhia Brasileira de Alumínio
CCA	Canadian Co-operative Association
CCEDNet	Canadian Community Economic Development Network
CEBI	Ecumenical Center for Bible Studies
CEO	chief executive officer
co-op	cooperatives
CONAQ	Coordenação Nacional de Articulação das Comunidades Negras Rurais Quilombolas
CUNY	City University of New York
CWCF	Canadian Worker Co-operative Federation
EAACONE	Articulation and Advisory Group for Black Communities/Equipe de Articulação e Assessoria às Comunidades Negras
ECD	Eastern Caribbean dollar
FHA	Federal Housing Administration
FSC	Federation of Southern Co-operatives
FSRA	Financial Services Regulatory Authority of Ontario
GTA	Greater Toronto Area
HOLC	Home Owners' Loan Corporation
ICA	International Co-operative Alliance
ILO	International Labour Organization
IPHAN	National Historical and Artistic Heritage Institute (Brazil)/Instituto do Patrimônio Histórico e Artístico Nacional
IT	information technology
JCA	Jamaican Canadian Association
LBGTQ	lesbian bisexual gay transgender queer
M4BL	Movement for Black Lives
MAB	Movement of People Threatened by Dams (Brazil)/Movimento dos Atingidos por Barragens
MST	Landless Workers' Movement/Movimento dos Trabalhadores Rurais Sem Terra
MXGM	Malcolm X Grassroots Movement
NAPO	New Afrikan People's Organization
NBPOC	non-Black people of color
NGO	non-governmental organization

NMIA	National Marijuana Industry Association (St. Vincent)
OCA	Ontario Co-operative Association
PPP	Paycheque Protection Program
PSW	personal support worker
ROSCAs	rotating savings and credit associations
SBA	small business association
SEWA	Self-Employed Women's Association
SNCC	Student Nonviolent Coordinating Committee
UNIA	Universal Negro Improvement Association
USD	U.S. dollar
USDA	U.S. Department of Agriculture
USFWC	U.S. Federation of Worker Co-operatives
WCBDI	Worker Co-operative Business Development Initiative

List of Contributors

Sol Aramendi is a community-engaged artist and researcher working with immigrant communities throughout New York City, and she is the Moving Walls Fellow at the Open Society Foundation. In her participatory practice "El Workers' Studio," she promotes change around fair labor and immigration conditions. She graduated with a Masters in Labor Studies at CUNY School of Labor & Urban Studies.

Tatiana Benjamin is Assistant Professor in the Department of Justice Studies at James Madison University. She is a scholar-practitioner with a long-standing commitment to centering the identities and experiences of the African diaspora. Her research interests include African diasporic history; immigration policy and advocacy; Caribbean American identity formation; transnationalism; intersectionality; and anti-Black racism.

Adotey Bing-Pappoe is a PhD in Economics and Politics at the University of Zambia and Development Economics in the Karl Marx University of Economic Sciences (now Corvinus University), Hungary. He worked as an economist for the government of Zambia, in publishing, and as a director of the Africa Centre in London. He is currently a faculty member at the University of Greenwich Business School. Dr. Bing-Pappoe has carried out numerous consultancies for African states, UNFAO, UNECA, and the Open Society Institute.

Patricia Campos Medina is a researcher and senior extension associate focusing on the intersection of race, immigration status, and workers' rights. She is of Mayan Indigenous ancestry from El Salvador. She is the Executive Director of the Worker Institute at the School of Industrial and Labor Relations at Cornell University where she leads research, policy innovation, and training to advance worker justice, collective bargaining rights, and the interest of workers in today's economy and society. She holds a BS and an MPA from Cornell and a PhD in Global Affairs, focusing on political science and immigrant integration, from Rutgers University, Newark, NJ. Follow her on Twitter @DrCamposMedina

Kesiena Mercy Ebenade is a Faculty member at the National College of Ireland. She has worked with Veolia Ireland, the French Environmental Services Company, for more than a decade. She holds a BA in French, a Higher Diploma in Business from Dublin Business School, a Masters of Science from the National College of Ireland, and a PhD from the University of Bolton in the United Kingdom. Her article published in the *Kybernetes Journal* won the highly commended Emerald Literati award for excellence.

Kevin Edmonds is Assistant Professor (teaching stream) in Caribbean Studies at the University of Toronto. His work focuses on Caribbean political economy, histories of alternative/illicit development, and foreign intervention. His dissertation, *Legalize it? A Comparative Study of Cannabis Economies in St. Vincent and St. Lucia*, examines the historical origins, as well as the cultural, political, and economic significance of the ganja (cannabis) industries of the Eastern Caribbean islands of St. Vincent and St. Lucia. His analyses on the Caribbean have been featured on TVO's The Agenda, CBC, NPR, the *Toronto Star*, Al Jazeera, NACLA, and the Black Agenda Report. Follow him on Twitter @Kevin_Edmonds

Caroline Shenaz Hossein is Canada Research Chair of Africana Development and Feminist Political Economy and Associate Professor of Global Development at the University of Toronto Scarborough. She is founder of the Diverse Solidarity Economies (DISE) Collective. She serves on the board of International Association of Feminist Economics, *The Review of Black Political Economy*, and Kerala's *Journal of Politics and Society*. Author of *Politicized Microfinance* (2016), co-author of *Critical Introduction to Business and Society* (2017), editor of *The Black Social Economy* (2018), co-editor of *Community Economies in the Global South* (2022) published by Oxford University Press, and editorial member of the *Encyclopedia of the Social and Solidarity Economy* (2022) for UNRISD. Her forthcoming solo-authored book, *The Banker Ladies*, is a story about Africa and its diaspora. Follow her on Twitter @carolinehossein

Ebun Joseph is Director of the Institute of Antiracism and Black Studies and she is a leading lecturer in Black Studies at University College Dublin in Ireland. She holds a PhD in Equality Studies which was jointly supervised by the UCD School of Social Justice (then named) and the School of Sociology in 2015. She has an M.Ed. in Adult Guidance and Counselling from Maynooth University; an IACP-accredited diploma in Professional Counselling, and a B.Sc. in Microbiology from the University of Benin. She has lived and worked in Ireland for two decades. Her recent book is *Racial Stratification in Ireland: A Critical Race Theory of Labour Market Inequality* (2020) with Manchester University Press and she co-authored *Challenging Perceptions of Africa in Schools: Critical Approaches to Global Justice Education*. Follow her on Twitter @EbunJoseph1

Esteban Kelly is the Executive Director of the U.S. Federation of Worker Cooperatives and has been involved in economic democracy and co-op movements for more than twenty years. He is a co-founder and worker-owner of Anti-Oppression Resource & Training Alliance, a worker co-op that builds capacity for social justice movements. He is the recent recipient of a Philadelphia Social Innovation Award for Public Policy.

Amina Mama is Professor at University of California Davis, and the Kwame Nkrumah Chair in African Studies at the University of Ghana, and she currently lives in Accra. She is a widely published scholar, writer, and activist and this includes more than 30 years of graduate and undergraduate teaching, at the Institute of Social Studies in the Hague (1989–91), and at the University of Cape Town (1999–2009). Her research interests include African politics and history, organizational development, higher educational transformation, radical pedagogy, and activist methodologies. She is widely published and has co-produced two films. Follow her on Twitter @AminaMamaAfrica

Erika J. Nava is a policy analyst and writes widely about immigration policy issues and how they relate to the economy of New Jersey and the United States. Erika holds a BA degree in political science and Latino studies from Douglass College at Rutgers University and she is a national McNair Scholar with a Masters' in Public Policy from Rutgers University's Edward J. Bloustein School of Planning and Public Policy. Currently, she is an Adjunct Lecturer at Rutgers University, New Brunswick, NJ.

Salewa Olawoye-Mann is Assistant Professor in the Business and Society program in the Department of Social Science at York University, Toronto. She holds a PhD in economics and social science consortium at the University of Missouri, Kansas City. Her research focuses on heterodox approaches to sustainable economic development through natural resources and monetary theory. Her research mainly focuses on these issues in the sub-Saharan African region, because she grew up in Lagos, Nigeria and was deeply impacted by what she saw there. She co-edited *Monetary Policy and Central Banking: New Directions in Post-Keynesian Theory* (2012) and she is working on a project about Central Banks and their responses to the COVID-19 pandemic in sub-Saharan Africa.

Silvane Silva is a researcher at the Center of African and Diaspora Cultural Studies, Catholic Pontifical University of São Paulo. She is also a member of the Study Group on Education at Education College of São Paulo University (FEUSP). For fifteen years she was a teacher in the public system and a coordinator of the Pedagogical Nucleus of the Educational Bureau of the city of Santos Region. Until 2017 she was a coordinator of Quilombola School Education and vice-president of the Quilombola School Education Council of the State of São Paulo fighting for equal and fair education. She holds a PhD and MA in social history from the Catholic Pontifical University of São Paulo. In 2018, she was a visiting researcher at the Center for Latin American Studies at the University of Florida.

Tiffany Willoughby-Herard is Associate Professor, African American Studies, University of California, Irvine where she researches Black political thought and the material conditions of knowledge production, Black movements, Black health advocacy, and raced gender consciousness and queer and trans sexualities internationally. Her book, *Waste of a White Skin: The Carnegie Corporation and the Racial Logic of White Vulnerability*, analyzes the political and historical impact and effects of the Carnegie Commission Study of Poor Whites in South Africa, 1927–32. She hails from Detroit, and she is also a poet, a reader, a mama, a member of a church choir, a teacher, and a Black lesbian feminist internationalist. Currently she is the President of the National Conference of Black Political Scientists.

Sharon D. Wright Austin is Professor of Political Science at the University of Florida. Her research focuses on African-American women's political behavior, mayoral elections, and rural African-American political activism. She is the author of *Race, Power, and Political Emergence in Memphis* (2000); *The Transformation of Plantation Politics in the Mississippi Delta: Black Politics, Concentrated Poverty, and Social Capital in the Mississippi Delta* (State University of New York Press, 2006); and *The Caribbeanization of Black Politics: Race, Group Consciousness, and Political Participation in America* (2018). She has also published articles in the *National Political Science Review*, *Political Research Quarterly*, *Social Science Quarterly*, the *Journal of Black Studies*, and *Politics and Policy*. Currently, she is editing *Political Black Girl Magic: The Elections and Governance of Black Female Mayors* for Temple University Press. Follow her on Twitter @SharonA82707528

Introduction

Taking Note of Informality in an Era of Racial Capitalism

Caroline Shenaz Hossein, Kevin Edmonds, and Sharon D. Wright Austin

> Marxism's internationalism was not global; its materialism was exposed as an insufficient explanator of cultural and social forces; and its economic determinism too often politically compromised freedom struggles beyond or outside of the metropole.
>
> Robinson (1983 [2000], I)

This book, *Beyond Racial Capitalism: Cooperatives in the African Diaspora*, discusses the contributions of Black people in countries around the world to the praxis of cooperativism. Racial capitalism is a system that derives value from the social and economic exploitation of another group's racial identity. The concept, popularized by political scientist Cedric J. Robinson (1983 [2000]), defines the manner in which capital is used by the dominant white elite social forces to control and exploit the labor of certain groups. We interpret Robinson's use of racial capitalism as one that exposes the historical truth that racism and capitalism were not revolutionary conventions, but that they existed and evolved out of the feudal system that preceded the global capitalist order.

It is Joshua Myers' (2021) fourth chapter title "Beyond Racial Capitalism" that we use as our own title to also show the varied ways in which the diaspora resists and organizes collective economies. In the neoliberal capitalist economy Black, Indigenous, and racialized people are those who are rethinking how to common and share our goods. The Black social economy is the emerging theory that we draw on to understand what going beyond racial capitalism actually means. The Black social economy is feminist, solidarist, and focused on politicized economic activity to bring social transformation by those who co-opt the goods. The international expansion of racial capitalism was dependent on "slavery, violence, imperialism and genocide"—building upon the practices of invasion, dispossession, settlement, slavery, and enclosure which had emerged initially *within* Europe (Kelley in Johnson and Lubin 2017). It is the African diaspora dealing with various forms of trauma and exclusion who are going beyond racial capitalism to do what they have always done: build economies that work from the ground up. To see this term in this way

Caroline Shenaz Hossein, Kevin Edmonds, and Sharon D. Wright Austin, *Introduction.* In: *Beyond Racial Capitalism.*
Edited by Caroline Shenaz Hossein, Sharon D. Wright Austin, and Kevin Edmonds, Oxford University Press.
 DOI: 10.1093/oso/9780192868336.003.0001

has helped us to frame our own empirical cases on cooperatives used by the African diaspora.

In *Rethinking Racial Capitalism: Questions of Reproduction and Survival*, Professor Gargi Bhattacharyya (2018) introduces ten theses on racial capitalism and points out that it is not enough to simply view racial capitalism as an "allegation of intentionality"; rather, there is a "coercive power" drawing people into this system. University of Toronto's Alissa Trotz's analysis of the writings of Andaiye shows that racism and sexism are interlocking oppressions through which capitalism assigns value and hierarchical order to economic and social exploitation (Andaiye 2020). Therefore, racial capitalism reveals the absurdity of the notion that capitalism can ever be a solution to racism, showing it instead to be the fertile soil in which racism and other forms of oppression grow (Akuno and Nangwaya 2017). The economist Lloyd Hogan (1984) in *Principles of Black Political Economy* also provides a comprehensive analysis of the way the capitalist system has profited from the institution of slavery and from the exploitation of Black labor that persisted after it ended. Further than this, Robinson's (1983 [2000]) concept of the Black radical tradition excavates the tradition of class resistance that grew out of the experiences of the peripheries: namely, enslaved Africans and peasant rebellions (Johnson and Lubin 2017; Bhattacharyya 2018; Jenkins and Leory 2021; Myers 2021).

The erasure of African knowledge, traditions, and history was central to the ongoing justification of colonialism, dispossession, and displacement to establish "civilized people." The first Europeans to visit the Great City of Benin marveled at its technological achievements and institutional organization (Koutonin 2016). The walls of the Great City of Benin covered an estimated 16,000 km and protected the 500 villages which were connected to the capital area (Darling and Agbontaen-Eghafona 2015, 342). Like the Great City of Benin, the Kingdoms of Kongo, Timbuktu, and Zimbabwe are examples of the politics of erasure from history (Rodney 1972; Thornton 2001; Kusimba et al. 2013; Iyatse 2021).

The denial of this history as a part of economic development and cooperation is precisely why the Black social economy theory seeks to acknowledge the contributions of what African-descended people have always been doing. It also means remembering the role that "extra nasty capitalism" has played in our history that means people would want to organize new collective systems (Bhattacharyya 2018). Erik Olin Wright (2019) also acknowledged that worker cooperatives are important in the anti-capitalist struggle, and are a way of forming viable alternatives. The takeaway to resisting racial capitalism can be found in the writing of Professor Beverley Mullings' (2021) "Caliban, Social Reproduction and Our Future Yet To Come," where she outlines the varied social economies that Caribbean people, wherever they find themselves, have had, outside of the continent. Much of this community-focused building is rooted in the hallmarks of many African Indigenous societies: communalism, commoning, mutualism, cooperation, and collectivity.

Going beyond Racial Capitalism

The people of the African diaspora have been organizing and protesting for as long as they have been forcibly displaced. Black diasporic people have had to turn inwards to cooperate with one another and to pool resources for their survival and beyond. Moreover, African concepts of cooperation have long been embedded in ancient philosophies of ujamaa (cooperation) and ubuntu (I am because you are). Africans in the diaspora know these ideas of cooperation, which have sustained their very survival in hostile lands (Mayoukou 1994). Robinson (1983 [2000], 121) reminds us, "African labour brought the past with it, a past that had produced it and settled on it the first elements of consciousness and comprehension." Enslaved Africans in the Americas carried with them their own terms of humanity: culture, language, beliefs, morality, and economic as well as monetary practices (Rodney 1972).

This body of work provides an extensive overview of Black political economy theories and of case studies on solidarity and cooperative economies. Black diasporic people have had to turn inwards to cooperate with one another and to pool resources for their survival and beyond. The authors of each chapter explain the manner in which they engage in trust and reciprocity when participating in Black-led social and economic efforts. To elaborate, participants in these cooperative economic efforts find ways to trust and network with each other and also to believe that each person will receive substantive benefits. The chapters apply the theories of racial capitalism, the Black radical tradition, and Black social (solidarity) economy to explain several cooperative economic efforts in local communities across a range of contexts.

Men and women around the world engage in these strategies as a way to counter the barriers posed by racial capitalism and to make more equitable economies for all. In each chapter, the authors will explain the manner in which the Black social economy operates and its contribution to the Black radical tradition. Each discusses the various economic efforts, but also provides insight into the societies and political structures where these efforts take place. The Black social economy argues that politicized cooperation is an effective way of mobilizing social change, mitigating economic exclusion, and ultimately confronting and transforming a global system of racial capitalism. The authors have conducted archival research, oral histories, and/or interviews to answer the following questions. How have people of color engaged in cooperative economic efforts and what have their experiences been? In addition, how do these efforts work in opposition to the logic and workings of racial capitalism?

The Black diaspora has for centuries been rooted in the African ancestral knowledge of cooperation. It is this way of being ubuntu that can inform us all on how to civilize the human economy. Because a book like this addresses the bias within the peer-review culture of academic journals, this edited book in a feminist series creates a space for scholars, many whom are Black. Authors in this book prioritize their empirical studies, and draw on the Black political economy—namely, the Black social economy—to engage with racial capitalism and ask why co-ops matter. Robinson's concept of the Black radical tradition has seen a resurgence, and authors are reading it with their own contextual lens to explain the case. The authors within this volume create theory together and examine cases using the cooperative model in today's economy.

Blackness in the Diaspora

Our discussion of cooperative economics provides information about the way in which Blackness is marginalized in the diaspora and the way that Black people respond to it. The African diaspora is composed of people of African descent residing all around the world. Some Black people were born and bred outside of Africa while others were born in African countries (on the African continent). Some of these latter individuals remained in Africa while others later moved to other countries. Historian Toyin Falola (2013) has recognized "old" and "new" diasporas to explain the dispersal and presence of Black people throughout the entire world because of their migration, both willingly and unwillingly, to countries outside of Africa.

All people of African descent are usually classified as Black in most countries. In the *Caribbeanization of Black Politics*, political scientist Sharon D. Wright Austin (2018) argues that Black immigrants living in major American cities such as Boston, Washington, D.C., Miami, and Chicago align on Black issues through a wider sense of group consciousness started by African Americans. The Black diaspora is far too diverse within countries and across countries for us to explore the fullness of African diasporic cooperativism here. In this book, we choose to embrace the term African diaspora to mean those citizens who live outside of the African continent. The book chronicles the stories of the Black diaspora in the United States, Canada, Ireland, Brazil, and the Caribbean. These groups connect through a Black diasporic identity that is both dynamic and rooted in cultural practices of African communal societies.

We apply the theory of the Black social economy to explain the economic, political, and social interactions of Black diasporic people. All contributors choose how they connect the Black social economy to define what they see as a form of community building. The contributions of these authors are so important because they are often silenced in other publications and other scholarly and professional spaces as being "too narrow." It is difficult for scholars studying and writing about anti-Blackness in the cooperative movement to get published. This book brings together these authors, giving them an uncensored space to share their critical political economy scholarship. The Black social economy is the home for Black scholar writing on political economy. The Black social economy is a burgeoning theoretical framework that pulls together long-standing threads of various liberatory theories in the Black political economy, focused on explaining how the African diaspora encounters violence in the economy and society (Astor et al. 2017). Through a process of working in solidarity, politicized communities in the Black diaspora can carve out humane systems of commerce and exchange.

The Black social economy is made up of potential sites for autonomous, sustainable Black communities that are separate from dominant, mainstream society. Black women are leading the Black social economy arena in important ways to change how we engage in the economy. More importantly, it is a place where existing oppressive social, political, and economic structures are rejected and replaced by a new system, in which "communities collectively and democratically" do for themselves and where resources and the means of production are put in the hands of the community itself.

Building Trust and Cooperating from Within

Many of the chapters in this book emphasize the important roles of Black women in individual and community economic efforts. However, these women who sustain their families and communities in the diaspora are often not valued for their contributions. In *Screwnomics*, Rickey Gard Diamond (2018) reveals how white men of privilege have been the ones to dictate how economics would unfold. Economist Nina Banks (2020) at Bucknell University has shown that while Black American women are leading community work, what they do remains unpaid despite its value. In October 2020, the Boston-Ujamaa Co-operative organized a #BLACKTRUST event focused on investment in Black lives. The Charles Tuck Arts and Lecture Series titled *The Black Social Economy: Valuing the Informal* focused on informal cooperative money systems called ROSCAs. ROSCAs are defined as mutual aid financing groups in which members of the group come together of their own volition to pool and to share money according to an agreed upon protocol (Ardener 1964; Ardener and Burman 1995). The rules and management are pragmatic, and all members have voting power, and hold values similar to cooperatives (Niger-Thomas 1996; Hossein and Christabell 2022).

Co-op building from within and for a community is about ensuring the agency and collective determination of communities of common interest. Economist Bina Agarwal (2020) has studied farming groups and cooperatives for decades and notes that top-down collectives fail when people are not in charge of these systems, and when women of different castes and classes come together, the cooperatives can thrive. The community residents we study also enhance their social capital by learning to work collectively, establishing trusting relationships, mobilizing resources for political action, and improving conditions in the areas in which they live (Austin 2006). As the authors of the chapters will explain, these informal efforts occur in both urban and rural communities. Oppressed and racialized community members design their own financial systems and economic institutions and therefore are in complete control of the systems and institutions they have created. For people new to the concept of ROSCAs and other types of cooperatives, a key point is that members are committed to democracy and share decision-making. Building consensus and practicing collective governance builds cohesion among members. This is especially true for Black people who have encountered economic exploitation and racism.

Many of the women cooperators are in communities that are not only racist, but patriarchal as well. This concept of racial patriarchy is not seeing the valued labor of Black and racialized women as contributing to solidarity systems. They are doing this work because they believe in it, and they are not being recognized or paid for it most of the time (Banks 2020). Then why do they take on this added work? Because of the obstacles they encounter when seeking to utilize their countries' financial establishments, cooperative economic initiatives provide them with beneficial shared resources.

Women participants receive a sense of autonomy when they engage in the social economy on their own terms and lead programs that they design (Hossein 2016). In some cases, the social issues women of color encounter may be complicated because of the dependence they have on others, and the worry they have if they leave an abusive relationship with regards to their economic well-being. In seeking independence and safety for themselves and their children, many women have benefited from solidarity economic initiatives that allow them to amass the funds necessary to take care of themselves and their families. By pooling their money with their allies, they are able to bypass banks that usually have refused to lend money to women from their racial, immigrant, and/or class backgrounds.

Purposefully Informal: The Nature of the Black Social Economy

At the very core of the Black social economy is cooperation and self-help. The systemic racism in the West has influenced people of color to depend on each other. Moreover, precolonial African Indigenous societies were by and large communal, interdependent, and cooperative in their worldview and organization. Thus, the pooling of economic resources is instinctive and has persisted as long as humankind has been thinking about livelihoods (Geertz 1962; Bouman 1995; Handa and Kirton 1999). The people of the Black diaspora take charge of local economies, and they continue doing what they have always done—making life vibrant and meaningful with the overriding goals of providing self-help to one another, embracing cultural traditions, and countering economic and societal exclusion. Pooling goods certainly helps excluded groups, minorities, and women cope with exclusion, but the cases in this book dare to present a narrative and make it clear that Black cooperation is a deliberate and pragmatic choice by people who descend from a very different worldview than the dominant Eurocentric one.

In this book, we show that cooperatives are quiet forms of revolution, where racialized women and minorities lead cooperative groups to bring about social change.

Some folks rebel against oppression in the open, and others quietly resist mainstream business systems. Guided by Cedric Robinson's (1983 [2000]) theory of racial capitalism and Hossein's (2013; 2018; 2019) concept of the Black social economy, this work examines how Black people choose to engage in cooperatives. *Beyond Racial Capitalism: Cooperatives in the African Diaspora* emphasizes women and minorities, including men, who use self-help and mutual aid in a calculated way to advance projects on their own terms (*Poto Mitan* 2008; Njie 2018). Black people are already conscious that what they do is heavily scrutinized, so they take care to honor these African systems while living in the West. A mutual understanding of the hazards in society and the history of white sabotage is motivation enough for Black people to keep their spaces of cooperation safe. This also speaks volumes to the level of complexity of what it means to be Black in the West.

Knowing the Value of Informality

The point of this work is to broaden the definition of cooperatives. Informal co-ops and ROSCAs are not underdeveloped nor do they engage with the state or private sector as other social economy institutions do. People who have been denied respect cannot participate in these sectors, and choose not to be interactive with the public or the private sectors. Ruth Wilson Gilmore (2017, 226) reminds us that enslaved people hid money in an emancipation pot because they knew that one day they would want something different. Black people who organize ROSCAs tend to be rooted in civil society far from formal state and non-state actors who are in the business of conforming. Black cooperators are often informal on purpose, and they reach alienated people so as to make a place where they can just be in their full humanity.

The members who organize Black cooperatives do so because economic cooperation is ancestral, cultural, and hereditary. These collectives are logical and feel right. Providing mutual support to people you trust is second nature to groups that have been ignored. The literature on solidarity and cooperative economies fails to see diaspora groups as leading in cooperation. For two centuries, Black people in the Americas have known about true bands, a cooperative system that helped refugees resettle when they fled from slavery. W. E. B. Du Bois (1907) often referred to the Underground Railroad as a cooperative system between Black and whites. This system of cooperation had to remain hidden because of the dangers involved in cooperating to end the enslavement of Black people. Some ROSCAs and cooperatives in the African diaspora have been (and still are) purposefully informal as a way to organize and to combat anti-Black racism in society. Jessica Gordon Nembhard's *Collective Courage* lays bare the history of white backlash and sabotage of Black-controlled cooperatives.

Beyond Racial Capitalism: Cooperatives in the African Diaspora reveals that the Black diaspora and other racialized groups are significantly (re)making and (re)defining the concept of cooperative economies. Russian philosopher Peter

Kropotkin (2012) studied mutual aid among animal life and found that all species collectively come together not just as a way to survive—especially during times of hardships—but also as a way to evolve. The cases in this book indicate that Black and excluded people create various forms of cooperatives not only to cope in an exclusionary racial capitalist environment, but also to contribute to social development. *Beyond Racial Capitalism: Cooperatives in the African Diaspora* draws on lived experience from Black feminist standpoints and also anchors this knowledge in racial capitalism. This book thus examines the globalized spaces where Black citizens and immigrants draw on lived experience to remake economies.

The idea of Black people pushing against an exclusionary market system is not new. Czech scholar Karl Polanyi (1944) in *The Great Transformation: The Political and Economic Origins of Our Time*, argues for a vision of society where the markets would not dominate how people lived. And when such markets caused disruption, there would be a "double movement," where those forces would resist business controlling their lives. For most people, living a rich social life meant that they cared about their interactions with each other and not about owning and working for firms in ways that troubled human life.

Making cooperative knowledge-making inclusive is about knowing community and context. The 2017 publication of *The Oxford Handbook of Mutual, Co-operative, and Co-Owned Business* by Jonathan Michie, Joseph R. Blasi, and Carlo Borzaga did not acknowledge the various kinds of cooperative institutions. Books like that miss a chance to recognize the contributions of Black and racialized minorities in co-op building. The late political science professor Elinor Ostrom (1990), who won the 2009 Nobel Prize, was recognized for her work in *Governing the Commons*, where she argued that people's behavior constituted more than focusing on their own "rational" interests and that value can be found in sharing and commoning resources, and that people were organizing goods to assist the community. The ROSCAs and cooperatives in this book are headed by primarily Black and Indigenous people, and they teach us that cooperatives attending to the membership are organized in a political way to mitigate the harms of the extreme variants of capitalism to create transformative economies that recognize the full humanity of castigated communities.

After reading this book, we hope that our readers will understand that collective honest work, where Black people take the time to organize and think through complex issues, exists all around us. Certainly, this work happens in some spaces more than others, but it is always going on. No matter how much wealth a nation has or how poor a nation is, the citizens of that country find ways to deal with matters of economic exclusion without the state or anyone—outside of the group—knowing. Most people have not even heard of cooperatives, but this does not make them any less important. Given the strains and alienation that the African diaspora experiences, they take it upon themselves to remake business, and they do so by forming cooperatives based on business cooperation and self-help to operate below the surface. This book is one intervention to activate more people and communities around cooperativism.

Bigotry inside the Capitalist Economic System

When capitalism first emerged in the sixteenth century, it was portrayed as a way to "develop" society and to make room for others to develop and increase the quality of life for people. The preceding feudal system in Europe exploited some groups and privileged a very small elite class (Bhattacharyya 2018; Jenkins and Leroy 2021). Life was socially tiered, and certain groups of people were viewed as less than others, such as the Slavs and Jews. This logic of inferiority permitted the elites to dominate and rule (Robinson 1983 [2000]). The mentality of those who were in charge found themselves in the dominant classes of a given society, and then believed that there were specific identities and characteristics that made them superior, and this understanding of social forces was used to structure human labor in the project for industrialization.

Venice at its height was the center of world trade and commerce because of its ideal location of canals connecting Europe to Asia. Through this global sense of commerce and trade, ruling elites felt they could advance the human life of Europe. Trinidadian Eric Williams' (1944 [1994]) *Capitalism and Slavery* offered a detailed history exposing the horrors of the human trafficking of African people, which was done for the sole purpose of making money and pushing a capitalist economic system that would help Europeans (Rodney 1972). African people in that system were used as captive labor, the profits of which would provide the lifeblood of the capitalist project. They were kidnapped, enslaved, and forced on a treacherous journey from slave ports such as Elmina, Ghana, Ouidah, Benin, Goree Island, and Senegal. An estimated 30 million African people—chained, tortured, and starved—miraculously made it to the Americas, even though hundreds of thousands are thought to have died on the voyage (UNESCO 2011). The terror continued in the Americas, where Africans were viewed as property to enrich the planter class. Early slave ships arrived in Haiti, with the majority of the enslaved landing in Brazil and many more brought by force to Latin America, the Caribbean islands, and the United States (Robinson 1983 [2000]). Planters raped women and tortured, killed, and terrorized African people for centuries. Moreover, slavery was state-sanctioned and deemed legal. Europeans felt they were justified in carrying out acts of terror by way of the law and the church because they were contributing to Europe's development and economic growth (Rodney 1972). In *Bankers and Empire: How Wall Street Colonized the Caribbean*, Peter James Hudson (2017) shows how commercial banks of today were heavily invested in plantation economies backed by loans. These capitalist firm-focused economies are entrenched in an immoral beginning, with enslavement and the plantations wreaking cruelty on African people in the diaspora (Williams 1944 [1994]).

Capitalism has always necessitated violence and oppression. The need for capital accumulation was used as perverted justification for Europeans to kill and enslave Black people. This was only possible because of the dehumanizing racialization of Black bodies. Plantations and trans-Atlantic trade were important in securing Europe's superior positioning in the world system (Cox 1959; 1964). The banning of slavery (1838 in the British colonies, 1862 in the United States, and 1888 in Brazil) did not completely demolish inhumane business systems, as Europeans simply renamed and reformed the systems. They replaced enslavement with indentureship systems to exploit the labor of southern peoples from China and India, and to extend the lifespans of the plantation economy to continue to generate profits. Colonization and indentured labor and carceral systems were practiced well into the twentieth century. This legacy of violence and harm remains for people of the African diaspora.

Racial Capitalism in Today's Economy

European thinkers on "capitalism" and its alternatives have often ignored race and racism, regarding Marx's sequencing of European modes of production as universal (Rodney 1972). This orthodox and narrow "class reductionist" approach continues to regard race and gender as real phenomenon, but are categorized and operationalized as secondary concerns, rather than as fundamentally interconnected. They do not speak about the racist roots of capitalism, and how colonialism, slavery, and genocide were central to its subsequent development and expansion. Scholars Eric Williams (1944 [1994]) and C. L. R James (1989) outlined the contradictions and the omissions, revealing how Europe's largest industrial complexes in the sixteenth and seventeenth centuries were actually the plantations and sugar mills of the Caribbean (Beckles 1997).

Building upon this radical tradition of Black scholarship, political scientist Cedric Robinson's *Black Marxism* (1983) was ignored—and continues to be similarly obscured. In *Black Marxism*, racial capitalism is defined as the organization and expansion of capitalist society along racial lines (Robinson 1983 [2000]). In other words, white capitalists exploit the forced labor of Black and racialized people to enrich themselves. Inevitably, racism permeates all social systems emerging from capitalism. In the updated version, Robinson (1983 [2000]) lays bare that just as Black capitalism is inherently problematic, so too is Marx's version of communism for the white proletariat. Joshua Myers' (2021) latest work, *Cedric Robinson: The Time of the Black Radical Tradition*, aims to show that Robinson's body of work was about seeing what was (is) possible, and not for Black political theory to be the sole authority on all matters but to see what can emerge from a dominant order. The Black Radical Tradition contests both the liberal view that anti-racism is possible without an anti-capitalist world *and* the Marxist view that class struggle and the general redistribution of wealth will not address racism or the specific violence inflicted upon racialized peoples.

White supremacy, racism, and the vestiges of slavery are so engrained in the fabric of Western and colonial states that anti-Black racism continues to thrive. Marx and Engels failed to adequately account for racism as a key factor in the economy with regard to property and labor. It is political theorist H. L. T. Quan's work that emphasized that in Robinson's work, capitalism and racism were intertwined, and that racism was needed to exploit the Black worker (Robinson 2019). Pan-Africanist and activist Marcus Garvey, who travelled the world, also questioned the white European Marxist perspective because of his own work experience. For Garvey, drawing on his lived experience in Costa Rica's banana plantations, on the dockyards of London, and as a construction worker on the Panama Canal revealed that anti-Black racism was at the core of the economic system (Lewis 1987).

Economist Curtis Haynes Jr (2018), in "From Philanthropic Black Capitalism to Socialism: Co-operativism in Du Bois' Economic Thought," spent decades studying W. E. B. Du Bois' support of cooperatives, including informal kinds. The body of work by Professor Robin D. G. Kelley (2015; 2021) demonstrates the effectiveness of adopting racial capitalism as a theoretical lens to understand the political dynamics of the United States, and in particular the white ruling class in the South who were intent on defeating Black workers, and ultimately sabotage the possibilities of biracial labor struggles. Guyanese feminist and activist Andaiye spent her life's work in formal politics and civil society organizations trying to include Black women's voices in how to develop a just world, and she made this point that challenged this historically reductionist approach:

> While we need organizing that is anti-capitalist and anti-imperialist, our organizing must also be anti-racist, anti-sexist, anti-homophobic, and anti-transphobic and against all forms of exploitation, subordination and discrimination. The Left says that identity politics is narrow, but the Left's definition of what is political and who is political has its own narrowness. (Andaiye 2020, 239)

The binaries of capitalism and Marxism are both European systems, devised by white men who did not understand the empirics of the African diaspora. It was not until the analysis of Trinidadian born Claudia Jones in the 1950s that correctives of race and gender were included in an otherwise class-reductionist approach (Davies 2007). Jones outlined the interconnected nature of race, class, and gender (seen in the super exploitation of the Black woman) to offer greater nuance and explanatory power to Marxism, providing a foundation for others to build upon. Unfortunately, Jones was largely written out of history and was regarded as a heretic within orthodox Marxist circles (Davies 2007). Jones, as a part of the Black radical tradition, challenged European Marxism to address the specific forms of harm and violence that racial capitalism inflicts on Black, racialized, and gendered peoples. African American economist Jessica Gordon Nembhard (2014) in *Collective Courage* reminded us that Black people turned to cooperation that was hidden as a means to resist neoliberal capitalist power of white Americans. This history and other cooperative practices throughout the Black diaspora must be recognized and celebrated as an integral part of the Black radical tradition.

The Need for the Black Social Economy

Being part of the Black diaspora is an experience of stigmatization and alienation. As a result, being in a community is essential to one's life. Racial capitalism and anti-Black racism are key parts of the context of cooperative development in the Black diaspora, though circumstances vary based on the location. The cases in *Beyond Racial Capitalism: Cooperatives in the African Diaspora* demonstrate that community is a site for resisting, organizing, and meeting livelihood needs. Some studies on co-ops seem progressive but they have obfuscated the stories of resistance. Other studies in cooperative economics emphasize the similarity of cooperative to conventional businesses rather than explaining the politics of differences. This book documents how Black people organize, often informally, and provides details of the mechanics of these groups in a specific cultural context.

The authors in this collection have come together with a sense of purpose and duty to showcase the many ways that Black people, mostly women, engage in co-ops. The case studies outlined in this book draw on the Black social economy and racial capitalism. The book widens the understanding of what cooperatives mean to Black diasporic people and moves toward an economics of possibility (Gibson-Graham 1996; Gibson-Graham et al. 2015). The goal is to shift the discourse from one of necessity to one of agency and collective determination, to present to the world collective organizing occurring from the ground up. Black people make a conscientious decision to opt for humane cooperative systems despite the hardships they encounter, and in doing so they show that they can decolonize economic institutions and sites of organizations. In this book, we advance the thesis that the practice of cooperatives by Black people (including cases of Mexicans and Indigenous people) is one that is deliberately informal and based on pragmatic decision making, trust, reciprocity, and self-help.

In a number of countries—including Canada, the United States, Ireland, Jamaica, Guyana, Haiti, Grenada, Trinidad, St. Vincent, St. Lucia, and Brazil—the people of the Black diaspora have turned to various forms of economic cooperatives to build a strong civil society. This book pushes against the silencing of Black people's co-ops because these organizations bring an enormous amount of knowledge on well-being, self-help, and care within economies. While Black and racialized people build co-ops from within, co-ops are also a quiet form of revolt—a means through which to reconcile the contradictions of racism and exploitation of everyday lives and the wildest dreams of Black liberation.

Unravelling Economic Exclusion through Cooperation

The authors of the cases in this book take an intentional stand to write from a Black perspective, drawing on literature such as Robinson's (1983 [2000]) racial capitalism but also work that comes out of the communities being examined. In Beyond *Racial Capitalism: Cooperatives in the African Diaspora*, we present scholarly material by Black people and diasporic groups, those who know first hand the struggle for solidarity in business and who are making tremendous efforts to change the notion of what business means. It is the informality of these self-help cooperatives that makes them so important to society. In *Collective Courage*, African American economist Jessica Gordon Nembhard (2014) points out that Black people who choose informal cooperatives are viewed as subversive.

Black cooperators are intentional. Black people who decide to cooperate in business are usually politicized and conscious of what they are doing. Many Black people choose cooperation because their group demands they do this to stem the violence in their everyday lives. We argue in this book that Black diasporic people make a conscientious decision to create co-ops because of trauma but also as a means to live out their values and dreams of liberation (Bhattacharyya 2018). Many of the cases in this book are places with democracies and that value justice and equality. The cases based in the United States, Ireland, and Canada received stinging peer reviews with somewhat racist undertones, because they dealt with the underdevelopment and exclusion of Black citizens in "developed" countries. This is a difficult fact to accept that racial capitalism exists in countries viewed as rich and "civilized." But it is a reality that the Black diaspora experience, especially those who are seen as minorities.

The nine case studies are anchored in anti-Black environments, where being Black can result in death. Cooperative systems ensure that Black people can turn inwards and rely on solidarity to meet their livelihood needs. The authors in *Beyond Racial Capitalism: Cooperatives in the African Diaspora* are Black and racialized scholars in the diaspora who focus on the work of Black cooperatives (and Mexican immigrants in one case) that take a stand, humanizing economics and showing that people can mobilize to help one another in some of the poorest places in the world.

Within the academe, research on cooperatives tends to highlight the work of white and formal institutions. Formal cooperatives dominate the literature, but this emphasis on formality ignores Black people who cannot formalize for a host of reasons. Black people often work below the radar on purpose. The authors in this book take professional risks documenting these stories, and they must be mindful of the people they interview and discuss, who could be endangered for revealing their identities. *Beyond Racial Capitalism: Cooperatives in the African Diaspora* is timely given the re-emergence of co-ops in mainstream societal conversations during the global pandemic.

Structure of the Book

The book is organized into two main sections. Part I: "The Black Americas: Varied Forms of Cooperativism in Canada and the United States," presents cases looking at ROSCAs and cooperatives in North America. In both Canada and the United States, serious issues of erasure and violence toward people of African descent have emerged. We provide an overview of the chapters below. Each explains the way that poor and middle-class people survive and empower themselves by developing cooperatives. In addition, these individuals are often the targets of both subtle and blatant racism that inhibits their abilities to achieve financial prosperity.

To engage in different economies the African dispora utilize the same kinds of African cooperative systems previously used by their ancestors (Wright Austin 2022). In doing so, they receive several benefits. First, these cooperatives allow them to fight their economic, political, and social oppression. Second, they enhance their collective well-being by trusting and aiding each other during their times of need. Finally, they use these cooperatives as an agent for social change in societies where they are ignored, dismissed, and discounted.

In the first chapter, Caroline Shenaz Hossein, a Black Canadian feminist political economist at the University of Toronto Scarborough, argues that there has been a deliberate erasure of the Black Canadian contribution in the cooperative sector. Even though Black Canadians have developed a myriad of cooperatives, they are ignored. Hossein discusses her empirical work interviewing hundreds of Banker Ladies over the past decade. These women are part of a legacy that has been engaged in organizing ROSCAs—also known as banking co-ops—for more than a century but they remain ignored.

Chapter 2 adds to this empirical work on ROSCAs in Canada with a comparative study of Nigerians living in Canada and the United States. Salewa Olawoye-Mann, a Nigerian Canadian economist at York University in Toronto, examines Ajo, a ROSCA used by Nigerian immigrants. Newcomers and first- and second-generation immigrants engage in saving systems in community economies as a way to cope with business and social exclusion in a society (Jerome 1991).

Many developed states make the "informal" look bad and illegal. For a number of months in 2017, the former U.S. president Donald Trump's Executive Order 13,769, titled "Protecting the Nation from Foreign Terrorist Entry into the United States," went into effect. Often referred to as the Muslim ban or the travel ban, it was operational for enough time to deny entry to people from Iran, Iraq, Libya, Syria, Somalia, Sudan, and Yemen. This is the kind of working environment that the authors in this edited book must navigate. Many of them are muzzled and cannot write freely about politics without the risks they may bring to the people they write about. They must hide the identities of the people they meet and interview for fear they will face the harassment that targets immigrants and minorities. They also are at grave risk of retribution for writing on the regimes under which they live, so we do not ask them to do this.

If this kind of trouble awaits people in the United States, one of the world's "most democratic" countries, imagine the horrors for those living in states that do not even avail themselves of democratic principles. We as editors have taken the liberty of editing and coding the names of subjects and places as much as possible. Writing on cooperatives is a political act. Choosing to upset entrenched money systems can upset elites, because it tells them that their systems are exclusionary and that people who are not in the same class can recreate their own collective systems to rival what is on offer. In Chapter 3, Tatiana Benjamin, a scholar of Jamaican American roots, and Sharon D. Wright Austin, an African American political scientist, bring together the Black American experience in banking co-ops. They recognize the expertise brought by both Black immigrants and African Americans to economic cooperation with a political purpose. Both political scientists argue that Haitian giving circles and ROSCAs in New York City and African immigrants in Washington, D.C., contribute to alternatives that not only help Black people cope with racism in the United States but also uplift their communities.

In Chapter 4, Patricia Campos Medina, who is Mayan from El Salvador, is Cornell University's director of the Worker's Institute, and her research assistants Erika Nava at Rutgers University and Sol Aramendi at the City University of New York consider the immigrant experience of Mexican immigrants who have been demonized in U.S. politics. These immigrants hide their informal cooperation in order to navigate a hostile and racist environment. Many low-income Mexican Americans, particularly those who are undocumented and of African and Indigenous descent, find themselves living in the same communities as Black Americans. This chapter offers a comparative analysis of these immigrants and Black Americans as a means to explain their use of the ROSCA Tandas. Pooling money helps people adjust and settle into their new country. Banking co-op systems based on mutual aid are thus the way that newcomers are able to live and find immediate financial support in America.

We, the editors, know the present dangers of doing research on co-ops because we see it in our own work and in the work of our contributing authors. Some U.S.-based authors have had to decline publication in this edited collection out of fear of the retribution they may encounter for publishing work about these vulnerable groups. The U.S. context shows signs of improving in terms of leadership, but the on-the-ground politics is still troubling in terms of safety when it comes to African Americans and immigrants. In Chapter 5, Amina Mama and Adotey Bing-Pappoe look at three cooperatives—the Federation of Southern Co-operatives, the Mandela Grocery, and Co-operation Jackson—exploring the use of cooperative organizing as a tool for transforming racial capitalism. These case studies in the West expose how racialized people living in white-dominated spaces have had to figure out how to recreate community economies that are humane and align with their visions of collective determination.

Part II, "Reflections: On Cooperation in the African Diaspora," contains two cases exploring the Caribbean and one case on the Brazilian experience in economic cooperation and one case on Nigerian Irish women. These cases show how the African diaspora copes in non-Western contexts to stem exploitation by local elites and the long-standing traditions of Black cooperation specific to the locales. Both the Caribbean and Brazil have rich cooperative traditions in ROSCA systems, such as Susu, Partner, Caixinha, and Boxhand. In Chapter 6, political scientist Kevin Edmonds, a Canadian of St. Lucian heritage, carries out empirical research on co-op economies in the Eastern Caribbean, a region that has experienced enslavement, colonization, and continual U.S. interference. In his chapter, Edmonds examines self-employed, predominately Rastafarian farmers to understand their cooperative economies of the ganja (marijuana) sector in St. Vincent and St. Lucia. The case of excluded groups in rural areas and small islands and among the Rastafarian community in the Caribbean shows how Rastas form co-ops and pool goods and resources as a way to politicize self-help and how collective economies were entered.

Chapter 7, by Silvane Silva of the University of Pontificia Catholic University, shifts the focus to Brazil. The Quilombolas are co-ops that were created by runaway slaves to build their own economy. Today, these marronage systems are legal. H. L. T. Quan (2005) has pointed out that Robinson's work saw marronage as a form of Black consciousness because enslaved people refused to accept their life in bondage (see Robinson 2019). Quilombolas continue to provide refuge for Blacks who risk death and exclusion (Ferreira 2021). The murder of leading Black women activists Beatrice Nascimento and Marielle Franco demonstrates that trying to cultivate a solidarity economy among Afro-Brazilians is dangerous work (Smith 2016). Silva, whose PhD thesis was about the Quilombola system, a cooperative economy organized by Afro-Brazilian women, takes a major risk writing about it. Brazil has made a major imprint on the concept of solidaria, starting with the Quilombolas as well as with the Movimento dos Trabalhadores Rurais Sem Terra (MST), or the Landless Workers Movement. The right-wing autocrat regime of Jair Bolsonaro has been reversing investments in the social economy, and minorities and Afro-Brazilians have been further marginalized. Silva's brave work educates the world on why the Black social economy is one of resistance and trouble-making to ensure that equity is included in business and society.

In Chapter 8, Nigerian-born Irish academics Ebun Joseph and Kesiena Mercy Ebenade focus on Ireland, specifically the use of Esusu, a ROSCA that has been used by Nigerians for centuries. Joseph and Ebenade's study is one of the first on Ajo and Nigerians living in Ireland. They uncover the racism within Irish society and show how Nigerians living in Dublin make use of Esusu to integrate into Irish society. In the last case study, Chapter 9, Hossein uncovers the story of Black Caribbean women cooperators in five countries valued for their business expertise to reach those who are excluded from formal finance. These women cooperators are building up community through Susus, Partner, and Boxhand systems without remuneration. They do this work to resist the racial capitalist economy and to propose a collective form of banking. ROSCAs are a traditional form of finance that they do because these women know and trust one another. In the final chapter, Wright Austin asserts that for people of African descent the solidarity is usually a place of contestation and those excluded are forming their own economies of care. And it is the faith in each other and sharing financial goods that is the antidote against racial capitalism and exclusion.

Conclusion

Haitian scholar Michel-Rolph Trouillot (1995) in *Silencing of the Past* reminds us of how the story of Haiti—the first Black people to topple a European colonizer and liberate themselves from slavery—was silenced to hide and sabotage the success of their emancipation. Black diasporic people, born and bred in this region, know this truth. The history of racial capitalism has interrupted Black lives in profound ways but it is not what defines people of African descent (Jenkins and Leroy 2021). Those who have come later to these lands have quickly learned about the horrors of enslavement, colonization, and systemic racism. People who are alienated, abused, and violated have learned to organize from within and below the surface.

ROSCAs are informal forms of cooperation to make do, build, and revitalize not only one's own life but those of others. Co-ops are by no means perfect, and they often arise out of crisis to help people. The Haitian people, the first liberated Black republic, organized and cooperated together to defeat the French colonizers for human freedoms. All of this struggle was hidden away and carried out where no one could see this politicized action. People take note of the informality, as a way to draw on African ancestral systems of collectivity, which also line up with cherished values of self-help and community building.

The co-op model should be considered a business model or method to decolonize the economy. The cases presented in this book are worth telling; Black people show how they contribute to co-op development as a way of throwing off fixation on the capitalist firm. People choose to cooperate in business, creating collectively owned democratic life-affirming institutions. More importantly, this book shows the myriad ways Black people invest in cooperative economic systems rooted in solidarity.

Works Cited

Agarwal, B. 2020. "A Tale of Two Experiments: Institutional Innovations in Women's Group Farming." *Canadian Journal of Development Studies* 41(2): 169–92.

Akuno, K. and A. Nangwaya. 2017. *Jackson Rising: The Struggle for Economic Democracy and Black Self-Determination in Jackson, Mississippi*. Wakefield, Quebec: Daraja Press.

Andaiye. A. D. 2020. *The Point is to Change the World: Selected Writings of Andaiye*, ed. Alissa Trotz. London: Pluto Press.

Ardener, S. 1964. "The Comparative Study of Rotating Credit Associations." *Journal of the Royal Anthropological Institute of Great Britain and Ireland* 94(2): 201–29.

Ardener, S. and S. Burman. 1995. *Money-Go-Rounds: The Importance of Rotating Savings and Credit Associations for Women*. Oxford: Berg.

Ashe, J. and K. J. Neilan. 2014. *In Their Own Hands: How Savings Groups Are Revolutionizing Development*. San Francisco: Berrett-Koehler Publishers.

Astor, M., C. Caron, and D. Victor. 2017. "A Guide to the Charlottesville Aftermath." *New York Times*, August 13. Available at https://www.nytimes.com/2017/08/13/us/charlottesville-virginia-overview.html?mcubz=0. Accessed September 7, 2017.

Austin, S. D. W. 2006. *The Transformation of Plantation Politics: Black Politics, Concentrated Poverty, and Social Capital in the Mississippi Delta*. Albany: SUNY Press.

Austin, S. D. W. 2018. *The Caribbeanization of Black Politics: Race, Group Consciousness, and Political Participation in America*. Albany: SUNY Press.

Austin, S. D. W. 2022. "Black Social Economy." In Yi, Ilcheong, et al. (eds.). 2022. *Encyclopedia of the Social and Solidarity Economy*. Cheltenham and Northampton, MA: Edward Elgar Publishing Limited partnership with United Nations Inter-Agency Task Force on Social and Solidarity Economy (UNTFSSE). Accessed July 28, 2022: https://www.e-elgar.com/textbooks/yi

Banks, N. 2020. "Black Women in the United States and Unpaid Collective Work: Theorizing the Community as a Site of Production." *Review of Black Political Economy* 47(4).

Beckles, H. 1997. "Capitalism, Slavery and Caribbean Modernity." *Callaloo* 2(4).

Bekerie, A. n.d. "Iquib and Idir: Socio-Economic Traditions of Ethiopians." Tadias Online. Available at http://www.tadias.com/v1n6/OP_2_2003-1.html. Accessed October 17, 2018.

Bhattacharyya, G. 2018. *Rethinking Racial Capitalism: Questions of Reproduction and Survival*. London: Rowman & Littlefield.

Bouman, F. 1995. "Rotating and Accumulating Savings and Credit Associations: A Development Perspective." *World Development* 23(3): 371–84.

Collins, D., J. Morduch, S. Rutherford, and O. Ruthven. 2009. *Portfolios of the Poor: How the World's Poor Live on $2 a Day*. Princeton: Princeton University Press.

Cox, O. C. 1959. *The Foundations of Capitalism*. New York: Philosophical Library Inc.

Cox, O. C. 1964. *Capitalism as a System*. New York: Monthly Review Press.

Darling, P. and K. Agbontaen-Eghafona. 2015. "Conservation Management of the Benin Earthworks of Southern Nigeria: A Critical Review of Past and Present Action Plans," in E. Korka (ed.), *The Protection of Archaeological Heritage in Times of Economic Crisis*, 341–54. Newcastle upon Tyne: Cambridge Scholars Publishing.

Davies, C. B. 2007. *Left of Karl Marx: The Political Life of Black Communist Claudia Jones*. Durham, NC: Duke University Press.

Du Bois, W. E. B. 1907. *Economic Co-operation among Negro Americans*. Atlanta: Atlanta University Press.

Falola, T. 2013. *The African Diaspora: Slavery, Modernity, and Globalization*. Rochester, NY: University of Rochester Press.

Ferreira, P. 2021. "Racial Capitalism and Epistemic Injustice: Blindspots in Theory and Practice of Solidarity Economy in Brazil." *Geoforum* 132: 229–37.

Gard Diamond, R. 2018. *Screwnomics: How Our Economy Works against Women and Real Ways to Make Lasting Change*. Berkeley, CA: She Writes Press.

Geertz, C. 1962. "The Rotating Credit Association: A Middle Rung in Development." *Economic Development and Cultural Change* 10(3): 241–63.

Gibson-Graham, J. K. 1996. *The End of Capitalism (As We Knew It): A Feminist Critique of Political Economy*. Oxford: Blackwell Publishers.

Gibson-Graham, J. K., J. Cameron, and S. Healy. 2015. *Take Back the Economy: An Ethical Guide for Transforming Our Communities*. Minneapolis: University of Minnesota Press.

Gilmore, R. W. 2017. "Abolition Geography and the Problem of Innocence," In Gaye Theresa Johnson and Alex Lubin (eds.), *Futures of Black Radicalism*. Brooklyn: Verso.

Gordon Nembhard, J. 2014. *Collective Courage: A History of African American Cooperative Economic Thought and Practice*. University Park, PA: Pennsylvania State University Press.

Hall, M. 2011. "'Sou-sou': Black Immigrants Bring Savings Club Stateside." *The Griot*. http://thegrio.com/2011/05/20/sou-sou-Black-immigrants-bring-savings-club-stateside/. Accessed October 10, 2017.

Handa, S. and C. Kirton. 1999. "The Economies of Rotating Savings and Credit Associations: Evidence from the Jamaican 'Partner.'" *Journal of Development Economics* 60: 173–94.

Haynes, C. Jr. 2018. "From Philanthropic Black Capitalism to Socialism: Co-operativism in Du Bois' Economic Thought." *Socialism and Democracy* 32(3): 125–45.

Hogan, L. 1984. *Principles of Black Political Economy*. Bloomington: Trafford Publishing.

Hossein, C. S. 2013. "The Black Social Economy: Perseverance of Banker Ladies in the Slums." *Annals of Public and Co-operative Economics* 84(4): 423–42.

Hossein, C. S. 2016. *Politicized Microfinance: Money, Power, and Violence in the Black Americas*. Toronto: University of Toronto Press.

Hossein, C. S. 2018. *The Black Social Economy in the Americas: Exploring Diverse Community-Based Alternative Markets*. Edited collection. New York: Palgrave Macmillan.

Hossein, C. S. 2019. "A Black Epistemology for the Social and Solidarity Economy: The Black Social Economy." *Review of Black Political Economy* 46(3): 209–29.

Hossein, C. S. and P. J. Christabell. 2022. *Community Economies in the Global South: Case Studies about Rotating Savings and Credit Associations and Economic Co-operatives*. Oxford: Oxford University Press.

Hudson, P. J. 2017. *Bankers and Empire: How Wall Street Colonized the Caribbean*. Chicago: University of Chicago.

Iyatse, G. 2021. "Reinventing the Ancient Benin Economy." *The Guardian* (Nigeria). August 16. Available at https://guardian.ng/business-services/reinventing-the-ancient-benin-economy/. Accessed November 24, 2021.

James, C. L. R. 1989. *The Black Jacobins: Toussaint L'Ouverture and the San Domingo Revolution*. London: Vintage.

Jenkins, D. and J. Leroy. 2021. *Histories of Racial Capitalism*. New York: Columbia University Press.

Jerome, T. A. 1991. "The Role of Rotating Savings and Credit Associations in Mobilizing Domestic Savings in Nigeria." *African Review of Money Finance and Banking* 2(1): 115–27.

Johnson, G. T. and A. Lubin. 2017. *Futures of Black Radicalism*. Brooklyn: Verso.

Kelley, R. D. G. 2015[1990]. *Hammer and Hoe: Alabama Communists During the Great Depression*. Chapel Hill: UNC Press.

Kelley, R. D. G. 2017. Part four. "Winston Whiteside and the Politics of the Possible." In Johnson, G. T., and A. Lubin. 2017. *Futures of Black Radicalism*. Brooklyn: Verso.

Kelley, R. D. G. 2021. "From Mississippi to Madrid: Models for the World." *The Volunteer*. November 16. Available at https://albavolunteer.org/2021/11/from-mississippi-to-madrid-models-for-the-world/

Koutonin, M. 2016. "Story of Cities #5: Benin City, the Mighty Medieval Capital Now Lost without a Trace." March 18. *The Guardian*. Available at https://www.theguardian.com/cities/2016/mar/18/story-of-cities-5-benin-city-edo-nigeria-mighty-medieval-capital-lost-without-trace

Kropotkin, P. 2012. *Mutual Aid: A Factor of Evolution*. USA: Courier Corporation. https://journals.sagepub.com/doi/full/10.1177/1473325020986017

Kusimba, C. M., S. B. Kusimba, and L. Dussubieux. 2013. "Beyond the Coastalscapes: Preindustrial Social and Political Networks in East Africa." *African Archaeological Review* 30(4): 399–426.

Lewis, R. 1987. *Marcus Garvey: Anti-colonial Champion*. Kent: Karia Press.

Marx, K. and F. Engels. 1978. *The Marx-Engels Reader*, 2nd edn., edited by Robert C. Tucker. New York: W.W. Norton.

Mayoukou, C. 1994. *Le systeme des Tontines en Afrique: Un systeme bancaire informel. Le case du Congo*. Paris: l'Harmattan.

Michie, J., J. R. Blasi, and C. Borzaga (eds.) 2017. *The Oxford Handbook of Mutual, Co-operative and Co-owned Business*. Oxford: Oxford University Press.

Mullings, B. 2021. "Caliban, Social Reproduction and Our Future Yet to Come." *Geoforum* 118: 150–8.

Myers, J. 2021. *Cedric Robinson: The Time of the Black Radical Tradition (Black Lives)*. Cambridge: Polity Press.

Niger-Thomas, M. 1996. "Women's Access to and the Control of Credit in Cameroon: The Mamfe Case," In S. Ardener and S. Burman (eds.), *Money-Go-Rounds: The Importance of Rotating Savings and Credit Associations for Women*, 95–110. Oxford: Berg. https://www.africabib.org/rec.php?RID=W00088214.

Njie, H. 2018. "Local Response to Poverty Alleviation: 'Osusu' as a Form of Peri-Urban Gambian Women's Valued Capability." Paper presented at the 60th African Studies Meeting, Chicago, Illinois, November 16–18. (unpublished)

Nyerere, J. K. 1966. *Nyerere on Socialism*. Oxford: Oxford University Press.

Ostrom, E. 1990. *Governing the Commons: The Evolution of Institutions for Collective Action*. Cambridge, UK: Cambridge University Press.

Polanyi, K. 1944. *The Great Transformation: The Political and Economic Origins of Our Time*. Boston: Beacon Press.

Poto Mitan: Haitian Women, Pillars of the Global Economy. 2008. Film; 60 minutes. Prod. Tet Ansanm, http://www.potomitan.net/

Quan, H. L. T. 2005. "Geniuses of Resistance: Feminist Consciousness and the Black Radical Tradition." *Race & Class* 47(2): 39–54.

Robinson, C. J. 1983 [2000]. *Black Marxism: The Making of the Black Radical Tradition*, 2nd edn. London: Zed Press.

Robinson, C. J. 2016. *In the Terms of Order: Political Science and the Myth of Leadership*. Chapel Hill: University of North Carolina Press.

Robinson, C. J. 2017. "It's Hard to Stop Rebels That Time Travel," In Gaye Theresa Johnson and Alex Lubin (eds.), *Futures of Black Radicalism*, 173–93. Brooklyn: Verso.

Robinson, C. J. 2019. *Cedric Robinson: On Racial Capitalism, Black Internationalism, and Cultures of Resistance*, edited by H. L. T. Quan. London: Pluto Books.

Rodney, W. 1972. "Tanzanian Ujamaa and Scientific Socialism." *African Review* 1(4): 61–76.

Rodney, W. 1972 [1983]. *How Europe Underdeveloped Africa*. London: Bogle-L'Ouverture Publications.

Rutherford, S. 2000. *The Poor and Their Money*. New Delhi: DFID/Oxford University Press.

Smith, C. A. 2016. "Towards a Black Feminist Model of Black Atlantic Liberation: Remembering Beatriz Nascimento." *Meridians: Feminisms, Race and Transnationalism* 14(2): 71–87.

St. Pierre, M. 1999. *Anatomy of Resistance: Anticolonialism in Guyana 1823–1966*. London: MacMillan Education.

Thornton, J. 2001. "The Origins and Early History of the Kingdom of Kongo, c. 1350–1550." *International Journal of African Historical Studies* 34(1): 89–120.

Tirfe, M. 1999. *The Paradox of Africa's Poverty: The Role of Indigenous Knowledge, Traditional Practices and Local Institutions*. Lawrenceville: The Red Sea Press.

Trouillot, M. R. 1995. *Silencing the Past: Power and the Production of History*. Boston: Beacon Press. https://www.penguinrandomhouse.com/books/246609/silencing-the-past-20th-anniversary-edition-by-michel-rolph-trouillot/

UNESCO. 2011. "In Remembrance of the 30 Million Victims of Slavery." March 25. Available at: https://www.ohchr.org/en/newsevents/pages/slaveryinternationalday.aspx

Vélez-Ibañez, C. G. and C. C. Vélez-Ibañez. 1983. *Bonds of Mutual Trust: The Cultural Systems of Rotating Credit Associations among Urban Mexicans and Chicanos.* New Brunswick: Rutgers University Press.

Williams, E. 1944 [1994]. *Capitalism and Slavery.* Chapel Hill, NC: University of North Carolina Press.

Willoughby-Herard, T. 2015. *Waste of a White Skin: The Carnegie Corporation and the Racial Logic of White Vulnerability.* Oakland: University of California.

Wright, Erik Olin. 2019. *How to be an Anticapitalist in the Twenty-First Century.* New York City: Verso Books.

PART I

THE BLACK AMERICAS

Varied Forms of Cooperativism in Canada and the United States

1

Black Canadian Cooperators and Countering Anti-Black Racism

Caroline Shenaz Hossein

1.1 Introduction

Cooperatives can be said to be part of the Canadian DNA, reflected in Canada's well-known legacy of cooperativism.[1] Most of the literature about cooperative economics and co-op history is anchored in Eurocentric knowledge that ignores Black people's contributions of economic cooperation. Leading Canadian cooperative scholars Lou Hammond Ketilson and the late Ian MacPherson (2001) argue that the story of cooperativism in Canada is based on the European history of the Rochdale weavers—a history not inclusive of people from different heritages. This story makes no mention of the collective and marronage past of Black people that was fundamental to Canada's own development. According to Robinson (1983 [2000]), marronage is at the root of Black consciousness for Black diasporic people. This concept of marronage is true in the Canadian context too.

One of the most important works on including Black voices on cooperative identity is Jessica Gordon Nembhard's *Collective Courage* (2014), which exposes the historical fact that African Americans made major contributions to the co-op movement. John Curl (2012) also credits Indigenous and African American people with their engagement in co-ops in U.S. history. Yet these works have been seldomly cited. In this chapter, I argue that this citation blindness on the part of scholars and Canadian cooperators is why anti-Black racism is unresolved in this sector. The failure to recognize and appreciate Black people's contributions is systemic racism—what I refer to as "anti-Black racism 101"—where those with power in the academe choose to reward their own networks with citations and anecdotes while neglecting to draw on studies using empirical evidence. Excluding the work of Black scholars and cooperators is not only unconscious bias, it is racist (and bad scholarship). This chapter reveals that the Canadian cooperative literature is limited because it is blind to the

[1] Permission has been granted by the journal editor Daphne Rixon on 23 March 2021 to reuse sections of a published paper. This chapter has been significantly revised from my published paper (December 2020) in the *International Journal of Co-operatives, Accounting and Management* at Saint Mary's University. The link to the original paper is here: https://www.smu.ca/webfiles/10.36830-IJCAM.202014Hossein.pdf

Caroline Shenaz Hossein, *Black Canadian Cooperators and Countering Anti-Black Racism*. In: *Beyond Racial Capitalism*. Edited by Caroline Shenaz Hossein, Sharon D. Wright Austin, and Kevin Edmonds, Oxford University Press.
 DOI: 10.1093/oso/9780192868336.003.0002

contributions of Black Canadian[2] co-operators, namely women. Citation blindness, ignoring the already published work on Black cooperators, is biased scholarship and a way to keep the canons trained on rewarding (white) men's expertise.

Canadian research on co-op development focuses almost exclusively on the Anglo and Francophone narratives, and mainly on white Canadians. White Canadians have also dominated the narration of the Indigenous experience. Robinson's (1983 [2000]) concept of racial capitalism is useful in showing how Black people in this country have had to come together informally because their culture demanded this. Even those who study Black people's cooperatives or "alternatives" turn to Eurocentric theories to explain why cooperation is vital for Black people. They fail to recognize that their European Marxist ideas cannot show Black people's need for self-determination in a racist working environment. Informal coming together should not be stigmatized but rather understood in the context of racial capitalism. The preoccupation with formally registered cooperatives is one way that white cooperators are able to exclude many Black Canadians, intentionally or unintentionally.

In this chapter, I discuss the important role Black cooperators play in countering anti-Black racism in Canada. This work questions the general thinking that the African diaspora is not familiar with cooperatives, especially when this is said by scholars who know little about the lived experience of Black people. Michi Saagiig Nishnaabeg scholar Leanne Betasamosake Simpson (2020) in her Chapter 4, "Nishnaabeg Internationalism," explains that radical resurgence is located inside the community and that Indigenous people have always had these solidarity practices, and that the goal of so many of their ceremonial practices has been about gift giving.

The knowledge making of collective organizing and helping each other is not new to Black people harmed by extreme forms of capitalism fixated on scarcity. For a long time, economist Jessica Gordon Nembhard's work (2014) was alone in reacting against the dominant view that African Americans were not cooperators, and she has dared to push against that narrative. A similar situation exists in the Canadian context, where the assumption has been that Blacks and immigrants are not informed about cooperatives. Because their cooperative expertise remains unacknowledged largely because of its role in the informal arena (see Hossein's Big Thinking lecture), I attempt to (re)define what cooperatives are, to expand the definition, and make room for Black Canadians who have also had strong leadership in the development and execution of cooperativism.

1.2 Redefining Cooperatives

Globally, more than 1.2 billion people belong to cooperatives. Many cooperatives are informal and grassroots groups. The International Co-operative Alliance (ICA) (n.d.) has defined cooperatives as

[2] See Joseph Mensah's (2010) definition of Black and the African diaspora in *Black Canadians*.

> people-centred enterprises owned, controlled and run by and for their members to realize their common economic, social, and cultural needs and aspirations. Co-operatives bring people together in a democratic and equal way. Whether the members are the customers, employees, users or residents, co-operatives are democratically managed by the "*one member, one vote*" rule.

This definition, accompanied by seven internationally agreed cooperative principles, suggests that these groups should be spreading the values in the cooperative movement, which does not deny anyone based on identity and race. I argue that to better capture the importance and impact of cooperatives among a variety of communities and peoples in Canada, our definition of cooperatives should include informal and formal cooperatives carried out by Black and racialized people. This would more adequately represent the sector and recognize the myriad forms and players. In addition, as part of the sixth principle of co-ops—cooperation among cooperatives—the onus should be on established co-ops to assist in the development of cooperatives organized by people of color.

According to the ICA website, cooperatives are collective, member-owned institutions organized by groups of people who are filling a gap in society and business. While applicable to any group using solidarity and self-help to address market failure, the current understanding of cooperatives ignores the contributions of non-Europeans. This limits its relevance to a diverse group of Canadians. The Canadian Co-operative Association produced a 2011 report on *Ethnocultural and Immigrant Co-operatives in Canada* that surveyed formal cooperatives among immigrants in English-speaking Canada. This preoccupation with formally registered cooperatives has led to the exclusion of many Black and racialized Canadians who have established cooperatives and collectives that are not formalized. In the United States, Gordon Nembhard (2014) has similarly found that to understand the traditions and legacies of solidarity, mutual aid, and cooperativism among Black Americans, it is important to study diverse examples of economic cooperation, not just formally incorporated cooperative businesses.

In the Caribbean context, my work (Hossein 2017a, 2017b) also notes the importance of studying the informal Black social and solidarity economy in order to understand not just economic survival but also financial cooperation and political control. At the core of what I coin the Black social economy are the informal ways people organize collectively to resist oppression. The mainstream North American literature on cooperatives ignores the purposefully informal cooperatives that Black people engage in; this reveals the systemic racial bias in determining what organizations are defined as cooperators. Furthermore, the literature does not address this bias. The cooperative literature thus does not count informal cooperatives as part of the ecosystem and this is left unchallenged in the academe.

Formal and established cooperatives have not been very helpful to Blacks in their efforts to set up cooperatives in Canada. The Canadian movement only recounts stories about how Black people have failed to make cooperatives "successful" financially, in this way missing many stories of cooperatives, most of them informal, that have been effective in what they set out to do. We need to expand what we mean by cooperatives in the Canadian context to include the Black perspective. By recognizing and valuing the cooperation of Black and racialized people, we problematize the Eurocentric values of success (financial profits, growth and expansion, formality) and show Black and immigrant people's views on what cooperatives should be.

Cooperatives are usually born out of crises. They often exist to fill a need in business and society (see Gordon Nembhard 2008, 2014; ICA n.d.). These organizations are democratic, with the rules determined by the members who created them (see ICA n.d.). The more we study cooperatives and solidarity economies, the clearer it becomes that people around the world have and are engaged in both formal and informal cooperatives. In a recent reflection, economist Curtis Haynes Jr. (2021) draws on Lloyd Hogan's (1984) work to explain that cooperative efforts by the diaspora to do something different is how we create just societies.

1.3 Black People's Expertise on Politicized Cooperation

Cooperatives are practiced around the globe. It is not clear where the idea of collectively organizing with the intention of helping others originated. Nici Nelson (1996) documents banking co-ops among Kenyans since the 1970s and she believes that this activity began well before colonial times. In researching Bahir Dar, Ethiopia, academics and leaders in community development argued that the Habesha people were the first in the world to create the idea of collectivity through Equub (Kedir and Ibrahim 2011), Indir, and Iqib, which are informal group systems of credit and savings (Bekerie 2003, 2008). Given that Abyssinia (today Ethiopia) is seen as the land of human origins, this theory is plausible.

India also has an ancient system of chits, cooperative businesses that help groups access funds. Laws regulating chit funds date back to the 1800s, before colonization (Sethi 1996). India's chit system and other self-help groups are some of the oldest cooperatives in the world (Datta 2000). In fact, India leads the world in the number of cooperatives. The first meeting of the ICA was held in India to mark this achievement and the country's expertise on a variety of cooperatives (Williams 2007). It is also difficult to determine the actual beginnings of cooperatives. Richard C. Williams (2007) has located some of the earliest forms in the Global South, in places like India and China, where self-help groups were common. Thomas Davies (2018), in his exploration of the historical development of NGOs, similarly argues that the world's NGOs and community organizations were first created in non-Western locations. And Chancellor Williams (1961 [1993]), 151) has argued that "the economic basis of African life was originally co-operative."

These findings, however, are rarely acknowledged in scholarly writings about cooperatives, which often only note important cooperative movements from the European context. Some of the earliest of these movements include fire insurance mutuals in the U.K., cheese cooperatives out of France, and Robert Owens' experiment of the New Lanark in Scotland—all of which envisioned systems of cooperatives to counteract corporatization. The ICA (n.d.) notes that the founder of the cooperative principles and the modern cooperative movement was the Rochdale cooperative in 1844, as memorialized by the association founded in 1895. Rochdale became a commercial firm at one point and then later returned to being a cooperative (BBC 1980).

It is the work of solidarity economy scholar Ethan Miller (2010) that attributes the concept of *economia solidaria* to people's movements in Latin America, specifically Peru, Chile, and Brazil, where Black and Global South people have relied on collectivity to protest against their unequal treatment by the colonizing white/ened elites. In Canada, Indigenous people have turned to potlatches and Wisdom Circles as ways to rethink cooperativism (Wuttunee 2010). Leanne Betasamosake Simpson (2020) has shared how the ancestors did not accumate capital; rather they relied on personal relationships with others rooted in reciprocity and trust. In the United States, W. E. B. Du Bois (1907) referred to the Underground Railroad of the 1790–1800s as a cooperative movement, where people made both economic and social commitments to risk their lives to move enslaved people into freedom.[3] Du Bois documented many examples of African American mutual aid. John Curl (2012, 4) concludes that U.S. "history documents how co-operatives were an integral part of numerous American communities in many time periods, and how the working people of this country turned time and again to co-operation for both personal liberation and as a strategy for achieving larger social goals," starting in the 1830s.

Not only does John Curl (2012, 15) include Black cooperative action in this history, he also recognizes that the first North Americans "to practice collectivity, co-operation and communalism were, of course, Indigenous. Cultural patterns of economic co-operation were clearly engrained in the fabric of every tribe." Curl (2012) provides early examples of economic cooperation from First Nations, including the Shoshone Nation, the Lakota, Southwest Pueblos, Northwest Coast tribes, and the Iroquois Confederacy. Wanda Wuttunee's foundational work *Living Rhythms* (2010) shows the importance of various collective systems and how people considered the environment, their livelihoods, and their spirituality in thinking through opportunities. Betasamosake Simpson (2020) further points out that concepts like "capital" and "excess" go against Nishnaabeg thought because the core of the thinking is about assisting neighbors, like when the Wendat and Rotinonhsesha:ka/Haudenosaunee people asked to hunt or farm on Nishnaabeg land.

Knowing that these ancient ideas of gift giving and sharing among Indigenous people occurs everywhere in deliberate ways demonstrates that corporatized notions of how to do business is not the norm for everyone. Millions of people around the globe participate in cooperatives as a way of sharing dividends and redistributing

[3] See more about the Underground Railroad at the Harriet Tubman Historical Society website: http://www.harriet-tubman.org/

goods among others. It is the informal nature of how these groups operate that makes them vital to reaching those most excluded in society. Omissions of informal cooperatives in research is counterproductive to understanding how we as people live and grow.

1.4 Learning about Black Theory for the Co-op Story

It is plausible that African people's collective and cooperative systems predate most systems in the world (see Williams 1961 [1993]). In the United States, Gordon Nembhard (2014) chronicles the many forms and practices of African American cooperativism and the impact of Black mutual aid and communalism on the larger U.S. community development movement (Sullivan 1969; Stewart 1984; Haynes 2010, 2018). In the 1700s, for example, an African interpreter for Europeans by the name of Mathieu de Costa brought knowledge and ideas about how to trade with the Indigenous people of Canada (Johnston 2001).

Black Canadians, however, are still seen as newcomers. Despite historical evidence of their presence, Black arrivants[4] to Canada are often missing in the literature and storytelling of Canada's settler experience (James et al. 2010). Indeed, Black Canadians are often viewed as recent migrants. Ryerson's Grace Galabuzi (2006) has found that contemporary immigration policy in Canada is biased against Black applicants, a situation that has existed for decades. Even though policy has diversified the groups of people emigrating to Canada, the integration of Black immigrants into the Canadian economy has been especially difficult. The racial capitalist theory has explained that certain groups are excluded and exploited for their labor and viewed as inferior in white-dominant countries.

This is why Black Canadians have created their own cooperative systems outside of the mainstream. The concept of the Black Social Economy focuses on how excluded groups, driven by intense forms of racism in the dominant economy, find refuge in the social economy (Hossein 2018). They attempt to remake the economy in a way that goes beyond interacting, and creates new forms of economic communities that reach those left out. Guyanese economist C. Y. Thomas (1974, 1988), in his research on small Caribbean countries, explains how small-sized economies like Guyana can outwit the extractive world system created by Europeans. This system has dispossessed precious raw materials from the Caribbean, leaving the local people dependent on imported food and other necessary goods. Thomas's (1974) body of work is important because it speaks to self-sufficiency and economic cooperation, making sense of the Caribbean diaspora. Thomas's (1974) work has influenced

[4] This term was first coined by the late Bajan scholar Kamau Brathwaite (1981) and is also used in Tiffany Lethabo King's recent work (2019), *The Black Shoals*.

community economic development in Canada, making it clear that Black perspectives have shaped Canadian ideas on collectively organizing economic goods (Rebel Sky Media 2018).

The late Canadian economist Jonathan Loxley (1985, 2008), who has a great deal of experience in community economic development in Manitoba, credited Thomas's work as the basis for the Neechi principles that determine how organizations engage in their own self-help and sufficiency in the economy. Significantly, an Afro-Guyanese scholar has influenced the very principles we use in community economic development in Canada and that are endorsed by the Canadian Community Economic Development Network (CCDNet). Yet anti-Black racism is so entrenched in society that it does not acknowledge this contribution, even when one of Canada's leading economists has supported it.

1.5 Shaking It Up! Who Counts as a Cooperator?

The cooperative sector has missed the opportunity to include Black people's contributions—both as scholars and as practitioners—to the cooperative sector. Many cooperatives in Canada follow the ICA's definition and are formally registered with the provincial government. This means that only institutions that meet ICA criteria are considered cooperatives. However, in the province of Ontario—and most likely across Canada—many informal cooperatives do not fit into this definition. To understand the cooperative experience related to the African diaspora and racialized minorities in Canada, we must expand the definition of cooperatives. We must include institutions that are voluntarily formed by groups of people, usually from the same socioeconomic group, who come together because they are excluded from mainstream business.

Richard C. Williams (2007, 2010) notes that cooperatives are fundamental to democratizing the market; however, they are in gradual decline in the Global North. In contrast, they are pervasive in the Global South, embedded in people's ways of life, although they are often relegated to the sidelines because of their informal nature. In Canada, formal cooperatives are led by white Canadians; and despite the great cultural diversity in major cities, these institutions have limited appeal for diverse groups. Black and other diaspora people have emigrated from places where cooperatives and credit unions are well known. Yet, in my research, I have found that in major cities such as Toronto and Montreal, where there are large numbers of Black and racialized people, they are not valued for having co-op expertise. However, these people can offer added knowledge about self-help groups, collectives, mutual aid, and rotating savings and credit associations (ROSCAs), which are all forms of cooperatives.

It is time to shake up who counts as a cooperator in Canada. Making cooperatives in Canada inclusive of Black contributions would be a start in undoing its dominating whiteness. As stated earlier, the goal of this chapter is to recognize Black

Canadians' participation in cooperatives. Their experience is rooted in the distinct expertise of operating cooperatives below the radar. By ignoring the contributions of racialized people in economic cooperation, the Canadian cooperative sector has also missed an opportunity to grow the cooperative sector and push against commercial firms.

1.6 Methods and Approach

In my work, it became clear that the literature, specifically the question of who is a cooperator, needed attention. In Canada, research defaults to Western (read white) ideas about cooperatives as a given, without acknowledging Black contributions in this sector. Teaching these works of literature made me complicit in furthering this knowledge. I took care in carrying out discourse analysis to re-read the texts and publications with an eye to equity and inclusion. I became acutely aware of the need to write a paper that challenges what we mean by a cooperator in Canada. It is also imperative to push the sector as a whole to be inclusive of the kinds of cooperatives Black and racialized people take part in.

For the past ten years, I have examined and thought about informal banking groups among the African diaspora in Canada and the Caribbean. My interest in Black cooperatives was first piqued while I was a doctoral student in Jamaica in 2008 and then again on a trip to Accra, Ghana, where I met Jamaican immigrants in Ghana using the Marcus Garvey Credit Union. In our exchange, they inquired about Black cooperatives and credit unions in Canada, but we had none. From that day on, I started to view ROSCAs and similar organizations as cooperatives and wondered why they were not included in the formal definition of cooperatives. The notion of viewing Black Canadian women's organization of ROSCAs as cooperators found support in the academic conferences I presented at because this material was missing.

The more I study these banking co-ops operated by Black women, the more convinced I am that they have been erased on purpose. Why have they been missing? And the narrative that immigrants "lack knowledge" about cooperatives needs to be corrected. Over the years, with the help of a team of research assistants, I collected papers and documented writings on cooperatives. I also saved newspaper stories on cooperatives run by the African diaspora. I noticed a disconnect between what Black people were doing and what was being included in knowledge-making. So my research assistants, all advanced doctoral students, carried out a sweep of the cooperative material in the field with an eye on those writings in Canada and globally. Most major credit unions—such as Equity, Meridian, and Ganaraska—serve the general public. A few have affinities with teachers, healthcare workers, local trade unions, and firefighters. They all seemed to be lacking in culturally diverse leadership at the executive levels and on their boards. To learn more about these organizations, one of my research assistants carried out detailed searches of the board of directors on LinkedIn and Twitter feeds of the executives and discovered that their networks were mainly white.

The practice of ignoring and not seeing Black women's labor is far from new in the social economy. In *Waste of a White Skin*, Willoughby-Herard (2015) reminds us of the long history of social sciences wiping away Black people's counteractions to make the world livable. Those who produce co-op knowledge want to see a certain version of knowledge shared. This means that co-ops that are not formal are seen as not worthy of study. In Section 1.8 I discuss the two main Eurocentric discourses that have weighed in on how co-ops are understood in Canada. Then, I introduce my theory of the Black social economy to introduce informal banking cooperatives and diversify the cooperative movement, particularly for the African diaspora.

1.7 Grounding the Black Cooperator Experience

The story of cooperatives in the Canadian context is often told from a Eurocentric view, ignoring the Black and Indigenous experiences. These two groups suffer some of the lowest scores in human development in Canada and many other places (James et al., 2010; National Council of Welfare Reports, n.d.; Timothy 2018). What Canada lacks is theoretical framing and knowledge-making in the study of the cooperative activities of racialized people.

Notably, outside of Canada, recognizing different forms of cooperatives is the norm. A recent International Labour Organization (ILO) webinar on gender equality and cooperatives hosted more than 175 people, including informal organizations like ROSCAs as cooperatives (April 27, 2021). The Self-Employed Women's Association (SEWA) presented expertise in building informal and formal cooperatives, each having a place in Indian society. In Canada, Indigenous scholar Wanda Wuttunee (2010) has located her own lived experience and first-hand knowledge about Indigenous cooperative businesses, which can be both formal and informal. My studies (Hossein 2013, 2018) involved extensive empirical work in the Global South and Canada to understand financial cooperatives among the Black diaspora. In tracing informal and formal Black cooperatives in the United States, Gordon Nembhard has argued that they are all part of the cooperative system. What is evident is that there is a gap in understanding the Black and racialized people's cooperative expertise in the West.

The literature review in this paper emphasizes the ways that Black and racialized people are engaged in the cooperative sector and have always been. It seems that the cooperative sector has erased what racialized people have done in building cooperatives. In *Rethinking Co-operatives: Japanese-Canadian Fishing Co-operatives*, Jo-Anne Lee, Brian Smallshaw, and Ana Maria Peredo (2017, 541) argue, "This privileging of dominant group co-operative experiences has resulted in an impoverished understanding of ethnic minority co-operatives and co-operative development more generally." Yet, a decline in co-op membership (and the struggle to attract members) points to a need to rethink cooperativism for racialized groups.

As noted earlier, cooperatives are defined as open and democratic structures that aim to fill a gap and meet the needs of people who are excluded from mainstream business. A fundamental role of a co-op is to help other co-ops develop and to spread the movement. Canadian Desjardins International has an international arm focused on growing the cooperative movement in the South. Yet cooperative building in Canada is limited in how it invests in and helps minorities in their cooperatives. Beyond the scope of this paper is the separate issue that co-ops themselves lack cultural diversity in terms of race and ethnicity.

Boards on cooperatives are not always equitable—a situation that exists in both Canada and the United States. In a *New York Times* article entitled "As Co-ops Spread, Discrimination Concerns Grow," Iver Peterson (1990) writes about the racist behavior of mainly white cooperative boards in Brooklyn and Queens. Several new worker cooperatives in the United States have been formed by racialized women because it is a way to restructure the power in a firm (Palmer 2019). The film *Shift Change: Putting Democracy to Work* (Dworkin and Young 2012) shows how U.S. worker co-ops such as Evergreen in Ohio are increasingly culturally diverse. This is also the case in cooperatives among African Americans and immigrants, who are aiming for urban revitalization and community economic development (Haynes and Gordon Nembhard 1999; Haynes 2010).

U.S. scholars Wei Li and Lucia Lo (2008) also find that when commercial banks cannot meet the needs of the ethnic minority business community because of racial bias, credit unions can. The authors focus on the financial sectors in Los Angeles and Toronto, cities that have dense and ethnically diverse immigrant populations. They find that Los Angeles has over thirty ethnic banks to meet the needs of its Asian populations; in contrast, Toronto has eighteen credit unions, many with a long European history. Other factors—including differences in national financial structures, immigration policies, and immigrant profiles—contribute to the disparities between the two cities in financial services for ethnic immigrants.

A number of associations, such as the Canadian Co-operative Association (CCA) and the Canadian Worker Co-operative Federation (CWCF), have tended to focus on formal cooperatives. While we do not see large numbers of immigrants leading formalized cooperatives, Black Canadians are developing informal ones. Lou Hammond Ketilson (2006, 3), in her work on Indigenous cooperatives, argued there is a need to expand the definition of cooperative, stating that "the culture of co-operatives stagnated as the co-ops paid too little attention to education and efforts to attract young people and immigrants." The cooperative movement in Canada is missing the contributions of racialized people—the so-called "minorities"—and much of this has to do with how the story of cooperativism has been told.

1.8 Understanding the Discourses on Co-ops in Canada

The history of cooperative development is Eurocentric and reflects mainly the English and French Canadian experience. As a result, it is grounded in theories that reflect a white settler experience. The dominant discourse on cooperatives stems from the English Protestant telling of these stories (Fairbairn 1994). The ICA (n.d.) names the Rochdale cooperatives that began in 1844 in England as one of the first prototypes for cooperatives. The history often references the Raiffeisen worker banks of Germany for the credit union model, citing their ability to address financial exclusion (Guinnane 2001). The ICA actually notes that the Fenwick Weavers' society in 1761 as the first cooperative, through which the people of Scotland sold basic food stuff to bypass commercial factories, again noting "pioneering" cooperatives to Europe and specifically to the UK. On its main web page, the ICA notes that many cooperatives started off as "small grassroots organisations." However, it only cites industrialized regions of the world—such as Western Europe, North America, and Japan—as points of origin for these organizations.

Knowledge about cooperatives in Canada is dominated by ideas from English Canada. The Guelph Campus Co-op, founded in 1913, is featured prominently by the Ontario Co-operative Association (OCA) as part of the origin story of the cooperative movement in Canada (OCA website; Wade et al. 1984, 16). In his book *One Path to Co-operative Studies: A Selection of Papers and Presentations,* Ian MacPherson (2007) documents that the first cooperative store was opened in Stellarton, Nova Scotia, in 1861. But Gordon Nembhard's (2014) work finds that the first communal co-ops in Canada were the self-sustaining Black farms in Wilberforce, Ontario, as early as 1831. This cooperation by Black people was a way for them to sustain themselves in a racist environment in which they were vulnerable.

The most renowned cooperative legacy for English-speaking Canada has been the Antigonish movement in Nova Scotia in the 1930s. This cooperative movement was led by two Catholic priests, Reverend Dr. Moses Coady and Reverand Jimmy Tompkins, who drew on Catholic social teaching to develop agricultural extension services and adult education. They intended to raise the consciousness of the fisher folk so they could protest against commercialization of the fisheries (Macaulay 2002, 46; Welton 2003, 80). This was a working-class struggle: the documentary film *Yes You Can Do It: The Story of the Antigonish Movement* reveals that fisher folk wanted fair prices for their goods and financial services that served community needs (Murphy 2009). While the film fails to include the minority experience in Canada and thus misses the opportunity to include knowledge of racialized Canadians in cooperatives, it does include the Ethiopian cooperative Just Coffee and connects it to the legacy of the Antigonish movement.

Western Canada, and particularly the prairie provinces of Manitoba and Saskatchewan, saw a similar struggle for the working class that resulted in the development of agricultural and farming cooperatives (Fairbairn 2004, 2005, 2007,

2009). Since 1896, Wawanesa Mutual in Winnipeg, Manitoba, has been rooted in cooperation to meet the insurance needs of farmers ("History of Wawanesa," 2020). Cooperatives, led by white Europeans in the 1930s, focused on the commercialization of food, principally in the wheat and fisheries sectors. These are significant struggles for the white working class. This English-speaking trajectory is framed in a very white and exclusionary narrative.

Another prominent narrative of Canadian cooperativism is the French-Canadian *economie sociale* experience in the province of Quebec. The struggle of class politics also preoccupies the social economy, and as in English Canada, in French Canada racial bias is ignored in this discourse. Historically, the 1900 Desjardins *caisses populaires* movement dominates the understanding of Quebec's social economy (Lévesque et al. 1997; Mendell 2009). In 1900, Alphonse and his wife Dorimene Desjardins learned about the German cooperatives from Friederich Reifeissen and Hermann Schulze-Delitzsch. They believed a *caisses populaires* (credit union) would meet the needs of a French-speaking minority in Quebec. Benoît Lévesque, Marie-Claire Malo, and Ralph Rouzier (1997) describe the integral connections between the socioeconomic development of French Quebec and the growth of the Desjardins movement to become the primary financial institution and the largest employer in the province of Quebec. The 1980s saw wide-scale support for the development of the *Chantier de l'economie sociale*, a provincial trust fund that received substantive funding of more than $50 million toward cooperative and social economy development. Desjardins is revered globally as a leading cooperative in the world.

Desjardins has an international arm that carries out technical assistance in developing countries to strengthen the cooperative sector. When doing doctoral research in Haiti in the early 2000s, I observed that Desjardins was hired as the technical provider to assist the local network, Le Levier, following a scandal there. Desjardins also invests in environmental sustainability and social innovation within Canada (Vezina et al. 2017, 265); however, to work with immigrant Canadians in Quebec, the organization has to call on its international arm working in developing countries.

I find it interesting that none of the Canadian-based Desjardins staff were able to work with language and racialized minorities, whereas the international staff who worked overseas were called in to assist in the projects because they "understood cultural diversity" and they were better trained to work with allophones and Black minorities living in Quebec (Focus groups, Little Burgundy and Cote des Neiges (Montreal), 2016). I learned that this is partly due to staff being unable to connect to non-white people, including the Haitians, its largest Black community (interview with a partner organization of Desjardins, name and location withheld on purpose, 2016). In the eyes of the Black Montrealers that I spoke to, Desjardins seems too white and an institution whose employees are mostly concerned with "Pure Laine"—white French-speaking people. And so, while the Desjardins *caisses populaires* has addressed the needs of a distinct minority of French Canadians, it seems as though it has had limited impact on Black and non-French minorities.

1.9 The Erasure of the Black Canadian Discourse in Cooperative Studies

In 2020 and after the Black protests for racial and economic justice, the need to diversify the membership in Canadian cooperatives has become greater than ever. The idea of remaking community economic development in Canada is also rooted in ideas of the Black diaspora, as seen in the influence of C. Y Thomas's (1974) self-sufficiency, local needs, and convergence theory. MacPherson (2012, 119), who played a leadership role in updating the ICA cooperative principles, has argued that we need to culturally diversify the interpretation of racialized people:

> An important point was the recognition, in the Voluntary and Open Membership principle, that co-operatives should be open to people without "gender, social, racial, or religious discrimination". Given the different attitudes towards gender equality around the world at the time, this was not achieved without debate, particularly in some southern countries. Similarly, the idea that race should not count was not always readily accepted in places where it demonstrably and historically did.

Some of Canada's largest credit unions, such as Meridian and Desjardins, have been able to conquer the exclusion of minority languages, but they have only a limited focus on Black Canadians. Alterna Savings and Credit Union, one of Ontario's oldest credit unions, offers a community investment portfolio (which used to be a microfinance program) that reaches mainly racialized people. But this unit is separate from its core business and has been sustained through the efforts of two Jamaican Canadian women.

Cooperatives in Canada seem to be preoccupied with whiteness, in this way excluding Black and other marginalized people. According to data from the Financial Services Regulatory Authority of Ontario (FSRA), Korean and Taiwanese organizations are the only non-white credit unions in Ontario. European immigrant communities—Ukrainian, Dutch, Finnish, Italian, Slovenian, Estonian, and Lithuanian—make up the remainder of the organizations. After reviewing these credit unions on LinkedIn and Twitter feeds as well as their websites, I found an absence of Black, South Asian, and Indigenous credit unions, and the leadership of the organizations present also lacks representation of Black Canadians. There has been, and continues to be, little consideration of the racism—in both the practice and the research—of cooperative institutions.

The two white discourses that explain co-ops in Canada thus reveal that Black people are missing from discussions about cooperatives. The revered Neechi principles, developed by an Indigenous worker co-op, are a set of values for sustainable and locally owned community economic development. These values are rooted in the convergence theory of self-sufficiency—producing what you can consume and taking an internal focus—which is built on the early thinking of Afro-Guyanese economist

C. Y. Thomas (1974). The idea of remaking community economic development in Canada for Indigenous people is rooted in ideas of the Black diaspora. Building on this connection, we need to add a fourth discourse to include the experiences of Black Canadians in cooperatives. These experiences will speak not only to an alternative model for business but also to the inequality and business exclusion in Canada.

1.10 Disrupting the Dominant Discourses on the Cooperative Experience

Ian Macpherson (1979, 2007, 2009, 2012), a leader in cooperative studies in Canada, recognized that the formation of cooperatives by non-white racialized immigrants came in waves. Japanese Canadians were particularly resourceful in developing marketing cooperatives, but they were forced off their lands during the Second World War. Lee et al. (2017, 552), for example, list a dozen Japanese Canadian fishing cooperatives that the Canadian government shut down as part of the process of confiscating property and interning Japanese Canadians during the Second World War. Macpherson (2007, 134) finds that Koreans, Filipinos, and Sikhs from India have formed cooperatives in banking, medical services, and job creation—diasporic contributions that are largely unknown. Macpherson argues that these co-ops reflect the ethnicities prevalent in different regions and often the "timing of different migrations." A pattern emerges from the cooperative development of ethnic minorities in Canada: namely, cooperatives that ethnic minorities establish for themselves become a means to access services and resources that are otherwise unfamiliar and inaccessible.

A number of scholars have explained that cooperatives in Canada have failed to open their membership to racialized groups—and open membership is an important principle for cooperatives. The housing cooperative sector presents particular challenges. Raphaël Fischler and colleagues (2013, 2017) describe the difficulties of social integration of immigrant households in cooperative housing, where new racialized immigrants come into conflict with existing housing cooperative residents in Montreal. Similarly, Gisele Yasmeen (1993) finds that there is a conflict between new racialized immigrants and existing cooperative members of a feminist housing cooperative in Montreal, citing "race relations" (92) and surveillance by other co-op members as some of the disadvantages of cooperative housing. Cultural and linguistic differences also serve as barriers between Haitian and French members. These barriers segregated the mutual aid opportunities and valuable networks intended by cooperative associations.

Guyanese development economist C. Y. Thomas (1974) contributes to tackling capitalism by looking at ways to "transform economies," and this may mean moving away from the binary of Marxism or capitalism to one that is considerate of the ways in which people can focus on their own well being. Many poor Black people in the Caribbean have decided to migrate elsewhere to be free from racially class-tiered societies (Thomas 1974). This is why Thomas' convergence theory to focus on self-sufficiency and for people to produce what they need in their own locales is meaningful, as it pushes against a raw capitalist system. The self-help and cooperative work for people of the African diaspora are culturally relevant. The many examples of the faltering of Black cooperatives in Canada signal that there is no help for Black co-ops in the country, and that established co-ops are not fulfilling the mandate of helping other co-ops. And those existing co-ops are not culturally diversified enough to meet the needs of newcomers.

There are, however, stories of success. Jo-Anne Lee, Nora Curry, and Ana Maria Peredo (2015) have discovered a successful housing cooperative by a primarily Chinese community in Vancouver. Jorge Sousa (2015, 67) describes the successful transformation of a social housing complex into the Atkinson cooperative by immigrant residents in downtown Toronto, the first complex of its kind in Canada. The Atkinson case highlights the role of cooperation in community development, specifically how cooperative principles can work to uplift marginalized communities. Canada's first Black paper for women, *Our Lives*, was started by the Black Women's Collective (1986–9) in Toronto. Members paid monthly dues, and the collective emphasized solidarity and education (Black Women's Collective Constitution 1988; Stikeman and Brand 1991; Haritaworn et al. 2018). In past issues of *Our Lives*, authors documented the racism in employment faced by Black women and housing issues. For the Black Women's Collective, it was pragmatic for the members to use cooperative structures to organize against racism and inequality.

Several works have examined the failed efforts of the Black diaspora in a number of domains in the country, and many of these limitations are due to the hostile racist environment (Du Bois 1907; Winks 1997; Clairmont and Magill 1999; Nelson and Nelson 2004). Examples of these cases include the Toronto United Negro Credit Union formed in the 1920s by members of Marcus Garvey's Universal Negro Improvement Association (Lewis 1987; Toney 2010), and the Commonwealth Cooperative Buying Club, the community collective credit initiative that the Toronto United Negro Association grew out of in the 1920s (Toney 2010). The Toronto United Negro Association, in turn, formed a Credit Union in the 1940s (Gooden 2019). Another credit union was formed through Canada's first Black Union, the Order of Sleeping Car Porters, as early as 1937 in Winnipeg, Manitoba (Chateauvert 1997; Mathieu 2001, 2002; Gordon Nembhard 2014). These associations were helpful during these difficult years of overt racism and discrimination.

More recently, the Black diaspora has tried to create its own credit unions. The first effort was made by the Jamaican Canadian Association in 1963 in Toronto, but it had to fold because of management issues ("Jamaican Canadian Association," n.d.). The Seaview Credit Union was created in 1969 in response to racism in the historical Black Canadian town of Africville, Nova Scotia. However, this bank did not last, because members did not repay loans, signaling that the credit union did not have the support needed to develop its capacity (Clairmont and Magill 1999, 14–15). These results amplify the failure of the established cooperative system to assist other cooperatives, which is a core cooperative principle (see ICA n.d.). In 1993, the Jamaican Canadian Association launched the Caribbean African Canadian Credit Union in Toronto (Hemeon 1993). But because of infighting and a lack of community support, as well as the withdrawal of state funding after a change in government, it closed down (Haliechuk 1993).

These cases among the diaspora have ended in failure. They show that while Black people want cooperatives and know the value of being cooperators, they have not received the needed support. The cases also raise the question of whether established credit unions have adhered to the ICA cooperative principles of aiding cooperative development. Meanwhile, in the United States, many Black cooperatives have been violently destroyed by "white competitors (who) used slander, violence, murder, physical destruction, and economic sabotage" (Gordon Nembhard 2014, 29). There seems to be no shortage of documentation that speaks to the failed cooperative experiences among the diaspora, but limited knowledge of cooperatives that have worked for Black and racialized people. Negative media reports on cases that have failed do not put these experiences within the context of racism and the challenges Black and non-white diaspora people encounter when forming cooperatives.

Credit unions that serve African Americans are reaching a group of people alienated by the formal financial sector. Curtis Haynes Jr.'s work (2018) highlights Du Bois' thinking about "the condition of Black America" (130), which called for Blacks to create their own economic means. A "racial isolation," Haynes argues, "transcended all other social differences" and underpinned Du Bois' ideas of racial cooperation (130). Haynes (2010, 172) hypothesizes that collective action by Black American communities is a means by which to respond to harsh socioeconomic conditions. The fact that there is no Black credit union or formal cooperative suggests that there is a lack of support for this group to create their own institutions.

The *Toronto Star* recently reported on the efforts of African Canadian organizations to develop a Pan-African Credit Union as an alternative to mainstream banking for Black Torontonians (Miller 2020). Addressing under- and unbanked people of color, the organization also aims to provide financial access to Black entrepreneurs and Black-owned businesses, recognizing the systemic barriers populations of color face. In July 2020, the Pan-African Credit Union had a steering committee meeting via Zoom to discuss some of the market study findings about what Black Canadians wanted regarding financial services. It was evident that a Black-led financial institution is long overdue. However, it is too early to tell if there will be support to develop a new Pan-African credit union, especially in terms of raising the required $5 million in capital.

1.11 Politicized Solidarity and the Black Cooperator Experience

There are reportedly about 200 million people of African heritage living in the Americas, and many of these people endure extreme forms of exclusion in business and society. The U.N. has dedicated a decade to observing the contributions of the African diaspora, a diaspora that is largely unknown in the cooperative experience. The Black social economy is an epistemology aimed at politicized work that co-opts business forms and makes them cooperative as a way to reach those left out of mainstream society (Hossein 2019, 2020). A review of the ILO website reveals limited material covering collective and informal cooperatives of racialized people in the West.

A political economy focused on racial minorities would benefit from drawing on theories that reflect the Black experience. Mutual aid was part of survival for enslaved and colonized Black people in the United States, Canada, and the Caribbean (e.g., Marcus Garvey's Universal Negro Improvement Association (UNIA) member-based movement). Black people in the diaspora are aware of this history and the continued ways group economics help them in dominant white societies (Hossein 2017b). Haynes (2018) has written a detailed article positing that W. E. B. Du Bois' commitment to cooperatives was a way to counteract a racist society; as early as 1907, Du Bois, a Harvard-educated African American, advanced the theory of group economics among Black people to withstand white racist power. In 1901, Booker T. Washington (1901 [2013]), imagining a world in which Black people did not have to fear lynching, devoted resources to anti-lynching campaigns. The Underground Railroad (1790s–1860s) organized covertly and moved slaves from the United States into Canada, and this is often viewed as a cooperative movement that faced many challenges (Gordon Nembhard 2014).

Black minorities, drawing on these ideas, have always used various forms of cooperation to cope in society (Rothschild 2009; Gordon Nembhard 2014; Haynes 2018). Hossein (2018) points out that ROSCAs, organizations primarily run by racialized people, are a form of cooperation that is often overlooked. The African diaspora in Canada, the United States, and Europe use these systems to combat exclusion. Through numerous interviews, Dutch academics Julie-Marthe Lehmann and Peers Smets (2019) have uncovered that Ghanaians and Nigerians in Amsterdam engage in ROSCAs as a form of group business and banking to help one another in an exclusionary environment. Black and racialized people in the West are thus actively engaged in cooperatives, but they are missing within the Western efforts to democratize banking.

1.12 The Underground Railroad (1790s–1860s) and the Use of True Bands

Banker cooperatives and ROSCAs are largely absent from academic literature. Stories that focus on racialized people in Canada are even harder to come by. Du Bois' (1907) research examined collective forms of African business, and this historical grounding inspires the Black diaspora outside of the African continent. The Underground Railroad is one example. Black Canadian scholar and owner of the Buxton Museum in southwestern Ontario, Bryan Prince (2004), explains that the Underground Railroad was a secret network of good-hearted people, Black and white, who risked their safety and lives to help fugitives find their way to Canada. Over 30,000 people are estimated to have found safety and a new home in Canada prior to the American Civil War and the constitutional amendment of 1865, which finally ended slavery in the United States.

Maroons' and slaves' refusal to be part of an inhumane system required that people collectively organize, and they did so by hiding what they were doing (Quan 2017). The Underground Railroad was, without a doubt, a cooperative. It relied on the pooling of economic resources and good will to help enslaved Black people escape. This form of cooperative had to be hidden because of the dangers of moving people into freedom. Robin D. G. Kelley (2017) linked the ideas of rebellion to his teacher Cedric Robinson's own life story, where he theorized from the ground up because he was mindful of the community that nurtured him when he had obstacles to overcome. When the Africans settled into Canada, "true bands" were created in towns like Buxton, Ontario, to help people receive the goods they needed to live.

The historical context for the development of Black cooperatives in Canada must include these precursors of formal cooperatives developed by free Blacks that settled in Canada. Gordon Nembhard (2014) describes self-sustaining communal Black farms and communes operating in Wilberforce, Ontario, as early as 1831, a finding that predates the Desjardins and Antigonish movements. Lia Haro and Romand Coles (2019) argue that true bands by Black immigrants had to operate underground because they would be seen as breaking the law and could endanger the newly arrived Black refugees. Benjamin Drew (1856, 236) documented some of the earliest first-hand accounts of cooperatives and Black folks who escaped slavery to Canada. He defined true bands as cooperatives: "A True Band is composed of coloured persons of both sexes, associated for their own improvement. Its objects are manifold: mainly these: the members are to take a general interest in each other's welfare; to pursue such plans and objects as may be for their mutual advantage."

Michael Hembree (1991) emphasized the importance of true bands for the integration of Black people—who did not want to be dependent on handouts or charity—in these communities. In 1853, a Black convention held at Amherstburg in Essex Country in Ontario established vigilance committees in eight communities to coordinate relief for the refugees. Its members funded the first true band society in Maiden in 1854; and by 1856, Black people had organized fourteen similar societies (Hembree 1991, 321). Shirley Yee (1994, 62) describes the critical role true bands played in the 1800s in the organizational networks that sustained Black communities who faced racism after settling in Canada through the Underground Railroad, stating that the "goal of the bands was to foster independence by raising money to improve schools, providing temporary assistance to needy Black families, and caring for the sick."

1.13 Counting ROSCAs as Cooperatives

It is difficult to locate the beginnings of mutual aid and cooperatives among the African diaspora in Canada. Black and racialized people living in Canada are aware of cooperatives, as many used them in their lands of origin. They have a great deal of experience in organizing informally in Canada. The African diaspora has had notable success with financial cooperatives in states that have assisted in their development. For example, in England, the Hornsey Co-operative Credit Union was formally registered by West Indian immigrants in 1962 and later merged with the London Capital Credit Union in 2013 (Greaves n.d.; O'Connell 2009). Caribbean immigrants in the U.K. were successful mainly because they had local knowledge of building ROSCAs. Similarly in the United States, many of the Black credit unions used by African Americans began as informal groups before they were legally registered (Haynes and Gordon Nembhard 1999; Rothschild 2009).

The data and reports on Black cooperatives in Canada are missing or very dated. The CWCF (Corcoran 2009) and the CCA (2011) published reports more than a decade ago explaining why non-white Canadians are not forming cooperatives. The findings of the CWCF report (Corcoran 2009) continue to be useful ten years later: a lack of awareness of what cooperatives are; a lack of support from other organizations; limited financial means; a lack of time; challenges with language, culture, and academic education; and differing cultural definitions of what it means to be a cooperative. One reason for these findings is the inaction of the sector to support other cooperatives (namely, non-white racialized ones). This is evident in the failed efforts to form the first-ever Pan-African credit union in the Greater Toronto Area (GTA). No state has made it a priority to mentor or finance Black cooperativism. Black and racialized people have their own conception of cooperative, and many of them have had to hide or carry out their cooperative activities discreetly for fear of being harassed.

ROSCAs are a conscientious form of economic cooperation—they are not simply underdeveloped cooperatives or credit unions. ROSCA members voluntarily join and work together to control the organizations, stressing the values of democracy, voice, and participation. But these people lack the technical and financial support to create diverse credit unions or build Black-owned credit unions. Research by John Maiorano, Laurie Mook, and Jack Quarter (2017) mapped the location of credit unions in the GTA to show that the credit union "difference" was limited in terms of helping minorities. Moreover, credit unions are not located in racially marginalized communities. A cursory view confirms this finding. For example, Alterna Credit Union has its headquarters on Bay Street and branches at York University and in the trendy Leslieville area—even though its community investment portfolio aims to assist low-income people. Meridian Credit Union, one of Canada's largest credit unions, is also located in affluent parts of the city, such as at Yonge and Sheppard, on Danforth, in the Beaches, and Vaughan. At the writing of this report, these two prominent credit unions were also limited in the cultural diversity of their management team and leadership.

1.14 ROSCAs by Black People Counter Racial Capitalism

A number of Black Canadian scholars (James et al. 2010; Mensah 2010) have noted the negative impact of the legacy of slavery in Canada on Black lives and the Black immigrants who continue to come to the country. These Black Canadians have been hiding in plain sight in terms of the cooperatives they run. As noted in Section 1.12, at least since the 1800s, Black minorities have carried out true bands and many other forms of economic cooperation in secret because they fear reprisal.

In eleven years of doing interviews with Black Canadian women, I have noticed that while they are not ashamed of what they do, they know the risks of making it public. Black Canadian women hide their ROSCAs because they are routinely discriminated against and treated as inferior (Smets 1998; Mintz 2010; Gordon Nembhard 2014; Hossein 2017a, 2018, 2020). The documentary *The Banker Ladies* (Mondesir 2021) shows how Black Canadian women participate in various forms of banking cooperatives to counteract being excluded from business and society (available to watch online at https://www.youtube.com/watch?v=fXMYRtLTYP0).

For centuries, Black women in the Caribbean and Canada have mobilized collectively in their low-income communities (Ardener and Burman 1995; Hossein 2017b, 2018). Jessica Gordon Nembhard (2014) has found that African American women in Alabama created the Freedom Quilting Bee Co-operative to feed, shelter, and help their families and communities meet their needs, as well as mitigate the harms of white supremacy. The Underground Railroad is a towering example of informal economic cooperation largely taken on by Black people moving out of slavery. This story needs to feature prominently in the cooperative narratives in Canada—and not only during Black history month events. Knowledge of the work of true bands is carried through oral history and includes many details to locate how these cooperatives helped slaves settle into Canada.

ROSCAs among the GTA's Black diaspora are diverse, with women representing countries in Africa and the Caribbean. Many other newcomers to Canada—from Pakistan, China, Korea, Mexico, Sri Lanka, Ecuador, and India, to name a few—also run and participate in ROSCA systems. "Natla," a 35-year-old married Sudanese-Canadian woman I interviewed, told me this system helped her settle into Canada:

> Who knows me here when I first come from Sudan [pause]. No one. I can't even speak English back then. Sandooq [an informal cooperative bank] gives me friends and a chance. I buy [bought] my airplane ticket back home and bring my children for there [for vacation]. Sandooq helped me so much when I came to Canada. I swear to my God for it. (Interview, "Natla," Toronto, March 26, 2015)

Documented experiences of the racist behavior of mainstream banks can explain why racialized people choose to participate in alternative banking services. In December 2014, Haitian Canadian Frantz St. Fleur was arrested on the suspicion that he was trying to deposit a fraudulent check by Remax at his Scotiabank branch in Toronto's east end, where he had been a customer for ten years (Alamenciak 2014; Hossein 2018); it turned out the check was credible. In January 2020, Maxwell Johnson and his 12-year-old granddaughter were handcuffed by police after the Bank of Montreal (BMO) wrongfully suspected them of illicit behavior (Sterritt 2020); in this case, as well, it turned out the suspicions were groundless. And in February 2020, Egyptian Canadian Dana Ramadan went into the Royal Bank of Canada in Toronto's west end, where tellers wrongly accused her of illegal activities (Paradkar 2020).

According to ACORN Canada, only 3 percent of the population (i.e., 842,000 Canadian) are unbanked, with no access to financial services (ACORN 2016). In 2014, I had an informal conversation with an analyst at the Bank of Canada in which she was unsure how many Canadians are underbanked. This term refers to people who have bank accounts but only engage with them minimally to receive a salary or deposit savings. Between banks' unconscious bias against them and their general trust issue with commercial banks, Black people who are a minority may be inclined to turn to ROSCAs to meet their livelihood needs.

Black Canadian women who are given a hard time in formal banks seem especially inclined to start their own ROSCAs. In fieldwork interviews, I spoke with "Fardowsa," a Somali-Canadian resident of Jane and Finch, who explained the cultural aspect to ROSCAs:

> We are bringing change through our own banking ways. It helps me to keep doing what I do when they [critics who do not know about informal co-operatives] look at us in a weird way to say it's our culture. We show we can do it [business] ourselves and also . . . is a social thing . . . We drink tea and talk. (Interview, "Fardowsa," Toronto, March 20, 2015)

This statement reveals that racialized and Black women opt to form and join ROSCAs because this informal cooperative meets all their needs. The meetings of ROSCA members are reminiscent of the kitchen meetings of the Antigonish movement. Women gather in the safe space of someone's home or the room of a local community center to discuss their lives and the politics of the day while enjoying a potluck of fish samosas and rice.

1.15 Conclusion: Banker Co-ops are a Part of Canada's Co-op System

The African diaspora has been leading cooperatives for a very long time (Stewart 1984; St. Pierre 1999). The timelines of their economic cooperation begin well before the Rochdale weavers of the U.K. The economic ideas of C. Y. Thomas were instrumental in forming the Neechi principles, which guide how cooperative economic development is carried out in Canada. Yet, we choose to forget this major contribution. The cooperative sector in Canada needs to widen its definition to ensure that ROSCAs and other mutual aid groups of the diaspora are included. Currently, Black and racialized people seem to be missing both in the literature and in actual membership of formal cooperatives. More work is needed to understand how credit unions and consumer co-ops in the city are working to include these groups.

ROSCAs are informal cooperatives used by non-white Canadians across the country. The work done by the women who organize ROSCAs is obscured, and they receive no support from formal cooperative associations or credit unions. Black Canadian women operate their ROSCAs out of the public view because they fear being arrested or having their funds confiscated, or to avoid being stigmatized for what they do. Why they feel a need to hide their community building is a matter that requires further investigation.

By ignoring the work of the African diaspora, the cooperative movement misses out on spreading the benefits of the ROSCA model for racial equity and justice. This may be the opening the declining cooperative sector needs to boost its membership. But the sector will first have to look at how to make its own institutions representative of the cultural diversity in Canada on every level and then evolve to recognize scholarship and practice of racialized people in cooperative development.

Works Cited

ACORN Canada. 2016. "It's Expensive to Be Poor: How Canadian Banks Are Failing Low Income Communities." ACORN Canada [website].

Alamenciak, T. 2014. "Banking While Black." *Toronto Star*, December 10. https://www.thestar.com/news/gta/2014/12/10/banking_while_black_toronto_man_accuses_scotiabank_of_racial_profiling.html

Ardener, S. and S. Burman. 1995. *Money-Go-Rounds: The Importance of Rotating Savings and Credit Associations for Women*. Oxford: Berg.

Aryeetey, E. and W. Steel. 1994. "Informal Savings Collectors in Ghana: Can They Intermediate?" *Finance and Development* 31(1): 36–7.

BBC Horizon. 1980. *The Mondragon Experience*. TV series.

Bekerie, A. 2003. "Iquib and Idir: Socio-Economic Traditions of the Ethiopians." *Tadias Online*. http://www.tadias.com/v1n6/OP_2_2003-1.html

Bekerie, A. 2008. "The Ethiopian Millennium and Its Historical and Cultural Meanings." *International Journal of Ethiopian Studies* 3(2): 23–31.

Betasamosake Simpson, L. 2020. *As We Have Always Done: Indigenous Freedom through Radical Resistance*. Minneapolis, MN: University of Minnesota Press.

Black Women's Collective Constitution. 1988. *Rise Up: A Digital Archive of Feminist Activism*. https://riseupfeministarchive.ca/activism/organizations/Black-womens-collective/. Accessed June 29, 2020.

Bouman, F. J. A. 1995. "ROSCA: On the Origin of the Species." *Savings and Development* 19(2): 117–48.

Brathwaite, K. 1981. *The Arrivants: A New World Trilogy (Rights of Passage; Islands; Masks)*. Oxford: Oxford University Press.

Buckland, J. 2012. *Hard Choices: Financial Exclusion, Fringe Banks, and Poverty in Urban Canada*. Toronto: University of Toronto Press.

Canadian Co-operative Association (CCA). 2011. *Ethnocultural and Immigrant Co-operatives in Canada*. Edited by John Anderson, Donna Balkan, and Lynne Markell. Ottawa: Canadian Co-operative Association.

Chateauvert, M. 1997. *Marching Together: Women of the Brotherhood of Sleeping Car Porters*. Champaign: University of Illinois Press.

Clairmont, D. H. J. and D. W. Magill. 1999. *Africville: The Life and Death of A Canadian Black Community*. Toronto: Canadian Scholars' Press.

Corcoran, H. 2009. *Strategies for Developing Immigrant Worker Co-ops*. Calgary: Canadian Worker Co-operative Federation.

Cox, O. C. 1959. *The Foundations of Capitalism*. New York: Philosophical Library Inc.

Cox, O. C. 1964. *Capitalism as a System*. New York: Monthly Review Press.

Curl, J. 2012. *For All the People: Uncovering the Hidden History of Co-operation, Co-operative Movements, and Communalism in America*. Oakland: PM Press.

Dana, L. P. 2010. "Nunavik, Arctic Quebec: Where Co-operatives Supplement Entrepreneurship." *Global Business and Economics Review* 12(1–2): 42–71.

Datta, R. 2000. "On their Own: Development Strategies of the Self-Employment Women's Association (SEWA) in India." *Development* 43(4): 51–5.

Davies, T. 2018. "Historical Development of NGOS." In Aynsley Kellow and Hannah Murphy-Gregory (eds.), *The Handbook on Research on NGOs*, 15–34. Cheltenham: Edward Elgar Publishing.

Drew, B. 1856. *A North-Side View of Slavery: The Refugee: Or, The Narratives of Fugitive Slaves in Canada. Related by Themselves, with an Account of the History and Condition of the Colored Population of Upper Canada*. Boston: JP Jewett.

Du Bois, W. E. B. 1907. *Economic Co-operation among Negro Americans*. Atlanta: Atlanta University Press.

Dworkin, M. and M. Young, prods. 2012. *Shift Change: Putting Democracy to Work*. [Film] Bullfrog: U.S.

Fairbairn, B. 1994. "The Meaning of Rochdale: The Rochdale Pioneers and the Co-operative Principles." Occasional Paper, 1–62. Saskatoon: Centre for the Study of Co-operatives, University of Saskatchewan.

Fairbairn, B. 2004. "History of Co-operatives." In Christopher D. Merrett and Norman Walzer (eds.), *Co-operatives and Local Development: Theory and Applications for the 21st Century*, 23–51. Armonk: M.E. Sharpe.

Fairbairn, B. 2005. "Canada's Co-operative Province: Individualism and Mutualism in a Settler Society 1905–2005." In *Reflections in Celebration of Saskatchewan's Centennial Year*. Saskatoon: University of Saskatchewan, Centre for the Study of Co-operatives.

Fairbairn, B. 2007. "A Century of Prairie and Saskatchewan Farm Co-operatives: Philosophy, Organization, and History." In Murray Knuttila and Bob Stirling (eds), *The Prairie Agrarian Movement Revisited*, 93–106. Regina: Canadian Plains Research Centre.

Fairbairn, B. 2009. "Canada's Co-operative Province: Individualism and Mutualism in a Settler Society." In Jene M. Porter (ed.), *Perspectives of Saskatchewan*, 149–74. Winnipeg: University of Manitoba Press.

Financial Services Regulatory Authority of Ontario (FSRA). "Ontario Credit Unions and Caisses Populaires." http://creditunion.fsco.gov.on.ca/english/

Fischler, R., R. Aubin, S. Kraemer, and L. Wiginton. 2013. "Co-operative Housing and the Social Integration of Immigrant Households." Quebec Metropolis Centre—Immigration and Metropolis, Working Paper No. 52. http://www.metropolis.inrs.ca/working-paper-no-52-co-operative-housing-and-the-social-integration-of-immigrant-households/

Fischler, R., S. Kraemer, and L. Wiginton. 2017. "A Place to Stand Up on Your Two Feet: The Community Housing in Immigrant Integration in Montréal, Quebec." *Revue canadienne de recherche urbaine* 26(2): 15–32.

Galabuzi, G-E. 2006. *Canada's Economic Apartheid: The Social Exclusion of Racialized Groups in the New Century*. Toronto: Canadian Scholars Press Inc.

Gooden, A. 2019. "African Canadian Leadership: Pan-Africanism, Transnationality, Community Organizing." In Tamari Kitossa, Erica S. Lawson, and Philip S. S. Howard (eds.), *African Canadian Leadership: Continuity, Transition, and Transformation*, 111–48. Toronto: University of Toronto Press.

Gordon Nembhard, J. 2008. "Co-operatives." In William A. Darity (ed.), *International Encyclopedia of the Social Sciences*, 2nd edn, 123–27. Farmington Hills: Macmillan Reference USA.

Gordon Nembhard, J. 2014. *Collective Courage: A History of African American Co-operative Economic Thought and Practice*. University Park: Pennsylvania University Press.

Greaves, E. n.d. "Board of Directors" [bio] Credit Union [website]. https://www.credit-union.co-op/content.asp?section=258

Guinnane, T. 2001. "Co-operatives as Information Machines: German Rural Credit Co-operatives, 1883–1914." *Journal of Economic History* 61(2): 366–89.

Haliechuk, R. 1993. "Credit Union Aims to Meet Black Needs." *Toronto Star*, June 5, Section B.

Hammond Ketilson, L. 2006. *Revisiting the Role of Co-operative Values and Principles: Do They Act to Include Or Exclude?* Saskatoon: University of Saskatchewan, Centre for the Study of Co-operatives.

Hammond Ketilson, L. and I. MacPherson. 2001. *A Report on Aboriginal Co-operatives in Canada: Current Situation and Potential for Growth*. Saskatoon: University of Saskatchewan, Centre for the Study of Co-operatives.

Haritaworn, J., G. Moussa, and S. Marcus Ware. 2018. *Queering Urban Justice: Queer of Color Formations in Toronto*. Toronto: University of Toronto Press.

Haro, L. and R. Coles. 2019. "Reimagining Fugitive Democracy and Transformative Sanctuary with Black Frontline Communities in the Underground Railroad." *Political Theory* 47(5): 646–673.

Harriet Tubman Historical Society website: http://www.harriet-tubman.org/. Accessed August 3, 2020.

Haynes, C. 2010. "Commentary on Black Political Economy." *Journal of Philosophical Economics: Bucharest* 3(2): 164–72.

Haynes Jr., C. 2018. "From Philanthropic Black Capitalism to Socialism: Co-operativism in Du Bois's Economic Thought." *Socialism and Democracy* 32(3): 125–45.

Haynes Jr., C. 2021. "India Walton, W. E. B. DuBois and Co-operative Enterprise Development." *The Challenger News*. Buffalo, NY. Accessed November 28, 2021: https://thechallengernews.com/2021/10/india-walton-w-e-b-dubois-and-co-operative-enterprise-development/

Haynes Jr., C. and J. Gordon Nembhard. 1999. "Co-operative Economics: A Community Revitalization Strategy." *Review of Black Political Economy* 27(1): 47–71.

Hembree, M. F. 1991. "The Question of Begging: Fugitive Slave Relief in Canada, 1830–1865." *Civil War History* 37(4): 314–27.

Hemeon, J. 1993. "Black Credit Union Gets $750,000." *Toronto Star*. July 21. Section B.

"History of Wawanesa". 1996–2020. Wawanesa Mutual Insurance Company [website]. https://www.wawanesa.com/canada/about-us/about-history.html

Hogan, L. 1984. *Principles of Black Political Economy*. Bloomington: Trafford Publishing.

Hossein, C. S. 2017a. "Fringe Banking in Canada: A Preliminary Study of the 'Banker Ladies' and Economic Collectives in Toronto's Inner Suburbs." *Canadian Journal of Non-profit and Social Economy Research* 8(1): 29–43.

Hossein, C. S. 2017b. "A Case Study of the Influence of Garveyism on the African Diaspora." *Social Economic Studies Journal* 66 (3/4): 151174.

Hossein, C. S. (ed.) 2018. *The Black Social Economy in the Americas: Exploring Diverse Community-Based Markets*. New York: Palgrave Macmillan.

Hossein, C. S. 2019. "A Black Epistemology for the Social and Solidarity Economy: The Black Social Economy." *Review of Black Political Economy* 46(3): 209–29.

Hossein, C. S. 2020. "Rotating Savings and Credit Associations (ROSCAs): Mutual Aid Financing." In J. K. Gibson-Graham and Kelly Dombroski (eds.), *The Handbook of Diverse Economies*, 354–61. Cheltenham: Edward Elgar Press.

International Co-operative Alliance (ICA). n.d. "Co-operative Identity, Values and Principles." https://www.ica.co-op/en/co-operatives/co-operative-identity

"Jamaican Canadian Association." n.d. Jean Augustine Political Button Collection. York University Library. http://archives.library.yorku.ca/exhibits/show/pushingbuttons/Black—caribbean-community/jamaican-canadian-association

James, C., D. Este, W. Thomas Bernard, A. Benjamin, B. Lloyd, and T. Turner. 2010. *Race and Well-Being: The Lives, Hopes and Activism of African Canadians*. Halifax: Fernwood Publishing.

Johnson, G. T. and A. Lubin. 2017. *Futures of Black Radicalism*. Brooklyn: Verso.

Johnston, A. B. J. 2001. "Research Note: Mathieu Da Costa along the Coasts of Nova Scotia: Some Possibilities." *Journal of the Royal Nova Scotia Historic Society* 4: 152–164.

Kedir, A. M. and G. Ibrahim. 2011. "ROSCAs in Urban Ethiopia: Are the Characteristics of the Institutions More Important Than Those of Members?" *Journal of Development Studies* 47(7): 998–1016.

Kelley, R. D. G. 2017. "Winston Whiteside and the Political of the Possible." In Gaye Theresa Johnson and Alex Lubin (eds.), *Futures of Black Radicalism*, 255–62. Brooklyn, NY: Verso.

Lee, J., N. Curry, and A. M. Peredo. 2015. "Research Summary: Strathcona Co-op Housing." Project: Co-operatives in Context: Race, Ethnicity, Displacement and Exclusion. http://ec.msvu.ca:8080/xmlui/handle/10587/1512

Lee, J., B. Smallshaw, and A. M. Peredo. 2017. "Rethinking Co-operatives: Japanese-Canadian Fishing Co-operatives." *Community Development Journal* 52(4): 540–57.

Lehmann, J.-M. and P. Smets. 2019. "An Innovative Resilience Approach: Financial Self-Help Groups in Contemporary Financial Landscapes in the Netherlands." *Economy and Space* 52(5): 898–915.

Lethabo King, T. 2019. *The Black Shoals: Offshore Formations of Black and Native Studies*. Durham: Duke University Press.

Lévesque, B., M-C. Malo, and R. Rouzier. 1997. "The 'Caisse de dépôt et placement du Québec' and the 'Mouvement des Caisses populaires et d'Économie Desjardins': Two Financial Institutions, the Same Convergence towards the General Interest?" *Annals of Public and Co-operative Economics* 68(3): 485–501.

Lewis, R. 1987. *Marcus Garvey: Anti-Colonial Champion*. Kent, UK: Karia Press.

Li, W. and L. Lo. 2008. "People-Money Co-movement and the Ethnic Financial Sectors in Canada and the U.S." *Migracijske i etnicke teme* 24(4): 301–22.

Loxley, J. 1985. "Regulation and Restructuring: Responses to the International Financial Crisis." *Contemporary Crises; Dordrecht, Etc.* 9(2): 103–25.

Loxley, J. 2002. "Sustainable Urban Economic Development: An Aboriginal Perspective." *Journal of Aboriginal Economic Development* 3(1): 29–32.

Loxley, J. 2008. *Doing Community Economic Development*. Toronto: Fernwood Publishing.

MacAulay, S. 2002. "The Smokestack Leaned toward Capitalism: An Examination of the Middle Way Program of the Antigonish Movement." *Journal of Canadian Studies* 37(1): 43–67.

MacPherson, I. 1979. *Each for All: A History of the Co-operative Movement in English Canada, 1900–1945*, Vol. 116. Toronto: McGill-Queen's Press-MQUP.

MacPherson, I. 2007. *One Path to Co-operative Studies: A Selection of Papers and Presentations*. British Columbia Institute for Co-operative Studies. Victoria: New Rochdale Press.

MacPherson, I. 2009. "What Has Been Learned Should Be Studied and Passed On: Why The Northern Co-operative Experience Needs to Be Considered More Seriously." *Northern Review* 30: 57–81.

MacPherson, I. 2012. "'. . .What Is the End Purpose of It All?': The Centrality of Values for Co-operative Success in the Marketplace". In Patrizia Battilani and Harm G. Schröter (eds.), *The Co-operative Business Movement, 1950 to the Present*, 107–25. Cambridge, UK: Cambridge University Press.

Maiorano, J., L. Mook, and J. Quarter. 2017. "Is There a Credit Union Difference? Comparing Canadian Credit Union and Bank Branch Locations." *Canadian Journal of Nonprofit and Social Economy Research* 7(2): 40–56.

Mathieu, S. 2001. "North of the Colour Line: Sleeping Car Porters and the Battle Against Jim Crow on Canadian Rails, 1880-1920." *Labour/Le Travail* 47(1): 9–41.

Mathieu, S. 2002. *Jim Crow Rides This Train: The Social and Political Impact of African American Sleeping Car Porters in Canada, 1880–1939*. PhD Thesis, Yale University.

Mendell, M. 2009. "The Three Pillars of the Social Economy in Quebec." In Ash Amin (ed.), *The Social Economy: Alternative Ways of Thinking About Capitalism and Welfare*, 17–209. London: Zed Books.

Mensah, J. 2010. *Black Canadians: History, Experience, Social Conditions*, 2nd edn. Halifax: Fernwood Publishing.

Miller, E. 2010. "Solidarity Economy: Key Concepts and Issues." In E. Kawano, T. Masterson, and J. Teller-Ellsberg (eds.), *Solidarity Economy I: Building Alternatives for People and Planet*. Amherst: Center for Popular Economics.

Miller, J. 2020. "Black Groups Seek to Launch Credit Union." *Toronto Star*, February 20, GTA section.

Mintz, S. 2010. *Three Ancient Colonies: Caribbean Themes and Variations*. Cambridge, MA: Harvard University Press.

Mitchell, M. 1996. *From Talking Chiefs to a Native Corporate Elite: The Birth of Class and Nationalism among Canadian Inuit*. Vol. 12. Toronto: McGill-Queen's Press-MQUP.

Mondesir, E., dir. 2021 (soft release in 2020). *The Banker Ladies*. [Film] Prod. DiSE Collective. https://www.filmsforaction.org/watch/the-banker-ladies/

Murphy, P., prod. 2009. *You Can Do It: The Story of the Antigonish Movement*. [Film] Sea Bright Productions.

National Council of Welfare Reports. n.d. *Poverty Profile: Special Edition*. Government of Canada.

"Neechi Principles." n.d. The Canadian CED Network website. https://ccednet-rcdec.ca/en/toolbox/neechi-principles

Nelson, C. and C. A. Nelson (eds.) 2004. *Racism, Eh?: A Critical Inter-Disciplinary Anthology of Race and Racism in Canada*. Vaughan: Captus Press.

Nelson, N. 1996. "The Kiambu Group: A Successful Women's ROSCA in Mathare Valley, Nairobi (1971 to 1990)." In S. Ardener and B. Sandra (eds.), *Money-Go-Rounds: The Importance of Rotating Savings and Credit Associations for Women*, 49–71. Oxford: Berg.

O'Connell, S. 2009. *Credit and Community: Working-Class Debt in the UK since 1880*. Oxford University Press on Demand.

Ontario Co-operative Association (OCA), website. https://ontario.coop/. Accessed on August 3, 2020.

Palmer, T. 2019. Worker Co-operative State of the Sector Report. Democracy at Work Institute and the US Federation of Worker Co-operatives.

Paradkar, S. 2020. "This Egyptian-Canadian Woman Went to Withdraw Her Own Money at RBC. What Happened Next is the Subject of a Lawsuit against the Bank and Peel Police." *Toronto Star*, February 6. https://www.thestar.com/news/gta/2020/02/06/this-egyptian-canadian-woman-went-to-withdraw-her-own-money-at-rbc-what-happened-next-is-the-subject-of-a-lawsuit-against-the-bank-and-peel-police.html.

Peterson, I. 1990. "As Co-ops Spread, Discrimination Concerns Grow." *New York Times*, February 25. https://www.nytimes.com/1990/02/25/realestate/as-co-ops-spread-discrimination-concerns-grow.html

Prince, B. 2004. *I Came as a Stranger: The Underground Railroad*. New York: Tundra Books.

Quan, H. L. T. 2005. "Geniuses of Resistance: Feminist Consciousness and the Black Radical Tradition." *Race and Class* 47(2): 39–53.

Quan, H. L. T. 2017. "It's Hard to Stop Rebels That Time Travel." In Gaye Theresa Johnson and Alex Lubin (eds.), *Futures of Black Radicalism*, 173–93. Brooklyn: Verso.

Quarter, J., L. Mook, and A. Armstrong. 2017. *Understanding the Social Economy: A Canadian Perspective*. Toronto: University of Toronto Press.

Quiring, D. 2006. "From the Bush to the Village in Northern Saskatchewan: Contrasting CCF Community Development Projects." *Journal of the Canadian Historical Association/Revue de la Société historique du Canada* 17(1): 151–78.

Rebel Sky Media. 2018. *The Inclusive Economy: Stories of CED in Manitoba*. [Documentary] Winnipeg. Produced by the Canadian Community Economic Development Network, the Canadian Centre for Policy Alternatives.

Robinson, C. J. 1983 [2000]. *Black Marxism: The Making of the Black Radical Tradition*, second edn. London: Zed Press.

Rothschild, J. 2009. "Workers' Co-operatives and Social Enterprise: A Forgotten Route to Social Equity and Democracy." *American Behavoralist* 52(7): 1023–41.

Sethi, R. M. 1996. "Women's Informal Co-operative Banks in Contemporary Indian Society." In S. Ardener and B. Sandra (eds.), *Money-Go-Rounds: The Importance of Rotating Savings and Credit Associations for Women*, 163–79. Oxford, UK: Berg.

Smets, P. 1998. "Money-Go-Rounds for Women: Finance as Instrument or as Ultimate Goal in Lottery ROSCAs." *Anthropos* 9: 209–15.

Sousa, J. 2015. "Realizing the Co-operative Advantage at the Atkinson Housing Co-operative: The Role of Community Development to Improve Public Housing." *Journal of Entrepreneurial and Organizational Diversity* 4(1): 52–74.

Sterritt, A. 2020. "Indigenous Grandfather and 12-Year Old Grand-Daughter Handcuffed in Front of a Vancouver Bank after Trying to Open a Bank Account." CBC, January 9. https://www.cbc.ca/news/canada/british-columbia/indigenous-girl-grandfather-handcuffed-bank-1.5419519

Stewart, J. 1984. "Building a Co-operative Economy: Lessons from the Black Experience." *Review of Social Economy* 17: 360–8.

Stikeman, G. and D. Brand. 1991. *Sisters in Struggle*. 1991. National Film Board of Canada. Film.

St. Pierre, M. 1999. *Anatomy of Resistance: Anticolonialism in Guyana 1823–1966*. London: MacMillan Education.

Sullivan, L. 1969. *Build, Brother, Build: From Poverty to Economic Power*. Philadelphia: Macrae Smith Co. Publishers.

Thiagarajan, K. 2019. "Millions of Women in India Join Hands to Form a 385-Mile Wall of Protest." NPR Radio, January 4.

Thomas, C. Y. 1974. *Dependency and Transformation: The Economics of the Transition to Socialism*. New York: Monthly Review Press.

Thomas, C. Y. 1988. *The Poor and the Powerless: Economic Policy and Change in the Caribbean*. New York: Monthly Review Press.

Timothy, R. K. 2018. "How Racism Impacts Your Health." Maclean's, March 1. Section: Society. https://www.macleans.ca/society/how-racism-impacts-your-health/

Toney, J. 2010. "Locating Diaspora: Afro-Caribbean Narratives of Migration and Settlement in Toronto, 1914–1929." *Urban History Review/Revue d'histoire urbaine* 38(2): 75–87.

Vezina, M., M-C. Malo, and M. Ben Selma. 2017. "Mature Social Economy Enterprise and Social Innovation: The Case of the Desjardins Environmental Fund." *Annals of Public and Co-operative Economics* 88(2): 257–78.

Wade, M., D. Linton, and V. Sharma. 1984. "Off Campus: Developing Co-operative Housing for Students." Occasional Paper No. 8, Institute of Urban Studies, University of Winnipeg.

Washington, B. T. 1901 [2013]. *Up from Slavery: An Autobiography*. Delhi, India: Ratna Sagar Press.

Welton, M. R. 2003. "Decoding Coady: Masters of Their Own Destiny under Critical Scrutiny." *Studies in Continuing Education* 25(1): 75–93.

Williams, C. 1961 [1993]. "The Economic Basis of African Life." In C. Williams, *The Rebirth of African Civilization*. Chicago: Third World Press.

Williams, R. C. 2007. *The Co-operative Movement: Globalization from Below*. Farnham: Ashgate Publishers.

Williams, R. C. 2010. *The Co-operative Solution: Toward a Just Economy*. Lanham: University Press of America.

Willoughby-Herard, T. 2015. *Waste of a White Skin: The Carnegie Corporation and the Racial Logic of White Vulnerability*. Oakland: University of California.

Winks, R. W. 1997. *The Blacks in Canada: A History*. Toronto: McGill-Queen's University Press.

Wuttunee, W. A. 2010. *Living Rhythms: Lessons in Aboriginal Economic Resilience and Vision*. Kingston: McGill-Queens University Press.

Yasmeen, G. 1993. *Mutual Aid Networks in Two Feminist Housing Co-operatives in Montreal, Quebec*. Master's Thesis, McGill University.

Yee, S. J. 1994. "Gender Ideology and Black Women as Community-Builders in Ontario, 1850–70." *Canadian Historical Review* 75(1): 53–73.

Interviews and Focus Groups (Ethical protocol was approved)

"Fardowsa," Focus group, Toronto, March 20, 2015.
Jane and Finch, Focus group (20 people), Toronto, March 20, 2015.
"Natla," Focus group, Toronto, March 26, 2015.
Scarborough, Focus group (26 people), Toronto, March 26, 2015.
Little Burgundy and Cote des Neiges, Montreal, focus group, 2016.
Montreal partner, Interview, 2016 (withheld on purpose).

2
Beyond Coping
The Use of Ajo Culture among Nigerian Immigrants to Counter Racial Capitalism in North America

Salewa Olawoye-Mann

2.1 Introduction

In 1845, Julia A. F. Carney wrote a poem called "Little Things." The first verse states, "little drops of water . . . make a mighty ocean." This refers to the greatness that can be achieved from seemingly small beginnings and contributions. This sums up the Ajo system. "Ajo" comes from the Yoruba word *akojo*, is used in southwestern Nigeria, and means "pooled contributions" (Adebayo 1994). The word refers to communal economic restoration—where a community of people pool monetary contributions that are then given to a different member every period in a cycle. This is then used to foster growth through investments that the individual small drops of contribution may not have achieved outside a community. For years, rural Nigerian women have relied on this centuries-old cooperative banking system that can also be defined as a rotating savings and credit association (ROSCA) where members voluntarily pool their resources, including cash, for financial empowerment through interconnected relationships (Ardener and Burman 1995; Fasoranti 2010).

The tradition of Ajo and money pooling has been passed on from generation to generation. West African enslaved people brought this tradition to the Americas during the trans-Atlantic slave trade. Since the slavery era, African immigrants and descendants from Africa have continued to maintain this ROSCA tradition all around the world, albeit with different names, and it has played a vital part in the Black social economy (Ardener and Burman 1995; Hossein 2018). The Yoruba Ajo has also been utilized in the Caribbean region for several years (Maynard 1996). Thus, Black people have resorted to this method of community building for years (Hossein 2018). This can be seen in the money pooling systems African immigrants brought with them to build themselves and their communities in their new countries.

The Ajo system is rooted in mutual aid and dependent on trust, and people all over Nigeria use it for financial access but also to assist one another. The goal of Ajo has always been to grow within the community by focusing on internal sustainability and self-sufficiency despite external limitations prevalent in patriarchal

Salewa Olawoye-Mann, *Beyond Coping*. In: *Beyond Racial Capitalism*. Edited by Caroline Shenaz Hossein, Sharon D. Wright Austin, and Kevin Edmonds, Oxford University Press. © Oxford University Press (2023).
DOI: 10.1093/oso/9780192868336.003.0003

Nigerian societies (Ogwezi 2016). Women in villages all over Nigeria have historically experienced financial exclusion, and this is why microfinance has emerged as a major new business in the country (Raddatz 2003; Ogunrinola and Ewetan 2005). The introduction of formal banks in Africa did not eliminate informal cooperative banks such as Ajo (also known as Esusu in southeastern Nigeria). Historically, Ajo has been tied to the close relationship between illiteracy and the financial underdevelopment of the economy in Nigeria, which led to the rapid growth of the country's informal financial sector (Ogunrinola and Ewetan 2005). In Nigeria, street traders and other rural settlers use Ajo because they do not trust formal microfinance institutions (Oloyede 2008). Ajo is relevant among Nigerian immigrants in developed economies, such as Canada and the United States, because of the business exclusion that exists there (Ogunrinola and Ewetan 2005; Hossein 2013; Mundra and Oyelere 2018). Ajo systems are part of the self-help groups immigrants use to adapt to their new lands despite different types of exclusion (Lehmann and Smets 2019).

In this chapter, I argue that Ajo is used among Nigerian immigrants in Canada and the United States because of the racial capitalism in these white-dominated economies. I then address how informal cooperation built on trust and community helps newcomers adjust and settle into their new countries. Black immigrants have a more difficult time assimilating into these societies and are the least likely of all U.S. citizens to accumulate wealth in the United States (Painter and Qian 2016a). I conducted empirical research and interviews of 130 Nigerian immigrants in Canada and the United States to understand how Ajo is deployed and why it is used. Just as Ajo is practised in Nigeria, the women who lead these groups in the new country bring pragmatic decision-making and contribute to cohesion and building friendships.

2.2 Know the Context: The Nigerian Immigrants' Experience and Ajo in Canada and the United States

According to the 2019 World Bank Database, Nigeria has an estimated population of 201 million—which makes it the most populous country in Africa. The 2019 American Community Survey reports that about 392,811 (±20,000 margin of error) U.S. residents were born in Nigeria, and 2016 Statistics Canada data reports about 42,430 residents born in Nigeria. Nigerians migrate for different reasons, including for education or employment, to be closer to family members who have migrated, or for security reasons (Kómoláfé 2002; Kirwin and Anderson 2018). In Canada and the United States, poverty rates have been especially high among recent immigrants because they earn less on average than workers born in these countries despite typically having higher levels of education (Agrawal 2013).

This signifies a failure to translate internationally obtained skills into equivalent compensation, as their foreign credentials are not fully recognized

(Zuberi and Ptashnick 2012). Therefore, because of the deskilling of the labor of immigrants and neoliberal policies that affect migration and immigrants, these immigrants are kept poor (Bauder 2003; De Bustillo, Muñoz and Antón 2011; Card and Raphael 2013; Root et al. 2014). Also, they have a lower quality of life than their natural-born counterparts (Williams et al. 2015). The ripple effect of this poverty can be seen in social issues around housing, mental health, the meeting of basic needs, and the health of the immigrants (Galabuzi 2006; Lai et al. 2017). Nigerian immigrants are not exempt from these immigrant experiences in Canada and the United States; and to reduce their effects, many Nigerian immigrants join ethnic organizations that are either national or tribal (Abbott 2006). Through these communities, they adopt traditional Nigerian practices, such as Ajo.

Historically, the Nigerian—and in general African—way of life has been one of predominantly communal living (Rikko and Gwatau 2011). Since the era of subsistence farming, people have borne a responsibility for each other. This is in stark contrast to the individualism that exists in the West. As a result, Nigerian immigrants, much like other immigrants, tend to build communities similar to what they were used to when growing up. These community clusters create an avenue for trust, friendship, and community, which are necessary ingredients for person-to-person lending (Greiner and Wang 2010). These help in the face of the limitations, including economic limitations, that these immigrants face in their new area of settlements. As a Nigerian immigrant in Toronto, I personally understand the need for familiarity in a foreign land.

However, I always wondered why people continued this tradition of Ajo after migrating to countries with developed credit systems. Through my research, I realized that the practice of Ajo is about much more than financial gain. I saw how people in the community help each other in a way that does not increase their debt burdens, from sharing job and business opportunities to interactive zoom meetings about survival in a foreign land to encouraging emails about community aid and development. I understood the benefits of inclusion and community from a non-financial angle. From a financial angle, Indigenous methods of saving represent an important way for marginalized communities to accrue assets for personal and business purposes (Stoesz et al. 2016). Thus, Ajo becomes a functional solution to family finance for the immigrant poor.

2.3 Methods and Approaches

I started this project in 2019. I reached out to clusters of Nigerian communities in Canada and the United States to conduct focus groups and found 100 interviewees. When this research actualized in March 2020, we were in the first wave of the COVID-19 pandemic. Since I conducted interviews at the beginning of the pandemic, I had to repeat the interviews for some respondents six months later, in August

Table 2.1 Nigerians interviewed about Ajo in Canada and the United States (2020)

	Women	Men	Total
Canada			
GTA	20	5	25
Montreal	12	0	12
Vancouver	8	3	11
Winnipeg	10	2	12
Total (Canada)	**50**	**10**	**60**
U.S.A.			
DMV	23	5	28
Kansas City	10	3	13
Philadelphia	7	2	9
Houston and Dallas	15	5	20
Total (U.S.A.)	**55**	**15**	**70**

2020. I did a second wave of interviews with respondents who expressed fear of the pandemic's impact on their Ajo communities. All of the interviews were conducted through WhatsApp, Skype, FaceTime, Zoom, and telephone calls, and I received ethical clearance to carry out my research remotely.

Between March 2020 and May 2020, I interviewed 130 Nigerian immigrants, sixty in Canada and seventy in the United States. Of the respondents in Canada, fifty were women and ten were men in the Greater Toronto Area (GTA), Montreal, Winnipeg, and Vancouver (see Table 2.1). Of the respondents in the United States, fifty-five were women and fifteen were men in the District of Columbia, Maryland, and Virginia (DMV) area, Kansas City, Philadelphia, Houston, and Dallas. These respondents belonged to different professions, from medical workers to administrative workers, information technology (IT) professionals, and entrepreneurs.

Questions asked during the interviews covered issues such as the general reason for joining an Ajo group, the incidences and consequences of default in payment, the possibility of continuing with an Ajo, the benefits of using Ajo, the confidence level people have in Ajo, how Ajo groups are created, the introduction of new members, Ajo in the COVID-19 era, and the specific reasons these participants chose to adopt the traditional Ajo system in countries with loan and credit card systems like Canada and the United States.

With over 200 million living in Nigeria, there is great diversity in terms of how people use Ajo, and these various uses and mechanics continue as people relate and move to other places. The Ajo groups were defined along group inclinations, meaning that members joined an Ajo through, for example, a church or a mosque. Other groups were made up of colleagues or people in similar professional fields: for example, nurses, hairdressers, personal support workers (PSW), IT professionals, bankers, or entrepreneurs. Many of the Nigerians I interviewed used electronic systems to carry out their Ajo payments via e-Interac, CashApp, and Zelle. By using these electronic systems, ROSCAs adapt their mechanisms to new systems yet maintain the core of how they function (Lehmann and Smets 2019). Since Ajo is not a cash system, group members did not have to be in the same state, city, or province, but were made up of professionals in similar jobs. For Ajo groups that spanned different vocations and professions, the members were all employed. This stable employment guaranteed members could make payments when they were due and greatly reduced the risk of default.

2.4 Using Ajo to Counteract Racial Capitalism

In the nineteenth century, Africans were viewed as inferior because they did not document history in a written form that Europeans could understand. Despite the prevalence of Africans' oral tradition, the fact that many African experiences before European trade and colonialism lacked documenation caused Europeans to view African practices as old traditions (Rea 2013). African social order and history were to a great extent denied (Rodney 1981; Robinson 1983). African tradition and history were then forced to subscribe to being anglicized (Iyasere 1975). Through a deliberate distortion of history to suit the fairy tale that benefited the colonialists and oppressors (Du Bois 1935), racism has thus thrived under capitalism from slavery to the current state of racial economic inequality.

Political scientist Cedric Robinson (1983) explains that racial capitalism has denied African Americans opportunities because of their race and that Marxist counter ideas do not resolve the racism within the economic systems. The capitalist economic system and its critique fail to engage with the history of enslavement and forced use of Black labor in the market. In fact, capitalism has been reproduced to extract value from the racially disadvantaged, especially Black people (Robinson 1983). This racial capitalism has excluded Black people in such a way that they are kept in a racially oppressive position that makes it easy to extort social and economic values from them. Nigerian immigrants in Canada and the United States experience the short end of the stick of racial capitalism because of the color of their skin. However, through the application of the Black radicalism framework, we focus on the largely ignored activities and cultures that Africans and enslaved people passed on through the years before the European invasion. This includes the Ajo culture.

There is also the issue of the systemic association of dark skin with enslavement and inferiority that is prevalent in these societies, which has affected how Black people are perceived and employed (Lavalley and Robinson Johnson 2020). Nigerian immigrants to Canada and the United States move to North America for many reasons, such as searching for a better life or reuniting with family. When these Nigerian immigrants get to Canada and the United States, they encounter racism for the first time. This has been made worse with the resurgence in white nationalism that came with the 2016 U.S. election (Tenold 2018). These Nigerian immigrants are now defined as Black and inferior, an experience that many did not encounter in Nigeria. As a way to cope and settle into their new society, Nigerians draw on familiar systems like Ajo as a tool for creating connectedness and pushing against exclusion.

Ajo is a centuries-old mutual aid and cooperative system created by Nigerian women (Fasoranti 2010). It is an offshoot of a pre-colonial money system that was based on services and farming. With the vast arable land Nigeria possesses, farming was prevalent before colonialism and before the discovery of oil (Inikori 2013). Nigeria became annexed by the British in 1861, and farming increased from producing for subsistence to producing cash crops for trade (Floye and Ekpoh 2007). Ownership of land, thus farms, was restricted to men. However, wives and children were responsible for farm activities, such as sowing and reaping. This led to men marrying multiple wives to have many children so they had enough women and children to work on their farmlands. As a result, agriculture-induced marriages became the predominant practice (Patel and Anthonio 1974; Ibrahim 2020).

Women discovered the power of community and how much they could achieve if they worked together. The women contributed services to farming projects through a rotation system. This meant that members of a community farming unit rotated their services among each other's farms during planting and harvesting seasons (Nwabughuogu 1984). By rotating services among their husbands' farms, women eased their workload, sped up the process of planting and harvesting, and also fostered friendships and relationships that benefitted them in other areas. The model worked so well that it was adopted by other services, such as construction. Eventually, it became the monetary system we recognize today as Ajo.

Ajo has evolved through the years from farming to the digitalized system, and the practical way it is carried out makes it easy for it to be adopted in the diaspora (Josiah 2004; Stoesz et al. 2016). Its success within Nigeria has led to it being modeled outside Nigeria by Nigerian immigrants in different countries. In Nigeria, Ajo has been popularized as an alternative to the discriminatory system of colonial formal banking. The high interest rates and discriminatory system of microfinance institutions (Izugbara 2004; Hossein 2016) contributed to the Ajo system continuing through the years. Similarly, Nigerian immigrants in the United States and Canada adopt Ajo as a coping mechanism against the racial discrimination and racial wealth inequality they and other Black immigrants experience in these countries. This includes a system of racial income inequality that gives Black immigrants the short end of the stick and a social structure that makes integration more difficult for Black immigrants in Eurocentric societies (Este 2008; Borch and Corra 2010; Painter and Qian 2016a, 2016b). Also, immigrants need systems that provide nurturing and nostalgia for a home-away-from-home experience (Light and Bonacich 1988). Ajo networks provide this experience for Black immigrants. However, it takes more than all these to build and continue Ajo communities in new settlements of migration. From my interviews, I discovered that Nigerian immigrants draw from their lived experiences or the lived experiences of people they knew in Nigeria and then use these to recreate their communities in their new settlements.

Racism is a barrier to successful integration in society. Despite Nigerians being one of the most educated immigrant groups in Canada and the United States, the Nigerian immigrant experience is not devoid of racism and exclusion (Imoagene 2017). In recent times, these have been worsened by overt displays of racism and white superiority. American lawmakers famously quoted former president Trump as stating, "Why are we having all these people from shithole countries come here?" (Dawsey 2018). This brazen display of racism towards immigrants from the number one citizen of the land included Nigeria. This overt verbal attack on Nigerian immigrants is one of the many issues they have to deal with in trying to settle in a foreign land. Others include housing segregation that prevents immigrants from assimilating (Vang 2012); deterrents in homeownership (Mundra and Oyelere 2018); the struggle to find a suitable job, which leads to the deskilling of labor (Creese and Wiebe 2012, Ette 2012); and the complex struggles they face in trying to recognize and redefine their social and work-related identities in the face of a complex social hierarchy (George and Selimos 2019).

These experiences are made worse through white supremacy that puts the onus of integration and incorporation on the racialized immigrants while ignoring the racial barriers (Treitler 2015). Having a responsibility to integrate despite the many racial barriers, Nigerian immigrants turn to the age-old Ajo system as a solution. Through Ajo, Nigerian immigrants gain access to bulk finances to invest in different avenues—such as financial instruments, businesses, and down payments for houses—that aid their incorporation into new societies.

2.5 The Use of Cooperativism through Ajo during a Pandemic

In March 2020, COVID-19 was declared a global pandemic by the World Health Organization (Spinelli and Pellino 2020). This led to a global panic about the economic consequences of the pandemic and the ensuing lockdown (Nicola et al. 2020). From the first wave of interviews that I conducted in March 2020, I discovered that Nigerian immigrants, like many people, were worried about the pandemic's economic impact on their livelihood and finances. One of the respondents in the United States, Mrs. Ade, expressed concern that the COVID-19 pandemic meant the physical church gatherings for her pooling community would have to stop, thus ending the continuous cycles of Ajo in her community. Mrs. Ade provided two reasons for her fear: first, the physical meetings were a gentle reminder for members to make their contributions, and second, a negative effect of the COVID-19 pandemic on the economy might translate into a loss of jobs for members in her Ajo group, affecting their ability to make biweekly payments. By the second wave of interviews in August 2020, not only did the cycles continue, but more hands were also offered. When asked why, she said that the only two people who had lost their jobs during the pandemic were helped by members of the Ajo community to get jobs as essential workers. Even though it meant a deskilling of their labor, it ensured they were able to "keep a roof over their heads." This shows that with Ajo, a person gets more than financial help: they also get a community where people look out for each other's welfare and success.

Although some of the Nigerian immigrants interviewed during the first wave of the COVID-19 pandemic expected a discontinuance of the Ajo cycles, the reality was the opposite—new hands and more groups were created by conveners. According to respondents, the increase in Ajo hands resulted from the pandemic's uncertainty, which made people in the Nigerian community realize the need to save for a rainy day. As a result, many people reduced their consumption so they could save more and reinvest. Five percent of the people interviewed said they downsized their accommodations to save more in case the pandemic's impact on their economic situations was greater than expected. However, the reasons for an increase in savings differed between Canada and the United States. While more Nigerian immigrants in the United States saved in case the expenses of their COVID-19-related medical needs increased, the Nigerian immigrants in Canada, who had government-provided healthcare, saved more to reinvest in markets that could be affected by the pandemic.

2.6 Findings: What Does Ajo Mean for Nigerian Immigrants in Canada and the United States?

I interviewed 130 people, about 80 percent of whom were women (see Table 2.1). In both countries, respondents provided similar reasons for joining Ajo groups. The main reason given was that it creates financial freedom that helps them navigate their way through the systemic blockages and exclusion that racism creates. About 50 percent of the respondents said they belonged to an Ajo group to raise bulk money to make a down payment on a house, which is a very common use of Ajo contributions (Mundra and Oyelere 2018). The other respondents said they belonged to Ajo groups to raise money to pay off car loans, travel costs, or credit card bills, or to start a new business or fund an existing business.

I also discovered that the reasons for being in an Ajo group changed in different time periods, depending on immigrants' stage of life. While some of the people being interviewed needed money to pay for first and last month's rent, others needed a car for their families or to start a small business. These people fell into the groups of Ajo contributors that made biweekly payments of between \$100 to \$250. The respondents with bigger needs, like a down payment on a house or funding a big business, belonged to groups that made biweekly payments over \$500. Depending on the urgency of their needs, some respondents belonged to more than one group. One respondent, Sola, belonged to two groups that made biweekly $500 payments. She said she had just bought a home in January 2020 but remained in the two Ajo groups because she wants to begin an automobile exporting business. She also told me that she relocated to Canada in 2010 in search of a better life and struggled economically for five years until a fellow Nigerian immigrant invited her to join her Ajo group. Through this group, she made connections that exposed her to better paying job opportunities, and she was also able to improve her credit rating enough to buy a house and live comfortably. Another respondent, "Chinwe," joined an Ajo community in the DMV with her husband and was able to save for their invitro fertilization. She said that after her baby was born, she received so much care from her Ajo groups that she referred to them as her "family in the U.S."

2.7 Business and Social Supports Embedded into Ajo among Immigrants

The group I interviewed in Kansas City named their Ajo group the Investment Club because people saw the coming together as a way of boosting their social standing and growing economically and socially. This Ajo had ten members who owned businesses such as restaurants and car dealerships. Each member paid $1,000 biweekly and the receipt was $10,000 per hand. When asked why they didn't make payments for their businesses or bills directly through a credit card or by saving in their bank accounts, respondents said that Ajo was a more convenient way of gaining capital without paying high interest rates. A member of the Investment Club, Seun, told me about an additional advantage of this Ajo group. Since they were all entrepreneurs, people were referred to the pool for goods and services rather than patronize "outsiders." He said that as a car salesman, he had sold at least five cars to Investment Club members. Like the other entrepreneurs in this particular group, Seun offers a "family discount" to Ajo group members. This way, they look out for each other and help to build the economic levels of the Nigerian immigrant community.

Ajo groups not only provide a community of like-minded people, but also ensure that they encourage each other through life, that they do not dip into their pockets and bank accounts at will or spend a lot on remittances. Remittances are a transfer of funds from foreign workers to people in their home country. They are an important outcome of the migration process and account for a large portion of the expenses of Nigerian immigrants. A great deal of research focuses on the recipients of remittances and the positive impacts on recipients (Osili 2008; Akanle and Adesina 2017). Many of those who send remittances are women who left their homes because of desperate economic conditions (Akinrinade and Ogen 2011). Twenty percent of the total respondents—21 women and 5 men—fell into this category of people working abroad to support their immediate families in Nigeria. They worked in the informal sector and had families back home that depended on them for everything from necessities to frivolities. The problem with this is that these women are forced to live in debt so that they can send these remittances home. Five of the women that I interviewed in the GTA shared similar stories of relocating to Canada to work and provide for their families back in Nigeria. They all admitted that prior to joining the Ajo club, they sent almost everything they made as remittances to Nigeria to different people and could barely put a roof over their heads in Canada until they joined their Ajo groups.

One of them in particular, "Tope," said that since joining an Ajo community, she realized she was actually making more than enough money to survive and still send some remittances home. Prior to this, she was in various forms of debt to survive while her husband threw parties in Nigeria with all the remittances she sent home. In her words, "I am glad I joined this Ajo because I did not know how hard I was working and how much I was being exploited. Now I am almost debt free, and I sleep better at night." Through her Ajo group, she was able to manage her finances better.

Overall, every person interviewed spoke well of the Ajo communities they belonged to. This suggests the possibility of almost no cases of default among Ajo communities in Canada and the United States. While some members had defaulted, the community bond built made members patient with each other. One Ajo convener in the United States known as "Alhaja" said that she limits default risks by finding commonalities, usually in occupation, and ensuring that members in her groups are legal immigrants who can work. She, like other conveners interviewed, create groups based on people's abilities and their need. They also build groups based on trust, and any new member has to have an existing and trusted member to act as a guarantor for them. When asked if she created groups along tribal or religious lines, "Alhaja" said,

> Religion or tribe are issues we deal with in Nigeria. Here, the white people see the Black skin first before any other thing. So, I focus on the individual's stage in life and their needs. Outside Nigeria, we are first Black, but since we are not fully accepted as Black by Black Americans because of our different lived experiences, we are Nigerian, not Igbo, Yoruba or Hausa. So, I do not create groups based on the very things that divided us back home. At best, I create groups based on the commonalities of occupation.

Another convener in Canada, "Iya Ibeji," said that she has had only six defaulters in ten years of running various Ajo groups because she makes groups based on commonalities. People who could not meet up with the payments came to her with their reasons, and they made arrangements to pay in the next round. According to her, "Brothers and sisters have to look out for each other since we all came here midway through our lives and have to compete with those who have been here for years." Natural-born citizens get a head start in the relay journey of life, one that immigrants have to find ways to close the gap in order to avoid poverty, which includes changing accents and even names (Smith and Ley 2008; Abramitzky and Boustan 2017). Ajo provides a way for Nigerian immigrants to help each other close that gap while still keeping their identities and names. These two Ajo conveners, "Alhaja" and "Iya Ibeji," interview people to know what their income level can accommodate and what groups to put them in. Their overall goal is to help the people in the Nigerian communities grow economically and socially in the face of many limitations, like the Banker ladies in the Caribbean (Hossein 2013).

I found out that the people involved in Ajo are mostly women of various ages and occupations. Despite the possibility of default, respondents still trust the Ajo system over the formal financial credit system because of the burden of debt they accrued as new immigrants, with sudden access to credit that was not available to them in Nigeria. Seventy percent of respondents I interviewed said that their credit was affected by the lure of loans and credit cards to new immigrants. They had to go back to the old and trusted credit system they grew up with, Ajo, to pay off their loans, fix their credit ratings, and work toward a more secure financial future. Therefore, pooling resources is beneficial to members of an Ajo, as it helps fund their different projects. It also has the added benefit of injecting savings back into the Nigerian community and the economy at large.

Finally, this research brought to light a very important point about the use of Ajo among Nigerian immigrants in Canada and the United States. This had to do with the sentimental reasons for joining or creating an Ajo group. Even though 40 percent of respondents had never joined Ajo in Nigeria before migrating, they had close families and friends who had engaged in Ajo back home. However, in addition to the need for a community and their personal reasons, respondents joined an Ajo community for the pro-Nigerian feeling it gave them. One respondent, Hauwa, said it makes her feel closer to home, and she loves the opportunity to speak her native dialect with people from her homeland. She said that as an immigrant nurse, she had to conform to an anglicized pronunciation of her name, deal with many natural-born Americans who could not understand her experience as an immigrant at work, and conform to the American standard. However, at her Ajo group events, she meets a community of people with whom she can be herself. She also said that in the Philadelphia suburb where she lives and works, she has to tone down what she calls her "Nigerianness," so being introduced to her Ajo group by a former schoolmate allowed her to "feel at home." Thus, being a member of an Ajo community contributes to the home-away-from-home experience and makes members feel closer to their roots.

2.8 Conclusion: Ajo as a Way to Help Black Migrants Live and Thrive

The age-old Ajo financial system is one that Nigerians in Nigeria and the diaspora are familiar with, either first hand or through the involvement of people close to them. In Nigeria, Ajo is used to circumvent discrimination in formal banking and as a system of communal financial aid. In Canada and the United States, Nigerian immigrants adopt Ajo as a way of bypassing systemic racism and the financial limitations new immigrants face as well as an avenue that helps Nigerian immigrants incorporate themselves into their new countries. It speaks to the resilience of Nigerians and their ability to keep pushing in the face of discrimination of any kind. For Nigerian immigrants, racism is a new concept they only experience when they relocate. They realize they are "Black" and suddenly experience the racial capitalism common to Blacks in Canada and the United States. Since the onus of integration falls on the immigrant, Nigerian immigrants turn to fellow immigrants with similar experiences for survival. Together, they turn to tested and trusted Nigerian ways of surviving discrimination and building from within. Thus, Ajo is used by Nigerian immigrants in Canada and the United States to survive systemic racism and aid their integration into their new countries.

Nigerian women are particularly at the forefront of Ajo practices. They are used to the discrimination of patriarchy in Nigeria and have relied on the communal help system of Ajo since the pre-colonial ages of subsistence farming in Nigeria. The Ajo conveners I talked to spoke more about the positive outcomes from the Ajo than the problems Nigerian immigrants face in Canada and the United States. They were more solution-oriented, which was evident in how they set up groups based on the needs of the people and the testimonials of the participants in these groups. As a result, they successfully created Nigerian immigrant communities that transcend monetary gains. Through these groups, Nigerian immigrants have been able to reclaim a heritage that years of European invasion and voluntary migration to the West have interrupted. They recreated communities they are familiar with and that have been passed on from generation to generation while helping each other in the process. These women are creating a system that puts people first by including and helping people excluded by racial capitalism to thrive.

Ajo helps Nigerian immigrants bypass a discriminatory formal system and achieve the financial growth they could not achieve otherwise. The same system of pooling resources for community aid that has been used in Nigeria has been adopted in Canada and the United States. As immigrants, Nigerians do not have the beginner's advantage that natural-born citizens do. Ajo helps remove some of the hurdles in the race toward settlement and growth. The practice of Ajo among Nigerian immigrants is thus a statement of pan-Africanism that creates an experience Indigenous to Africa in a foreign land while closing the gap in growth that immigrants face.

Works Cited

Abbott, C. 2006. "Nigerians in North America: New Frontiers, Old Associations." In K. Konadu-Agyemang, B. K. Takyi, and J. A. Arthur (eds.), *The New African Diaspora in North America*, 141–65. Washington, DC: Lexington Books.

Abramitzky, R. and L. Boustan. 2017. “Immigration in American Economic History.” *Journal of Economic Literature* 55(4): 1311–45.

Adebayo, A. 1994. “Money, Credit, and Banking in Precolonial Africa: The Yoruba Experience.” *Anthropos* 89(4): 379–400.

Agrawal, S. 2013. “Economic Disparities among South Asian Immigrants in Canada.” *South Asian Diaspora* 5(1): 7–34.

Akanle, O. and J. O. Adesina. 2017. “International Migrants’ Remittances and Kinship Networks in Nigeria: The Flip-Side Consequences.” *Journal of Anthropological Research* 73(1): 66–91.

Akinrinade, S. and O. Ogen. 2011. “Historicising the Nigerian Diaspora: Nigerian Migrants and Homeland Relations.” *Turkish Journal of Politics* 2(2): 71–85.

American Community Survey. 2019. “Place of Birth for the Foreign-Population in the United States.” https://data.census.gov/cedsci/table?q=ACSDT5YAIAN2015.B05006&g=0100000US&tid=ACSDT1Y2019.B05006. Accessed December 5, 2020.

Ardener, S. and S. Burman. 1995. *Money-Go-Rounds: The Importance of Rotating Savings and Credit Associations for Women*. Oxford: Berg.

Bauder, H. 2003. “‘Brain Abuse’, or the Devaluation of Immigrant Labour in Canada.” *Antipode* 35(4): 699–717.

Borch, C. and M. Corra. 2010. “Differences in Earnings among Black and White African Immigrants in the United States, 1980–2000: A Cross-Sectional and Temporal Analysis.” *Sociological Perspectives* 53(4): 573–92.

Card, D. and S. Raphael (eds.) 2013. *Immigration, Poverty, and Socioeconomic Inequality*. New York: Russell Sage Foundation.

Carney, J. 1845 [1995]. “Little Things.” In Martin Gardner (ed.), *Famous Poems from Bygone Days*, 36. New York: Dover Publications.

Creese, G. and B. Wiebe. 2012. “‘Survival Employment’: Gender and Deskilling among African Immigrants in Canada.” *International Migration* 50(5): 56–76.

Dawsey, J. 2018. “Trump Derides Protections for Immigrants from ‘Shithole’ Countries.” *Washington Post*, January 12.

De Bustillo, R. M. and J. Antón. 2011. “From Rags to Riches?: Immigration and Poverty in Spain.” *Population Research and Policy Review* 30(5): 661.

Du Bois, W. E. B. 1935. “Inter-Racial Implications of the Ethiopian Crisis: A Negro View.” *Foreign Affairs* 14(1): 82–92.

Este, D. 2008. “Black Canadian Historical Writing 1970–2006: An Assessment.” *Journal of Black Studies* 38(3): 388–406.

Ette, E. U. 2012. *Nigerian Immigrants in the United States*. Washington DC: Lexington Books.

Fasoranti, M. M. 2010. “The Influence of Micro-Credit on Poverty Alleviation among Rural Dwellers: A Case Study of Akoko North West Local Government Area of Ondo State.” *African Journal of Business Management* 4(8): 1438–46.

Floye, B. N. and I. Ekpoh. 2007. "Transforming Traditional Agriculture: Historical Background to Modern Agricultural Development in Nigeria." *Global Journal of Social Sciences* 6(2): 97–102.

Galabuzi, G. 2006. *Canada's Economic Apartheid: The Social Exclusion of Racialized Groups in the New Century*. Toronto: Canadian Scholars Press.

George, G. and E. D. Selimos. 2019. "Searching for Belonging and Confronting Exclusion: A Person-Centred Approach to Immigrant Settlement Experiences in Canada." *Social Identities* 25(2): 125–40.

Greiner, M. E. and H. Wang. 2010. "Building Consumer-To-Consumer Trust in E-Finance Marketplaces: An Empirical Analysis." *International Journal of Electronic Commerce* 15(2): 105–36.

Hossein, C. S. 2013. "The Black Social Economy: Perseverance of Banker Ladies In The Slums." *Annals of Public and Co-operative Economics* 84(4): 423–42.

Hossein, C. S. 2016. *Politicized Microfinance: Money, Power, and Violence in the Black Americas*. Toronto: University of Toronto Press.

Hossein, C. S. 2018. *The Black Social Economy in the Americas: Exploring Diverse Community-Based Alternative Markets*. Edited collection. New York: Palgrave Macmillan.

Ibrahim, F. M. 2020. "Tracking Agriculture-Induced Fertility among Yorùbá Farmers of Southwestern Nigeria." *Issues in Ethnology and Anthropology* 15(2): 533–549.

Imoagene, O. 2017. *Beyond Expectations: Second-Generation Nigerians in the United States and Britain*. Oakland: University of California Press.

Inikori, J. E. 2013. "The Development of Commercial Agriculture in Pre-Colonial West Africa." *African Economic History Network Paper Series 9: Stockholm, Sweden*, 1–40.

Iyasere, S. 1975. "Oral Tradition in the Criticism of African Literature." *Journal of Modern African Studies* 13(1): 107–19.

Izugbara, C. O. 2004. "Gendered Micro-Lending Schemes and Sustainable Women's Empowerment in Nigeria." *Community Development Journal* 39(1): 72–84.

Josiah, B. P. 2004. "Creating Worlds: A Study of Mutuality and Financing among African Guyanese, 1800s–1950s." *Journal of Caribbean History* 38(1): 106–27.

Kirwin, M. and J. Anderson. 2018. "Identifying the Factors Driving West African Migration." *West African Papers* 17: 1–21.

Kómoláfé, J. 2002. "Searching for Fortune: The Geographical Process of Nigerian Migration to Dublin, Ireland." *Ìrìnkèrindò: A Journal of African Migration* 1(1): 1–17.

Lai, D. W. L., L. Li, and G. D. Daoust. 2017. "Factors Influencing Suicide Behaviours in Immigrant and Ethno-Cultural Minority Groups: A Systematic Review." *Journal of Immigrant and Minority Health* 19(3): 755–68.

Lavalley, R. and K. R. Johnson. 2020. "Occupation, Injustice, and Anti-Black Racism in the United States of America." *Journal of Occupational Science*: 1–13.

Lehmann, J. and P. Smets. 2019. "An Innovative Resilience Approach: Financial Self-Help Groups in Contemporary Financial Landscapes in the Netherlands." *Environment and Planning A: Economy and Space* 52(5): 898–915.

Light, I. and E. Bonacich. 1988. *Immigrant Entrepreneurs: Koreans in Los Angeles.* Berkeley: University of California Press.

Maynard, E. 1996. "The Translocation of a West African Banking System: The Yoruba Esusu Rotating Credit Association In The Anglophone Caribbean." *Dialectical Anthropology* 21(1): 99–107.

Mundra, K. and R. U. Oyelere. 2018. "Determinants of Homeownership among Immigrants: Changes during the Great Recession and Beyond." *International Migration Review* 52(3): 648–94.

Nicola, M., Z. Alsafi, C. Sohrabi, A. Kerwan, A. Al-Jabir, C. Iosifidis, M. Agha, and R. Agha. 2020. "The Socio-Economic Implications of the Coronavirus Pandemic (COVID-19): A Review." *International Journal of Surgery* 78: 185–93.

Nwabughuogu, A. I. 1984. "The Isusu: An Institution for Capital Formation among the Ngwa Igbo: Its Origin and Development to 1951." *Africa* 54(4): 46–58.

Ogunrinola, O. and O. Ewetan. 2005 "Informal Savings and Economic Status of Rural Women in Nigeria." *Journal of Economic and Financial Studies* 2(1): 10–26.

Ogwezi, J. O. 2016. "Women in Traditional Banking in Africa: The Nigerian Experience." *Journal of Social and Management Sciences* 1(1): 118–23.

Oloyede, J. A. 2008. "Informal Financial Sector, Savings Mobilization and Rural Development in Nigeria: Further Evidence from Ekiti State of Nigeria." *African Economic and Business Review* 6(1): 35–63.

Osili, U. O. 2008. "Understanding Migrants' Remittances: Evidence from the US–Nigeria Migration Survey." *Africa's Finances: The Contribution of Remittances* 57(77): 57–77.

Painter, M. A. and Z. Qian. 2016a. "Wealth Inequality Among New Immigrants." *Sociological Perspectives* 59(2): 368–94.

Painter, M. A. and Z. Qian. 2016b. "Wealth Inequality Among Immigrants: Consistent Racial/Ethnic Inequality in the United States." *Population Research and Policy Review* 35(2): 147–75.

Patel, A. U. & Anthonio, Q. B. O. 1974. "Farmers' Wives in Agricultural Development: The Nigeria Case," *International Journal of Agrarian Affairs*, International Association of Agricultural Economists, 1–14.

Raddatz, C. 2003. *Liquidity Needs and Vulnerability to Financial Underdevelopment.* Washington, D. C: The World Bank.

Rea, W. 2013. "'Our Tradition is a very Modern Tradition': From Cultural Tradition to Popular Culture in Southwestern Nigeria." In Stephanie Newell and Onookome Okome (eds.), *Popular Culture in Africa: The Episteme of the Everyday*, 47–66. Florence: Routledge.

Rikko, L. S. and D. Gwatau. 2011. "The Nigerian Architecture: The Trend in Housing Development." *Journal of Geography and Regional Planning* 4(5): 273–8.

Robinson, C. J. 1983. *Black Marxism: The Making of the Black Radical Tradition*, 2nd edn. London: Zed Press.

Robinson, C. J. 2019. *Cedric Robinson: On Racial Capitalism, Black Internationalism, and Cultures of Resistance*, edited by H. L. T. Quan. London: Pluto Books.

Rodney, W. 1981. *A History of the Guyanese Working People, 1881–1905*. London: Heinemann Books.

Root, J., E. Gates-Gasse, J. Shields, and H. Bauder. 2014. "Discounting Immigrant Families: Neoliberalism and the Framing of Canadian Immigration Policy Change." Ryerson Centre for Immigration & Settlement (RCIS) Working Paper No 7.

Smith, H. and D. Ley. 2008. "Even in Canada? The Multiscalar Construction and Experience of Concentrated Immigrant Poverty in Gateway Cities." *Annals of the Association of American Geographers* 98(3): 686–713.

Spinelli, A. and G. Pellino. 2020. "COVID-19 Pandemic: Perspectives on an Unfolding Crisis." *British Journal of Surgery* 107(7): 785–7.

Statistics Canada. 2016. "Immigrant Population by Selected Places of Birth, Admission Category and Period of Immigration, Canada, Provinces and Territories, Census Metropolitan Areas and Areas Outside of Census Metropolitan Areas, 2016 Census." https://www12.statcan.gc.ca/census-recensement/2016/dp-pd/dv-vd/imm/index-eng.cfm. Accessed December 5, 2020.

Stoesz, D., I. Gutau, and R. Rodreiguez. 2016. "Susu: Capitalizing Development from the Bottom Up." *Journal of Sociology & Social Welfare* 43(3): 121.

Tenold, V. 2018. *Everything You Love Will Burn: Inside the Rebirth of White Nationalism in America*. New York: Bold Type Books.

Treitler, V. B. 2015. "Social Agency and White Supremacy in Immigration Studies." *Sociology of Race and Ethnicity* 1(1): 153–65.

Vang, Z. M. 2012. "The Limits of Spatial Assimilation for Immigrants' Full Integration: Emerging Evidence from African Immigrants in Boston and Dublin." *ANNALS of the American Academy of Political and Social Science* 641(1): 220–46.

Williams, A., P. Kitchen, J. Randall, N. Muhajarine, B. Newbold, M. Gallina, and K. Wilson. 2015. "Immigrants' Perceptions of Quality of Life in Three Second-or Third-Tier Canadian Cities." *Canadian Geographer/Le Géographe Canadien* 59(4): 489–503.

World Bank. 2019. *Population Total—Nigeria*. https://data.worldbank.org/indicator/SP.POP.TOTL?locations=NG. Accessed December 5, 2020.

Zuberi, D. and M. Ptashnick. 2012. "In Search of a Better Life: The Experiences of Working Poor Immigrants in Vancouver, Canada." *International Migration* 50(s1): e60–e93.cs.

3
The Black Social Economy
Black American Women Using Susu and Cooperatives as Resistance

Tatiana Benjamin and Sharon D. Wright Austin

3.1 Introduction

Throughout the world, people in the Global South and North participate in rotating savings and credit associations (ROSCAs), which are also called money pools, giving circles, and Susus.[1] Although both men and women invest in these entities, we primarily focus on African and Caribbean women living in the United States in this chapter. Through ROSCAs, these women are able to save money, pool their resources, allocate money to each other, purchase necessities, and increase their wealth. These associations allow groups of people to pool their money as a method of reaping increased returns. Every month, each person contributes the same amount of money. Also, every month, one group member receives the untaxed funds, which are referred to as the "hand" (Hossein 2020). Thus, they allow members to avoid banking fees, loan interest, and bureaucracy (*Grio* staff 2011). After each group member has received funds, the group then decides whether any changes need to occur in terms of the composition of the group, amount of funds contributed, etc. These ROSCAs have been particularly useful in countries with either few banks and financial institutions or hostile banking institutions.

In this chapter, we examine Susus by Caribbean, African, and African American women in the United States. These women have also been referred to as "Banker Ladies" because of their ability to assist women disadvantaged by their immigrant status, credit history, racial identity, or socioeconomic status (Hossein 2016, 2018). For these reasons, these women encounter difficulties getting loans from American financial institutions. In recent years, women have established more sophisticated ROSCAs in the form of start-ups that are geared to women from all socioeconomic backgrounds. These ROSCAs also exist in rural and urban areas (Ardener and Burman 1995; Barclay et al. 2019).

Cooperation is a key factor for Black women in the United States because they continue to face marginalization along multiple lines. This includes racial and gender discrimination seen in the lack of adequate healthcare and lower wages. According

[1] We use the terms ROSCAs and Susu interchangeably in this chapter.

Tatiana Benjamin and Sharon D. Wright Austin, *The Black Social Economy*. In: *Beyond Racial Capitalism*. Edited by Caroline Shenaz Hossein, Sharon D. Wright Austin, and Kevin Edmonds, Oxford University Press. © Oxford University Press (2023). DOI: 10.1093/oso/9780192868336.003.0004

to the American Association of University Women (AAUW) the average family wealth for Black people is less than non-Black people of color (NBPOC) and white households. Last year, due to COVID-19 the unemployment rate for Black women rose from 5.4 to 12.7 percent, higher than all other racial and ethnic women (AAUW 2020). Black women also face disparities in access to adequate healthcare that are not absolved due an increase in socioeconomic status. For instance, "African American women are three to four times more likely to die from childbirth than non-Hispanic white women" (Chalhoub and Rimar 2018). Even as Black women advance economically and socially, they are still facing inadequate services that do not account for racial and gender disparities. Black women are more likely to have high blood pressure and live in areas that do not have adequate maternity wards (Chalhoub and Rimar 2018). Black women demonstrate that even when we account for economics, racism and sexism are still key factors. Both the wealth gap and disparities in the U.S. healthcare system demonstrate that racism has always been part of capitalism. Cedric Robinson's (1983 [2000]) racial capitalism theory highlights how an economic system seen as an equalizer was actually an internalized racial and economic system that continues to place African Americans on the margins.

As a theoretical framework, this research employs Hossein's (2013, 2018, 2019) concept of the Black social economy, Cedric Robinson's racial capitalism theory (1983 [2000]; see also Robinson 2019), and the concept of Black social capital (Orr 1999). We examine the benefits and risks associated with group financial empowerment efforts by focusing on ROSCAs in Brooklyn and Washington, D.C., through case study analysis of Black women-led Susus, ROSCAs, and cooperatives. In these cities, ROSCAs are a form of economic cooperation that assists women entrepreneurs—many of whom are immigrants, with poor or limited credit, low credit, or no credit—to invest funds and seek funding from banks. Women of various socioeconomic classes, including professional classes, also participate in ROSCAs (Ardener 2010). By examining this topic, we want to demonstrate how Black women pursue group-based initiatives and cooperatives to financially empower their communities. The main questions we consider are: How have Black women in America used Susus to their benefit? And what successes/challenges have they encountered when trying to do so?

3.2 Anti-Black Capitalist Racism in American Society

Anti-Black racism in the United States begins with the colonization of Indigenous land and the enslavement of African peoples. The arrival of European colonizers in the Americas during the seventeenth and eighteenth centuries resulted in the pillaging of land, mass murder, and the enslavement of African peoples in order to build an economic system dependent on their labor. During enslavement African descents were violently forced to work on plantations, picking cotton and growing tobacco for white slave masters. Even after the end of slavery, the exploitation of Black people continued into the nineteenth and twentieth centuries (Hogan 1984). Although freed Black people were no longer enslaved, white legislatures still determined and restricted their access to land, work, and profit through the implementation of Black codes. These codes limited access to voting, traveling, and jobs. Jim Crow laws extended Black codes into a system referred to as "separate but equal." This resulted in separate facilities such as restrooms, neighborhoods, schooling, access to loans, and legislation that attempted to block the right to vote. The socioeconomic ramifications of the Jim Crow era included banks refusing to provide loans for Black business owners.

The post-civil rights era ushered in a period of anti-Black racism anchored in color-blind ideology. Color-blind racism puts forward the idea that race is no longer a primary factor in the disadvantages African Americans face in this country. It acknowledges that race exists, but it refuses to see the structural ramifications of racism. Even in today's post-racial society, African Americans fare worse than their white, Latino, and Asian American counterparts. Current business models call for initiatives that increase minority ownership but do not eliminate the racial stratifications that reproduce racial and economic inequality faced by Black Americans (Nopper 2011). Yes, there is an increase in Black businesses through the U.S. Small Business Association (SBA), but African Americans still lag behind other minorities in the profits gained. In the 1960s, the SBA advanced initiatives that specifically targeted African American small businesses, but today their strategies and approaches center on all minorities. However, these strategies do not account for the fact that NBPOC have more economic capital than African Americans. Additionally, the SBA's distribution of loans allows the total offered to include "any combination of minorities, which includes white women" (Nopper 2011, 658). The results of the SBA stopping measures that specifically target Black communities has meant a decrease in Black-owned businesses. The practices of the SBA reflect how anti-Black racism results in the continuous cycle of political, social, and economic disenfranchisement experienced by African Americans.

However, Black people consistently create structures and systems to combat the restrictions imposed by white supremacist capitalist patriarchal institutions and structures (Hogan 1984). During the modern civil rights movement, Black people protested and created organizations that led to the overturn of *Plessy v. Ferguson* and the integration of the U.S. school systems. Organizations such as the Student Nonviolent Coordinating Committee (SNCC) were developed in order to combat segregation, gain the right to vote and political power, revitalize communities, and establish economic initiatives. Emily Stoper (1977, 15) described SNCC as an organization "not held together by a bureaucracy or bureaucratic incentives. Almost all of its members were activists in the field, and the office staff was kept a bare minimum." The lack of bureaucracy speaks to how Black people have consistently used the principles of cooperation to build what their communities needed. A non-hierarchical structure allowed everyone to provide input in the creation and governance of its two independent political parties, labor unions, agricultural cooperatives, and schools (Bond 2000). SNCC's organizing was not top down nor did it curry favour with white elected officials. It instead sought to work from within the member base and their communities.

A Black social economy is built on group-based initiatives and economics. It is tied to the survival that comes from within Black communities in order to combat racial, economic, and social exploitation by state and government agencies (Hossein 2018). A Black social economy ensures that Black people are not dependent on aid from the state but instead produce their own resources and funds. Black cooperative economics have served a number of purposes that include buying one's freedom, purchasing land to grow food, stopping the exploitation of inflated prices, and creating credit unions to provide loans because white banks refused to service African Americans (Gordon Nembhard 2014). More specifically, Black women have created cooperatives that provide resources and jobs and that address the racism and sexism they face. Activist Fannie Lou Hamer stated the following, "Guess what? We can't win the political struggle until we have economic independence. And how can we have economic independence? We have to own our own land, control our own food production—and we have to do it through co-ops" (Nzinga Ifateyo 2014). When Black people fight against inequality, whites then lock them out of the social economy. In order to survive, they have created a Black social economy. The following analysis of Susus and cooperatives demonstrates how Black women in the United States have used the principles of trust, solidarity, group collective organizing, and the pooling of resources to resist the consequences of market fundamentalism, anti-Blackness, and anti-immigration.

3.3 African Origins and the Usage of Rotating Savings and Credit Associations

Susu is one of the many African terms used to describe mutual aid and economic cooperation. Susus are formally known as ROSCAs. The term Susu and its practice originated in West Africa, some say Ghana and others say Nigeria or the Dahomey (Benin). The Yoruban term is Esusu and refers to the savings accumulated from the pooled money of several people (*Grio* staff 2020). In many countries, ROSCAs are the only financial option for individuals to access a lump sum of funds to invest in their projects because formal banks will not lend to them. By pooling their money with others, they possess the ability to bypass banks that have historically refused to lend money to women from their racial, immigrant, or class backgrounds.

In the United States, the growth of ROSCAs remains an unexplored research area because the focus has been in the Global South. But to what extent have American ROSCAs been influenced by citizens from other parts of the world who live in the United States? These ROSCAs utilize the same general concept but have different names, such as Equip and Idir in Ethiopia, Susu in Ghana, Hagbad or Ayuto in Somalia, Restourne in the Congo, Jangui in Cameroon, Esusu or Ajo in Nigeria, Itega in Kenya, Tontines in the francophone West Africa, Sandooq in the Sudan, Gama'yia in Egypt, Cheetu in Sri Lanka, Chits in India, Community in Pakistan, Hui in Vietnam, Arisan in Indonesia, Jou in Japan, or Kye in Korea (Hossein 2020, 355). In America, these groups are also referred to by the names given by diaspora communities, such as the Mexican Tanda, Peruvian Panderos, Bahamian Asousous, Bajan Lodge, Haitian Sol, Trinidadian Susu, Dominican Republic Sociedad, Guyana Box hand, or the South African Stokvel (*Grio* staff 2011; Mtshali 2017; Hossein 2018). Anthropolgist Faye V. Harrison (1988) argues that Jamaican "higglers" have invested in the Partner banks for their financial livelihood since slavery, and as a way of ensuring that they were providing for a people that were alienated in the society. Lastly, women in the extremely impoverished Cite Soleil area of Haiti invest in Sols to save money for needed purchases and to develop businesses (Hossein 2020, 356). As people move from these locations to major cities, they bring their own local habits and money systems to the United States.

More specifically, how do these American ROSCAs work? There is no one set way for these systems to operate. Some are biweekly, monthly, or weekly deposits, and the "hands" (deposits) can be small or large. The period of time is fixed and decided by the group (Gigante 2017). The group selects a treasurer who collects the funds, selects the date(s) funds will be distributed (unless members have requested that they receive their hand on a certain date), and determines the amount to be contributed and by whom (Mtshali 2017). ROSCAs operate through consensus and voting, which are key principles of a democratic society in which Black people are on the outskirts. ROSCAs address the failures of capitalism and democracy by creating a space that is equitable and accessible regardless of class, gender, or racial status. Members also have the option of doubling their contribution and receiving two hands in one cycle (Mtshali 2017). A "fund manager" then distributes the hand to a different contributor every month until the pool is empty (Hossein 2020). The "banker" also takes responsibility for when a member does not pay their hand. The "banker" will pay the missed hand if a member of the circle does not (Faber and Friedline 2020). One analyst described the process in this way, "If 12 people put $1,000 in, 12 people get $1,000 back, with zero interest paid or earned. For those who receive their lump sum early in the distribution cycle, it's an interest-free loan. For those who get their share toward the end, it's a form of forced savings" (Mtshali 2017).

Viewing the Susu as forced savings is important when we considered the unpaid labor performed by Black women. Both married and single Black women are usually the primary caregivers in their families. They are also paid less than their male counterparts, white women, and NBPOC, which can make it difficult to save when bills are piling up and caring for family members becomes a burden. In these circumstances, a forced savings allows Black women to care for themselves when daily and familial financial commitments do not allow. Susus have also been described as similar to an insurance policy because something has to happen before you reap the benefits.

Receiving permanent residency as an immigrant still does not provide all the benefits of citizenship. Black immigrant women are often stuck in low-wage jobs that do not allow for social or economic mobility. Being able to be part of a Susu has allowed immigrant women in the United States to gain the funds to place a down payment on their first home or start a small business or economic cooperative.

3.4 Methods and Approach

This article uses case study analysis that examines how Black women in the United States employ ROSCA strategies to create community and combat racial capitalism. The term Susu can be spelled in various ways, and we use the spelling commonly used among the diaspora. We use newspaper clippings and public interviews to examine how Marie Lumen Clersaint and Fonta Gilliam have used Susus to aid Black women in saving, advancing financially, and creating initiatives that also combat the socioeconomic disparities faced by Black communities. We examine how these two Black cooperatives employ group voice and shared resources to create sustainable wealth and financial systems. Analyzing how Black women use Susus and cooperatives to gain economic stability demonstrates how they are able to gain social and political power. The ROSCA emphasis on autonomy from American institutions, shared responsibility, and trust has been used to push against racial capitalism.

3.5 The U.S. Context: The Business of Exclusion of Black Americans

Traditionally, discrimination toward African Americans has also included Black immigrants. After arriving in America, these immigrants are classified as Black because of an antiquated one drop rule that defines every individual with even the slightest drop of Black blood as Black (Austin 2018, 21). In this sense, Black means African American.

Racial capitalism relegates Black people to the bottom of the economic ladder by embedding racism in America's laws and policies. African Americans have attempted to build wealth since the earliest days of America's origin. Yet, blatant and suble forms of resistance have impeded their efforts

> beginning with 246 years of chattel slavery and followed by Congressional mismanagement of the Freedman's Savings Bank (which left 61,144 depositors with losses of nearly $3 million in 1874), the violent massacre decimating Tulsa's Greenwood District in 1921 (a population of 10,000 that thrived as the epicenter of African American business and culture, commonly referred to as "Black Wall Street"), and

> discriminatory policies throughout the 20th century including the Jim Crow Era's "Black Codes" strictly limiting opportunity in many southern states, the GI bill, [and] the New Deal's Fair Labor Standards Act's exemption of domestic agricultural and service occupations. (McIntosh et al. 2020)

Throughout history, African Americans have also been disadvantaged by redlining—an illegal practice of denying bank loans to individuals seeking mortgages for properties in areas with large Black populations or to African American applicants generally (Satter 2009). During President Franklin Delano Roosevelt's New Deal administration, the Federal Housing Administration (FHA) (1934) and the Home Owners' Loan Corporation (HOLC) (1933) were created to provide opportunities of homeownership through the allocation of mortgage loans. However, these federal policies deprived African Americans of these loans and therefore of homeownership (Rheingold et al. 2001). The HOLC encouraged redlining through its categorization of neighborhoods as being good and bad risks for mortgage loans. The lowest category was coded with the color red and was usually applied to African American areas (Massey and Denton 1993). After these areas were redlined, it was virtually impossible for applicants desiring to purchase properties there to receive loans.

The FHA also contributed to this discrimination. It only awarded mortgages to "financially stable applicants"—that is, those buying newer properties in "racially stable" (translation white) neighborhoods (Massey and Denton 1993, 54). In support of this practice, the FHA strongly supported racially restrictive covenants that barred Jewish people and people of color from owning property in certain areas (Jones-Correa 2000–1). These agreements preserved the racial homogeneity of neighborhoods and their property values. Most FHA loans went to white families buying homes in the suburbs (Massey and Denton 1993). The U.S. Supreme Court invalidated these covenants in the 1948 *Shelley v. Kraemer* decision (Jones-Correa 2000–1, 5). The United States officially banned the practice of redlining in 1968 (Hackett 2020).

Unfortunately, discriminatory practices persist in today's banking industry in a subtler form of redlining known as fringe banking. Law Professor Mehrsa Baradan points out that the failure of the banking industry lies in the fact that large banks are able to get a bailout while underfunded and underserved communities are forced to fend for themselves. For the past 30 years, the banking industry has been able to operate unregulated and commit to their bottom line of profit. Deregulation has resulted in the failure of community banks and resulted in fringe banking. The fringe banking system is a muddy process of borrowing that charges high interest rates that leaves you in a cycle of borrowing that can take a decade to pay off. Low- and middle-income wage earners are usually those exploited—for example, when a sudden health crisis or loss of job makes it difficult for them to pay a bill. Before long they need to borrow another short-term loan with high interest to pay back the previous loan. Banking is a system that continues to privilege the rich and exploits the poor. People who have less money are forced to use alternatives to banking that can result in higher fees that take years to pay off (Barandarn 2015).

In 2020, the government distributed loans to small businesses for assistance during the period of their closure during the COVID-19 pandemic. The Paycheck Protection Program (PPP) awarded loans to "sole proprietorships." However, African American and Hispanic small business owners were the last to receive them (Hackett 2020). Class action lawsuits also have recently alleged racially discriminatory banking practices. In 2017, a California class-action lawsuit alleged that Wells Fargo employees opened accounts and lines of credit in the names of undocumented immigrants without their consent and then charged them fees on the closed accounts they never authorized (Faber and Friedline 2020). Wells Fargo was fined over $100 million for these practices, and had previously received a $1 billion fine associated with their discriminatory auto insurance and mortgage lending practices in 2018. Finally, J. P. Morgan and Chase settled a $55 million racial discrimination lawsuit that accused lenders of charging higher mortgage interest rates for African American and Hispanic borrowers (Faber and Friedline 2020).

Other less obvious forms of banking discrimination have also been evident. Banks have disproportionately opened and operated branches in white communities both nationally and within metropolitan areas. Between 2009 and 2014, banks closed at higher rates in majority minority areas, with some Black and Hispanic communities losing half their branches (Faber and Friedline 2020). In an article entitled "The Racialized Costs of Banking," the author points out,

> The uneven distribution of bank branch locations exacts a cost on residents of communities of colour in the forms of greater travel distance and time to the nearest banking facility. These practices also create "banking deserts" in which payday lenders, check cashers, and other non-bank services thrive, thereby implicating banks in facilitating a market dynamic whereby the financial services environments in communities of colour are dramatically different—in terms of quality and expense—from those in white communities. (Faber and Friedline 2020)

Both Black immigrants and naturalized citizens have been the target of the United States' discriminatory and anti-Black practices. American anti-Blackness against Black immigrants is present in former president Donald Trump's anti-Black and anti-immigrant statements. He referred to Haiti, El Salvador, and African countries as "shithole" countries (Kendi 2019). Ibram Kendi reminds us that it was not just a verbal offense but also reflective of America's racial hierarchy. Kendi states, "He placed whites over Asians, and both over Latinos and Blacks from 'shithole' countries" (Kendi 2019). America's racial hierarchy places Black immigrants outside of the social economy. Additionally, Trump's comments are a response to the immigrant rights movements, specifically Black immigrants. Racial capitalism is afraid of radicalism. The Black Lives Movement is rooted in the Black radical tradition of resistance. Black immigrant issues have been a key component of this contemporary fight for Black rights. Trump's verbal attack is part of the larger goal of racial capitalism that seeks to eliminate any form of activism in order to maintain the racial and labor hierarchy.

The Muslim Ban targeted both Middle Eastern and African refugees by not allowing entry for up to 120 days. The first Muslim Ban in 2017 included Iran, Iraq, Libya, Somalia, Syrian, Sudan, and Yemen. In 2020 Trump targeted more African countries, including Nigeria and Eretria, by refusing new immigrant visas. The Muslim Advocates group issued a statement on February 20, 2020, directly addressing the anti-Blackness of the Muslim Ban:

> America is a nation where people of all races and religions are entitled to equal protection under the law, yet the expanded Muslim Ban is another attack on the rights, the dignity and the identity of Black communities. As the expanded Muslim Ban includes people from Nigeria, Eritrea, Somalia, Sudan, Tanzania and Libya, even more Black families will needlessly suffer from a policy with no legitimate justification. (Muslim Advocates 2020)

Donald Trump's policies align with a longer history of immigration policy and reform that locks out and punishes Black immigrants. Black (un)documented immigrants are kept in low-paying jobs, detained, and deported at higher rates than other immigrants of color. His statements also reflect racial capitalism theory because African immigrants are regulated to the bottom of the social and economic ladder in order for whiteness to maintain its power and privileges. This reinforces white supremacist ideas of Black people being disposable and at the same time extracting material wealth from African territories. The Muslim Ban shows the racial violence embedded within a nation that claims multicultural liberalism and diversity.

The legacy of this discrimination's entirety is evident. A 2020 study revealed that income gaps between Blacks and whites are as high as they were in 1968 (Long and Van Dam 2020). Another 2020 study discussed the magnitude of racial wealth disparities by stating that "the typical White family has eight times the wealth of the typical Black family and five times the wealth of the typical Hispanic family" (Bhutta et al. 2020).

3.6 ROSCAs: At the Root of the Black Social Economy is Self-sufficiency

ROSCAs empower Black women financially, but serve an even greater purpose because they are based in community. They allow women to enhance their social and economic capital (at times in communities where they lack political capital). Nina Banks reminds us that the collective action taken up by Black women is not for profit. Women also engage in this type of resistance for the collective benefit of their communities (Banks 2020). Robert D. Putnam (1993, 167) defines the concept of social capital as "features of social organization, such as trust, norms, and networks that can improve the efficiency of society by facilitating coordinated actions." By strengthening their social capital ties, African Americans can develop strong networks within their communities and accomplish more, working together in community empowerment groups while continuing to elect Black officeholders (Austin 2006). Intergroup or bridging social capital involves a system of cooperation and negotiation among individuals of different races. Bonding social capital ties are those that are present among the residents of communities (Austin 2006).

Ardener and Burman in *Money-Go-Rounds* (1995) point out the role of ROSCAs in building social and economic capital for the most marginalized. According to their research, women around the world establish ROSCAs as a way of amassing funds, but also of networking with one another. In *Politicized Microfinance*, Caroline Shenaz Hossein (2016) discusses the challenges "marginalized women" face when seeking assistance from financial institutions. Given the obstacles these women encounter, money pools and ROSCAs provide them with the benefits of shared resources and a sense of autonomy in addition to tools for financial wealth.

Politicized microfinance comes in two forms: one that is most often used in Jamaica, Trinidad, and Guyana and another that is used as a way to enlighten people about the discrimination endured by people of African descent (Hossein 2016; see the Haiti and Grenada cases). Professor Hossein (2016, 12–13) explains,

> The concept of politicized microfinance refers to the clientelistic politicking and partisanship of the "Big Men," who further oppress the entrepreneurial poor. In the positive cases, politicized microfinance can refer to managers who agitate for social change by making financial resources available to excluded groups. Here, politicized microfinance requires the people in charge of this resource to be politically conscious, activist, and conscientious about the work they do—to the point of taking deadly risks.

The social capital used by ROSCA participants is an example of Black social capital. In *Black Social Capital: The Politics of School Reform in Baltimore, 1986–1998*, Marion E. Orr (1999) refers to the bonding social capital in African American neighborhoods as Black social capital. African Americans have enhanced their social capital ties in churches, civil rights organizations, community development organizations, fraternities and sororities; historically Black colleges and universities, and social, civic, and political groups (Orr 1999). These institutions have allowed them to socialize with each other, address community problems, and educate each other both during and after their formal exclusion from white institutions (Austin 2006). Most Black social capital research discovers that African American neighborhood activists increase their bonding social capital ties first, then improve their bridging social capital relationships when attempting to address their communities' ills (Austin 2006).

In America, Black women have often been able to "make a way out of no way." A popular quote used to describe the Black experience is: "Our God can *make a way out of no way* . . . He can do anything but fail" (Swann-Wright 2002, vi). After emancipation, the master–slave relation was transformed into an employer–employee relationship as the institution of slavery was replaced with the peonage system. Black sharecroppers worked hard and earned little money, but they saved money as a way to make a way out of no way (Swann-Wright 2002). Sharecropping is an arrangement in which property owners allow tenants to farm a piece of land in exchange for a share of the crop (Austin 2006). Black sharecroppers remained impoverished during this time mainly because of their dependency on the plantation elites for their farming supplies, food, housing, and other needs. Usually, the landowner furnished sharecroppers with the necessary supplies, deducted the costs from their pay at the end of the season, and gave them a portion of the harvest at settlement (Austin 2006). Sharecropping was widespread in the South during the Reconstruction era, after the Civil War. It was a way for landowners to still command labor, often by African Americans, to keep their farms profitable. This system faded in later years because of agricultural mechanization, especially the widespread usage of mechanical cotton pickers, and the mass exodus of workers from the rural South (Austin 2006). On many occasions, sharecroppers pooled their money with other family members to purchase homes and other necessities (Klein 2018).

After the turn of the century, W. E. B. Du Bois suggested that African Americans cooperate with each other for their own economic good. Initially, he believed that African Americans should emphasize political activism, but later he advocated economic cooperation as a way of gaining economic self-sufficiency. Black capitalism is defined as the use of economic self-sufficiency and consumer cooperation to obtain economic advancement (Haynes 2018). After the Great Depression, Du Bois contended that if African Americans were to have economic security, the group must invest in their industrial development. He asserted that if they did not, and waited to get their share of industry, racism would inhibit their contribution while keeping them in an unstable situation (Haynes 2018). In *The Philadelphia Negro*, Du Bois (2007) argued that African Americans must cooperate with each other in institutions such as churches, beneficial societies, and schools as a way of gaining self-sufficiency in economics. Moreover, political power is virtually meaningless without economic power (Haynes 2018).

Black elected officials usually pursue the same types of agendas as white elected officials in cities and counties. Regardless of their race, elected officials emphasize economic development strategies that benefit the middle class and the business community, often at the expense of the poor (Austin 2006). The ROSCA experience indicates the willingness of African Americans and Black immigrants to enhance their social capital for economic gain. Black cooperatives were also member-led organizations formed through economic autonomy and stability. The formation of cooperatives served the purposes of political, social, and economic gain. Cooperatives were also used to back political campaigns that enabled changes and regulated the market. ROSCAs and Black cooperatives have been responses in addressing racial capitalism, but they are limited in what they can do. These models still do not fix the underlying structures that produce underemployment and low wages in Black communities.

3.7 Susus in American Cities: Benefits and Risks

Susus and cooperatives are methods for economic advancement in an anti-Black society. They are forms of collective resistance produced when the state fails the Black community (Banks 2020). These alternative methods are a response to a lack of trust in banking and a building block for social, political, and economic gain. Nia Evans, Director of the Boston Ujamaa Project, advocates for the democratic model of cooperatives for addressing being locked out of the banking industry. Evans states, "Rather than paying big banks to invest our city funds in Wall Street, we could democratically invest in Main Street through a municipal public bank . . . While a 'ride-to-the-bottom' market inevitably shapes us; we can also organize to shape it back" (Simon 2019).

Susus and cooperatives are equitable systems that are actively engaged in reshaping and meeting the needs of all who participate. They are formed through communities that members know or feel connected to, which provides a foundation for trust. Participating in a Susu also allows members to avoid paying high interest, to secure housing, and to build connections. Cooperatives invest in the community through the pooling of resources as well as by creating sustainable institutions that train, educate, and create jobs inside the community. In what follows, we provide an analysis of how Susus continue the long history of economic cooperation as a key principle of the Black social economy. Both Marie Lumen Clersaint and Fonta Gilliam show how ROSCAs can be a liberatory practice used by marginalized communities.

Brooklyn case: Marie Lumen Clersaint, a Haitian American

How have Black women in American cities used ROSCA-like strategies to their benefit? For many years, Marie Lumen Clersaint, a Haitian immigrant, has been one of the most powerful women in Brooklyn, New York. She works for Caribbean Air Mail (CAM), a chain of money transfer stores in Brooklyn. More importantly, she oversaw a local Sol in 2011 that was utilized mainly by Caribbean and African immigrants. In later years, she continued to be known as "Brooklyn's reigning queen of sou-sous" (Time for an Awakening Media 2013). In 2011, one of her funds had amassed $20,000 and the other $10,000 (*Grio* staff 2011). A 2011 article in *The Grio* described her two Sou-sou groups as follows,

> They have 40 and 20 members, respectively. Each member puts in $500 bi-weekly. Every two weeks one member of each Sou-sou will receive their group's entire payout, until each person gets a turn. The $20,000 Sol runs for 18 months, the $10,000 saving club lasts ten months. For the person who gets the first disbursement, it's an

> interest-free cash advance and for the last payee it's a no-interest savings plan. And for those in the middle, it's a combination of both. There are no checks or money orders involved. It's all cash all the time. (*The Grio* staff 2011)

Women like Lumen Clersaint empower women financially, but in other ways as well. They help women in both urban and rural communities to end their isolation from fiscal resources. They give them a way out of abusive or exploitative relationships by providing the funds they need to improve their situation. Married women receive financial independence from their husbands. These women also have less stress and humiliation after being denied assistance from mainstream financial institutions. Although some dismiss ROSCAs and Susus as "under-the-mattress" and "archaic" saving methods, others realize their importance: as Lihle Mtshali (2017, 1) explains, "If you need a lump sum but cannot get a credit card or loan from a traditional financial institution due to a bad credit history, a Sou-sou may also be your answer."

The Washington, D.C., Sou-Sou group

Some Susus have become modernized and are called lending circles. The Sou-Sou Group of Washington, D.C., is a fintech start-up company that uses the same strategies as other ROSCAs in the sense that an individual receives the hand after a set period of time (Gilgore 2018). Fonta Gilliam is the CEO of this Susu. In 2015, she co-founded it after developing working relationships with banks in D.C. and New York (Gilgore 2018). Gilliam discusses how the Susu has been modernized:

> This isn't a module that we invented. This is a model that 80 percent of the world uses. What we're doing is modernizing it, and scaling it. It's one of the few things that is proven to work regardless of country. This idea of using village savings and loan models and using peer accountability encourages people to save. It uses peer accountability to get people to pay into the circle. Plus, we track the positive credit they're building from the loan to the credit rating agencies to help the members build credit. (Mocharko 2018)

Like the traditional Susu, the start-ups allow individuals with poor credit histories or who would have difficulty getting loans with a method to borrow money (Mocharko 2018). Yet, it goes further. This group allows its participants to receive credit lines from banks. It is primarily designed to assist women who have been ignored, disregarded, and disrespected by banks. Women can use their Susu app to find banks and to suggest ways for women with both lower and average credit scores to increase them (Mocharko 2018). According to Gilliam, this Susu model now operates in Tanzania and the United States. It is expanding its efforts to assist immigrants, refugees, and others who are struggling financially and moving to a new environment with their credit and finances (Mocharko 2018).

The D.C.-based Susu start-up is now a legitimate business that operates like a cooperative bank. It has assisted more than 100 entrepreneurs in the United States over the past year, has contracts with twenty-four financial institutions, and earned over $15,000 in revenue in 2018 (Gilgore 2018). This Susu reminds us of a key critique of racial capitalism, which is its lack of focus on gender analysis. Gilliam's start-up has successfully found a way to subvert the oppression of Black women in the labor market by providing banking that is usually denied to many of them, especially if they have lower incomes and lack financial resources.

What challenges have ROSCAs encountered? It is important to note that they are almost completely unregulated by any laws, background checks, or credit checks and thus leave many opportunities for fraud and corruption. Because of the risks involved, it is important for group members to know and trust each other. They must develop strong social capital relationships so that they know they will not be exploited. Usually, Susu members are from the same family or residential community (Mtshali 2017). In Brooklyn, Lumain Clersaint carefully screens the investors in her funds. She allows individuals to participate in her money pools only if she knows and trusts them. If by chance anyone "defaults on their contributions," she must compensate the other investors (*Grio* staff 2011). According to her testimony, she has never had to do this.

Nevertheless, corruption is inevitable. Investment schemes that resemble ROSCAs—such as "The Circle Game," "Blessing Loom," and "Money Board"—have emerged. These are fraudulent pyramid schemes that solicit donations from donors but primarily desire to continuously recruit individuals. When they are no longer able to attract investors, the pyramid collapses. This means that individuals who have not collected funds never will (Hobbs 2020). Some individuals have invested hundreds and thousands of dollars in these schemes with the belief they will earn sizable profits (Johnson 2020). Alexis Johnson (2020, 1) describes how they work:

> Participants are being asked to invest anywhere from $100 to $1,350 with an assurance to make a profit within just a few weeks. The catch is that the only way to keep the money circulating within the group is to recruit more people into it, which often time leaves the well dry before everyone involved gets paid out. The collection of money combined with mostly empty guarantees of a profit have all the makings of an illegal pyramid scheme in which those at the top, or members who sign up early, are rewarded with large payouts while those who are last to join usually aren't as lucky. Traditional Susus, however, are not meant to turn a profit for its members. Rather, they act as a collective savings account that is rotated among trusted family members or friends and help to bring people together.

Lumen Clersaint and Gilliam show us how the foundational principle of cooperation pushes against individualism, which is a key component of the Black social economy. The Black social economy argues that community partnership is what will build up African American communities and bring about racial, social, and economic liberation. Black communities have to stop internalizing individualism in order to build the trust needed to sustain cooperatives and start-ups. Individual wealth is limited, whereas collective wealth can provide the surplus needed to address social ills such as poor nutrition, the housing crisis, predatory lending, and poor quality education. These Susu are creating the environment and space that build the foundation of trust for the Black social economy.

3.8 Conclusion: Black Americans Contribute to Economic and Social Development

Through their participation in ROSCAs, women engage in self-help and solidarity. Black women enhance their social capital relationships and build trusting networks with each other for their own financial gain. Also, ROSCAs provide independence and financial stability, which are important components in the concepts of the Black social economy and racial capitalism. Caroline Shenaz Hossein (2020, 356) adequately summarizes their importance in this respect: "Because the women who organize them are local residents in the community, they are highly vested in bringing social change, drawing on the Indigenous systems they know and trust. They refuse to leave it to the control of a corporation to dictate how they run their own lives, homes and communities." Regardless of whether they are used by poor immigrant women or by more affluent women, ROSCAs are contributing to economic and social development in many U.S. communities.

The people of the Black diaspora continue to use informal savings methods and cooperatives to combat the alienation designed by racial capitalism. Marie Lumen Clersaint and Fonta Gilliam have continued the legacy of cooperation passed from generation to generation. They have refashioned Susus and cooperatives to meet the needs of our contemporary time. A Black social economy remains necessary in an economic system designed to treat African peoples as disposable. Although state and government agencies continue their attacks on Black communities, they keep renewing through reinvestment, commitment to solidarity, and the unpaid labor of Black women. These two case studies are only a piece of how Black women in the United States are resisting anti-Blackness. More work needs to be done on how the African diaspora in the United States is building wealth in order to gain political access and refuse invisibility, because the system of capitalism is not an equalizer. Racial capitalism is designed to lock Black people out of the social economy. The Black social economy is how the African diaspora survives alienation and premature death (Gilmore 2007). This economy remains autonomous by using mutual aid and cooperation to help those who have been left out.

Works Cited

Ardener, S. 2010. "Microcredit, Money Transfers, Women, and the Cameroon Diaspora." February 2010; *Afrika Focus* 23(2):11–24.

Ardener, S. and S. Burman (eds.) 1995. *Money-Go-Rounds: The Importance of Rotating Savings and Credit Associations for Women*. Oxford: Berg.

Association for the Advancement of University Women (AAUW). 2020. "The Simple Truth about the Gender Pay Gap: 2020 Update." AAUW. https://www.aauw.org/app/uploads/2020/12/SimpleTruth_2.1.pdf. Accessed December 16, 2020.

Austin, S. D. W. 2006. *The Transformation of Plantation Politics: Black Politics, Concentrated Poverty, and Social Capital in the Mississippi Delta*. Albany: State University of New York Press.

Austin, S. D. W. 2018. *The Caribbeanization of Black Politics: Race, Group Consciousness, and Political Participation in America*. Albany: State University of New York Press.

Banks, N. 2020. "Black Women in the United States and Unpaid Collective Work: Theorizing The Community as a Site of Production." *Review of Black Political Economy* 47(4): 343–62.

Baradaran, M. 2015. *How the Other Half Banks: Exclusion, Exploitation, and the Threat to Democracy*. Cambridge, MA: Harvard University Press.

Barclay, A., K. Fullwood, and T. Webb. 2019. "The Sweetness of Circles." Black Giving 365, March 26. https://medium.com/@Blackgiving365/the-sweetness-of-circles-f718a7433660. Accessed October 13, 2020.

Bhutta, N., A. C. Chang, L. J. Dettling, J. W. Hsu with assistance from J. Hewitt. 2020. "Disparities in Wealth by Race and Ethnicity in the 2019 Survey of Consumer Finances". September 20. https://www.federalreserve.gov/econres/notes/feds-notes/disparities-in-wealth-by-race-and-ethnicity-in-the-2019-survey-of-consumer-finances-20200928.htm. Accessed on November 28, 2021.

Bond, J. 2000. "SNCC: What We Did." *Monthly Review* 52(5). October 1. https://monthlyreview.org/2000/10/01/sncc-what-we-did/. Accessed July 28, 2021.

Chalhoub, T. and K. Rimar. 2018. *The Health Care System and Racial Disparities in Maternal Mortality*. Center for American Progress. https://www.americanprogress.org/issues/women/reports/2018/05/10/450577/health-care-system-racial-disparities-maternal-mortality

Du Bois, W. E. B. 2007. *The Philadelphia Negro*. NYC, NY: Cosimo.

Faber, J. and T. Friedline. 2020. "The Racialized Costs of Banking." Washington, DC: New America. https://www.newamerica.org/family-centered-social-policy/reports/racialized-costs-banking/the-racialized-costs-of-banking/. Accessed October 13, 2020.

Gigante, S. 2017. "Tanda, Hui, or Ayuuto? The Money Pool Way." [Blog] Mass Mutual, September 22. https://blog.massmutual.com/post/money-pools. Accessed October 7, 2020.

Gilgore, S. 2018. "Startup of the Week: Meet Sou Sou." *Washington Business Journal*, November 15. https://www.bizjournals.com/washington/news/2018/11/15/startup-of-the-week-meet-sou-sou.html. Accessed October 13, 2020.

Gilmore, R. Wilson. 2007. *Golden Gulag: Prisons, Surplus, Crisis, and Opposition in Globalizing California*. Berkeley: University of California Press.

Gordon Nembhard, J. 2014. *Collective Courage: A History of African American Cooperative Economic Thought and Practice*. University Park: Pennsylvania State University Press.

Grio staff. 2011. "'Sou-Sou': Black Immigrants Bring Savings Clubs Stateside." *The Grio*, May 20. https://thegrio.com/2011/05/20/sou-sou-Black-immigrants-bring-savings-club-stateside/. Accessed October 7, 2020.

Hackett, R. 2020. "Banking While Black: How A New Generation of Leaders Is Overcoming a Legacy of Discrimination and Mistrust." *Fortune*, June 19. https://fortune.com/2020/06/19/banking-while-Black-financial-discrimination-redlining/. Accessed October 13, 2020.

Harrison, F. V. 1988. "Women in Jamaica's Informal Economy: Insights from a Kingston Slum." *New West Indian Guide* 3(4): 103–28.

Haynes Jr., C. 2018. "From Philanthropic Black Capitalism to Socialism: Co-operativism in Du Bois's Economic Thought." *Socialism and Democracy* 32(3): 125–45.

Hobbs, K. 2020. "A Real or Fake Savings Club?" *Federal Trade Commission*, August 10. https://www.consumer.ftc.gov/blog/2020/08/real-or-fake-savings-club. Accessed October 7, 2020.

Hogan, L. 1984. *Principles of Black Political Economy*. Bloomington: Trafford Publishing.

Hossein, C. S. 2019. "A Black Epistemology for the Social and Solidarity Economy: The Black Social Economy." *Review of Black Political Economy* 46(3): 209–29.

Hossein, C. S. 2013. "The Black Social Economy: Perseverance of Banker Ladies in the Slums." *Annals of Public and Co-operative Economics* 84(4): 423–42.

Hossein, C. S. 2016. *Politicized Microfinance: Money, Power, and Violence in the Black Americas*. Toronto: University of Toronto Press.

Hossein, C. S. 2018. *The Black Social Economy in the Americas: Exploring Diverse Community-Based Alternative Markets*. Edited collection. New York: Palgrave Macmillan.

Hossein, C. S. 2020. "Rotating Savings and Credit Associations (ROSCAs): Mutual Aid Financing, Section 5." In J. K. Gibson-Graham and Kelly Dombroski (eds.), *The Handbook of Diverse Economies*. Cheltenham: Edward Elgar Press.

Johnson, A. 2020. "Investor Beware: Traditional African Sou Savings Clubs Have Become the Latest Pyramid Scheme." *Pittsburgh Post-Gazette*, August 20. https://www.post-gazette.com/local/region/2020/08/20/sou-sou-pittsburgh-savings-collective-economics-africa-pyramid-scheme-money/stories/202008190075. Accessed October 13, 2020.

Jones-Correa, M. 2000–1. "The Origins and Diffusion of Racial Restrictive Covenants." *Political Science Quarterly* 115(4): 541–68.

Kendi, I. 2019. "The Day *Shithole* Entered the Presidential Lexicon." *The Atlantic*, January. https://www.theatlantic.com/politics/archive/2019/01/shithole-countries/580054/. Accessed December 10, 2020.

Klein, A. 2018. "This Family Grew up Picking Cotton in South Carolina. Decades Later, They Return to the Place as Homeowners." *Greenville News*, January 25. https://www.greenvilleonline.com/story/life/2018/01/25/family-grew-up-picking-cotton-south-carolina-decades-later-they-returned-place-they-sharecropped-hom/1065203001/. Accessed October 12, 2020.

Long, H. and A. Van Dam. 2020. "The Black–White Economic Divide is as Wide as it was in 1968." *Washington Post*, June 4. https://www.washingtonpost.com/business/2020/06/04/economic-divide-Black-households/. Accessed on November 28, 2020.

Lyons, A. 1975. "Conventional Redlining in Chicago: A Case Study." In Urban-Suburban Investment Study Group, Center for Urban Affairs (ed.), *The Role of Mortgage Lending Practices in Older Urban Neighborhoods: Institutional Lenders, Regulatory Agencies and Their Community Impacts*. Evanston: Northwestern University.

Mcintosh, K., E. Moss, R. Nunn, and J. Shambaugh. 2020. "Examining the Black–White Wealth Gap." *Brookings*, February 27. https://www.brookings.edu/blog/up-front/2020/02/27/examining-the-Black-white-wealth-gap/. Accessed on November 28, 2021.

Massey, D. and N. Denton. 1993. *American Apartheid: Segregation and the Making of the Underclass*. Chicago: University of Chicago Press.

Mocharko, George. 2018. "How Fintech Startup Sou Sou Is Empowering Women Entrepreneurs." *Technical.ly*, July 12. https://technical.ly/dc/2018/07/12/how-fintech-startup-sou-sou-is-empowering-women-entrepreneurs/. Accessed October 13, 2020.

Mtshali, L. Z. 2017. "Everything You Ever Wanted to Know about Those Sou-Sou Savings Clubs African and Caribbean Women Love." *Essence*, January 18. https://www.essence.com/news/money-career/what-is-a-sou-sou-savings-club-facts/. Accessed October 7, 2020.

Muslim Advocates. 2020. "Major Civil Rights Groups Condemn Imminent Ban on Black Immigration, Call for Congressional Action." *Muslim Advocates*, February 20. https://muslimadvocates.org/2020/02/major-civil-rights-groups-condemn-imminent-ban-on-Black-immigration-call-for-congressional-action/. Accessed December 10, 2020.

Nopper, T. K. 2011. "Minority, Black and Non-Black People of Colour: 'New' Colour-Blind Racism and the U.S. Small Business Administration's Approach to Minority Business Lending in the Post-Civil Rights Era." *Critical Sociology* 37(5): 651–71.

Nzinga Ifateyo, A. 2014. "Black Co-ops Were A Method of Economic Survival: An Interview with Professor Jessica Gordon Nembhard." *Grassroots Economic Organizing*, May 27. https://geo.co-op/story/Black-co-ops-were-method-economic-survival. Accessed December 14, 2020.

Orr, M. 1999. *Black Social Capital: The Politics of School Reform in Baltimore, 1986–1998: Studies in Government and Public Policy*. Lawrence: University Press of Kansas.

Putnam, R. D. 1993. *Making Democracy Work: Civic Traditions in Modern Italy*. Princeton: Princeton University Press.

Rheingold, I., M. Fitzpatrick, and A. Hofeld Jr. 2001. "From Redlining to Reverse Redlining: A History of Obstacles for Minority Homeownership in America." *Clearinghouse Review* 34 (January-February): 642–54.

Robinson, C. 1983 [2000]. *Black Marxism: The Making of the Black Radical Tradition*. Chapel Hill: University of North Carolina Press.

Robinson, C. J. 2019. *Cedric Robinson: On Racial Capitalism, Black Internationalism, and Cultures of Resistance*, edited by H. L. T. Quan. London: Pluto Books.

Rutherford, S. 2000. *The Poor and Their Money*. New Delhi: DFID/Oxford University Press.

Satter, B. 2009. *Family Properties: Race, Real Estate, and the Exploitation of Black America*. New York: Macmillan.

Simon, M. 2019. "Kwanzaa Meets Capital: Meet Boston's New Democratic Investment Fund." *Forbes*, January 3. https://www.forbes.com/sites/morgansimon/2019/01/03/kwanzaa-meets-capital-meet-bostons-new-democratic-investment-fund/?sh=6e97f102ec1e. Accessed December 18, 2020.

Stoper, E. 1977. "The Student Nonviolent Coordinating Committee: Rise and Fall of a Redemptive Organization." *Journal of Black Studies* 8(1): 13–34.

Swann-Wright, D. 2002. *A Way Out of No Way: Claiming Family and Freedom in the New South*. Charlottesville: University of Virginia Press.

Time for an Awakening Media. 2013. "'Sou-sou': Black Immigrants Bring Savings Club Stateside." August 20. Time for an Awakening Media Radio Media/News Company. https://www.facebook.com/TimeForAnAwakeningRadio/posts/sou-sou-Black-immigrants-bring-savings-club-statesideits-like-karmic-cash-you-ge/354536801346615/. Accessed July 28, 2021.

Tippins, K. 2020. "Expanded Muslim Ban Takes Effect, National Groups Respond to the Expansion of the Muslim Ban Targeting More Black Immigrants." Lawyers Committee for Civil Rights Under Law, February 20. https://lawyerscommittee.org/statement-from-the-lawyers-committee-for-civil-rights-under-law-and-undocuBlack-network-on-the-expansion-of-the-muslim-ban-to-target-more-Black-immigrants/. Accessed December 12, 2020.

4

Tandas and Cooperativas

Understanding the Social Economy of Indigenous Mexican Immigrants Settled in Perth Amboy, New Jersey and Staten Island, New York, U.S.A.

Patricia Campos Medina, Erika Nava, and Sol Aramendi

4.1 Introduction

For migrants around the world who are displaced from their place of origin, their ability to thrive in a new country is dependent on their ability to integrate, adapt, learn, and re-create economic systems that sustain their livelihoods within hostile environments. Their agency in their economic survival leads to the narrative of some migrants as less or more successful than others. However, such characterization does not consider any of the specific conditions of each group's immigration pathway and economic reality once they arrive in their new environment.

For immigrants from the Global South, the specific reason for their entrance into a new country or the conditions of their arrival into local economies (i.e., the legality or illegality of their immigration) are irrelevant to the native political discourse determining access to the right of belonging in local communities (i.e., the right to belong and a path to citizenship). In the United States, the legality or illegality of a new immigrant is often pre-determined by foreign political interest beyond the control of the immigrant. But such predetermination of legality sets the stage that denies or offers immigrants access to the tools of integration that determine their ability to thrive in the new society: education opportunities, a permit to work (which affords legality), and access to housing and healthcare.

In mainstream political science, the granting of rights to new members of any society is left to the state, which sets the rules that determine who enters the society with or without rights and who is a visitor or a resident. In liberal societies, the state is elected by the citizens who have the right to vote. Since the founding of the United States, however, who has the right to vote has a contested history because European colonizers set different rules at different times to exclude different sets of people from voting based on racial and economic considerations (Cole 2000; Clarke et al. 2014).

The innate paradox of this power is that while the state demands adherence to a process of legality, it changes that process haphazardly and often fails to treat similarly

Patricia Campos Medina, Erika Nava, and Sol Aramendi, *Tandas and Cooperativas.* In: *Beyond Racial Capitalism.*
Edited by Caroline Shenaz Hossein, Sharon D. Wright Austin, and Kevin Edmonds, Oxford University Press.
 DOI: 10.1093/oso/9780192868336.003.0005

situated immigrants under the same rules. Laws of entry into the United States have historically been connected to the unrelenting expansion of western European capitalism: from the dispossession of lands from the Native American population, to the imposition of enslaved labor as a form of land development, to the subjugation of the former Spanish colonies (i.e., natives from the former Mexican and the rest of Latin American tribes), to today's imposition of illegality that leads to the cheap labor of undocumented workers from the Global South. The result continues to be the exploitation of Native Americans[1] and African descendants as the source of wealth accumulation for the colonizers and their descendants.

Since the creation of the United States, the contestation of citizenship rights for all non-western Europeans became a political predetermination made by the white capitalist entrepreneurial class to control distribution of land and wealth. However, it also became a complex political dilemma to manage given the need to cohabitate with those excluded from rights in a political system that claims equality as its founding ethos. Political scientist Cedric Robinson called this practice "racial capitalism" because it purposely created exclusionary systems to deny any future descendants of all Native tribes and African slaves first their rights as human beings for freedom and later their rights to equal rights (Robinson 1983). Under this predetermined racial capitalist cast, western European settlers awarded to themselves the top of the racial hierarchy and the ownership of the wealth of the new colonized lands (Jenkins and Leroy 2021). The economic survival of all non-western Europeans in the new American territories, therefore, has historically been defined by each group's ability to survive and adapt to rules in a society that limits their humanity and economic welfare.

The two case studies explored in this chapter examine the experience of Native/Indigenous undocumented immigrants from Mexico in two cities in the New York–New Jersey (NY–NJ) metro region: Staten Island, N.Y., and Perth Amboy, N.J. Using a qualitative ethnographic approach (Creswell 2013), we authors engage in a process of immersion and participant observation to develop a theory of economic interaction grounded on the social economy model described by Canadian feminist economist Caroline Shenaz Hossein (2016, 2018). Through individual interviews, both case studies explore how these Indigenous Mexican immigrant groups tap into their cultural heritage of the communal economy to survive the oppressive reality of their daily lives as undocumented laborers in these two U.S. cities. Similar to the cultural heritage of Afro-Caribbean immigrants, Indigenous Mexican immigrants in the United States tap into their cultural practice of the social economy by engaging in Tandas and cooperativas to cobble together enough economic resources to meet the essential needs of their families.

The two case studies analyzed here use the theory of the Black social economy to observe and give meaning to the myriad of ways in which undocumented Indigenous

[1] Native American is the most common and neutral term in the United States, while First Nations is the preferred term in Canada. However, each Indigenous American group prefers to be called by their own specific name (e.g., Cherokee, Lakota) (Pauls n.d.).

people from Mexico draw on their own ingenuity, their cultural heritage, and their knowledge of the social economy to survive economically and thrive socially. Mexican immigrants, many who are also descendants of African descent, have an ancestral legacy of communal living, and they express it through the practice of Tandas and worker-led cooperativas. This communal economic practice results in the creation of a social-support system to aid in this group's agency of survival as they attempt to function without legality within the American economy. The anti-Black sentiment of the American experience is intertwined with the anti-immigrant environment of the current American political system because those in control of the state, who are mainly descendants of white European colonizers, still create laws that limit non-whites' ability to gain access to the right to vote. Systemic denial of citizenship access to Mexican undocumented immigrants who are essential to the economic activity of American society is a continuation of the racist capitalist enterprise described by Cedric Robinson.

4.2 Racial Capitalism and How Indigenous Immigrants to the United States Push Back

Since its founding, the history of the United States has been defined over and over again by the contestation of rights of different groups in American society. The struggles of survival of the displaced Native/Indigenous American tribes, the indenture servitude of eastern European migrants, the kidnapping and subsequent slavery of African natives, and today's experience of the exploitation of undocumented migrants from Mexico and the Global South are a continuation of the history of the contestation of rights of all non-whites since the colonization of the American territories.

The most defining contestation of belonging in U.S. society continues to be the struggle for the freedom of African-descended people. This 400+ years struggle and demand for freedom became a direct challenge to the capitalist enterprise of western European expansion to the new world. Cedric Robinson (1983, 113 and 199–200) notes that "Karl Marx's assessment of European power" was valid when it described the practice of slavery as "the chief momenta of primitive [capital] accumulation ... that sustained the emergence of Europe as a world economic power." African free labor, Cedric argues, sustained the emergence of Europe as a world market that eventually fueled the industrial production of the twentieth century.

This point of embedded racism within the market economy is crucial in understanding the construction of power relations. According to Robinson (1983), therefore, the economic foundations of the United States are a prime example of ruthless economic capitalist domination: land dispossession of all natives, plus the imposition of slavery as an economic model of economic growth fueled by land production and the expansion of the American Anglo-Saxon colonies. Despite the end of slavery in the 1800s, however, this system of labor exploitation continued in the modern era with the implementation of oppressive political systems that trapped the majority of former slaves into economic systems that push them to become "peasants ... tenant farmers ... migrant labourers, day labourers ... domestic servants and [providers of] low wage labour" (Robinson 1983, 120).

As the movement for civil rights of former slaves took hold in the twentieth century, the descendants of freed slaves forced the state to acknowledge their freedom through the Civil Rights Law of the 1960s, which codified political rights to vote into law. Hence, enslaved people eventually were able to gain political rights that gave them more power to demand better education and access to economic mobility, subsequently making their labor more expansive. In the twenty-first century, the cheap labor of African people eventually became replaced by the cheap labor of land-dispossessed Indigenous people previously colonized by Spain in Mexico, the Caribbean, and Central and South America.

In this chapter we examine Tandas co-op banks for Indigenous and Mexican immigrants to the United States. According to Drew professor Maliha Safri (2015), she has described in her work in Asbury Park in New Jersey that the social and solidarity economy is where excluded racialized Americans and immigrants are creating cooperatives, as a way of creating their own jobs. The Black social economy theory is one that exposes a tension occurring where there is this supposed arena for excluded people to seek support, but when these subsidies don't flow, people will come together of their own accord to build their own economies. These efforts to organize Tandas by newcomers is their way of politicizing the (social) economy and directly countering the impact of racial capitalism on their lives.

4.3 Methods and Approach

The two case studies examined are located in two major cities of the NY–NJ metropolitan region: Perth Amboy, N.J., and Staten Island, N.Y.

Case study 1: Tandas in Perth Amboy, N.J.

This case study focuses on Tandas, a non-interest loaning system and saving strategy used by immigrants from Mexico. The study uses qualitative methods comprising face-to-face semi-structured voluntary interviews with women from the Mexican community in Perth Amboy, an immigrant urban hub with the highest share (79 percent) of Latinos in New Jersey. The author of this case study is Erika Nava. She grew up in Perth Amboy, and became aware of Tandas through her personal experience of being the daughter of Mexican immigrants. The choice of methodology includes empirical review of existent scholarly work, recorded authorized interviews of voluntary subjects, and the author's own lived experienced in her childhood community knowing that her relatives and friends engaged in the social economy. Erika Nava is an established field researcher and policy analyst working for recognized think-tanks and legislators where she examines the immigrant experience in New Jersey and in the United States. She is a trained prime investigator on human subject qualitative and empirical data analysis.

The case study has some limitations. It was subject to empirical and quantitative data constraints. At present there is no comprehensive examination of New Jersey's Latino community's informal saving systems. These article conclusions do not attempt to be comprehensive, but rather give a snapshot illustration of how immigrants who lack proper documentation in urban cities in New Jersey participate in the formal economy. The case study focuses on the personal experience of the women who engage in Tandas, with the goal of illustrating why racialized Indigenous migrants from Mexico turn to their transnational and cultural practices of the social economy to survive and help their children thrive in their new lives as undocumented immigrants.

Case study 2: Cleaning workers cooperative in Staten Island, N.Y.

This case study focuses on the experiences of undocumented Mexican workers who organize themselves into a worker-owned cooperative home-cleaning venture. This case study was written by Sol Aramendi as part of her master thesis for the City University of New York (CUNY). She is a socially engaged artist who applies a social-participatory action model of field research. She combines empirical analysis of published data and qualitative ethnographic analysis of human subject interviews. Her participatory model prioritizes the subjects' experiences to help workers construct their own narrative. Her methods include immersion into the lives of the community by working as a volunteer on local organizations projects, which includes observation of member meetings to understand group dynamics and art and film expression that captures and prioritizes the workers' experiences. Her approach includes three phases of participatory research: a listening phase; a worker studio phase; and a public engagement phase, where she shares the findings with her subjects.

Due to the precarity of workers' lives and the dangers they face as undocumented workers, both authors use aliases for the names of the people they interviewed. Confidentiality and anonymity of the workers' stories is part of building trust with these marginalized populations, who live in constant danger of being deported by authorities of the U.S. federal government. The NY–NJ region is the second largest recipient of undocumented Mexican immigrants, second only to California, and therefore these two case studies can serve as a snapshot of how these undocumented Mexican

Indigenous immigrants use the social economy to survive in the United States' largest metropolis.

4.4 Racial Capitalism and Undocumented Labor from Mexico

U.S. history's ruthless capitalism, fueled and sustained by slavery and the cheap labor of racialized people, continues to shape the experience of Latin American migrants arriving in the United States as undocumented migrants today. According to the 2021 Migration Policy Institute report on the undocumented, there are 11.5 million immigrants who are "illegal" or migrant workers who entered the United States without legal authorization. Sixty percent of these undocumented workers are Mexican nationals.

These racialized immigrants move into already poorly resourced American urban centers and enter into direct competition for economic survival with African American workers looking for housing and low-wage jobs. Without legality, these workers become engaged in the U.S. economy often as day laborers or restaurant or domestic workers. Some become small entrepreneurs providing services to co-nationals who are more formally employed. Undocumented immigrants therefore become the cheap labor that drives economic activity in the low-wage service economy of the U.S. today.

The contestation of rights for immigrants has taken on different dynamics historically: from social movement protest for the undocumented to the eventual local political integration of legal immigrants. For example, after previous periods of social movement protest connected to the Civil Rights and Farm Worker movements of the 1960s, the children of undocumented racialized workers gained some rights and access to minimum protections under U.S. labor laws. This limited set of rights laid the foundation for other social movements that have emerged, such as the DREAMers, or the movement of undocumented children demanding a path to legality for themselves and their parents (Nichols 2013). It is important to understand that only legality via a permit to work removes the threat of deportation and family separation from the everyday experience of immigrant families. Only access to citizenship rights gives equity of opportunity for immigrants, allowing them to find ways to build a stable family unit while surviving economic limitations familiar to poor working Americans. Before achieving a path to legality or citizenship, racialized immigrants live in a form of alien citizenship (Bosniak 2006).

This means that while undocumented, these immigrants are permitted to engage in numerous legal economic activities, such as buying a home, owning a business, having a bank account, renting an apartment, sending their children to school, working, and paying taxes. Their ability to engage in these activities as alien citizens, however, depends on the willingness of the local political actors to accept them as participants in the economic activity of the community. Despite the acceptance of their existence in the margins of the local society, however, any group's ability to economically survive and thrive depends upon their familial and social networks allowing them to generate enough economic support to meet their families' basic needs.

Racialized immigration laws constrain the social and economic interactions of new immigrants upon their arrival in the United States. This leads to limited economic opportunities in local familial networks that already exist in limited economic enclaves in urban cities, like those examined in the two case studies in this chapter. This reality elevates the importance of social networks and the social economy as a means to survive an initial hostile environment upon arrival in the United States. The failure of the state to grant legal rights to new entrants allows these same groups (i.e., Mexican Indigenous immigrants) the opportunity to exercise agency over their lives and in this way redefine their own relationship with the economy and the state. It is in the contention over the right to belong to a new society that alien citizen immigrants ultimately define the rightfulness of their belonging in American society (Clarke et al. 2014).

4.5 The Hidden Social Economy for Indigenous Immigrants in the United States

The United States lacks a formal system of incorporation for non-political refugees. Throughout history, all non-political immigrants relied solely on informal networks of co-ethnics and family to gain access to a pathway of economic success: jobs, housing, education, training, and economic opportunity upon arrival. The level of economic capital any ethnic group has to offer to their future co-ethnic arrivals determines how long a newer group of migrants spends stuck in economic insecurity. The fewer resources their previous compatriots have to support newer arrivals into the United States, the more difficult it becomes for them to integrate into American society.

This strategy of informal integration is known as "ethnic–social–capital integration," and in the United States this model is best exemplified by Cubans who arrived in the United States in the 1960s fleeing the Cuban revolution. For the most part, these Cuban immigrants were the white elite descendants of Spaniards. Because of foreign policy considerations of the time, they were granted legality and had a clear path to citizenship rights upon entrance into the United States. In *Fragmented Ties*, Cecilia Mejivar explains how other Indigenous working-class Latin Americans who arrived in the United States at the same time were systematically denied legality. The results of this unequal policy action was that Cuban immigrants achieved economic mobility and social integration within same generation, building a stable white ethnic enclave with legal rights to vote and participate in the political affairs of the U.S. polity (Menjivar 2000).

Indigenous Mexican immigrants, however, have for generations contended with illegality, working as undocumented laborers in the land of their ancestors. There is an emerging U.S. solidarity economy network that is centering the experiences of vulnerable people, especially newcomers (Borowiak 2010). The result of people not understanding this third sector economy has been the slow integration of this group of migrants and the formation of poor ethnic enclaves in urban centers, like those observed by this chapter's case studies. In a recent lecture "Mapping the U.S. Solidarity City: Spatializing Diversity, Difference and Social Justice," Maliha Safri (2021) stated explicitly that Black and racialized Americans in New York and New Jersey are growing the solidarity economy sector through the expansion of worker cooperative sectors.

It is the limited access to economic mobility and legality that has forged a process of ethnic identity formation where some members apply their ancestral heritage of the social economy to develop systems of mutual aid to survive and help their children adjust to American society. Just as the descendants of African eslaved people had to do before them, some members of Indigenous Mexican enclaves also join the social economy by forming Tandas or creating worker-owned cooperativas. Both of these practices rooted in mutual aid and self-help allow people to collectively bring their agency within the formal U.S. capitalist system that excludes them.

4.6 The Black Social Economy and its Relevance for Mexican Indigenous Immigrants

The Black social economy is focused on the economic needs of people racially excluded from mainstream economics. Hossein (2018) argues that the socioeconomic practice of marginalized people is not a new phenomenon and that these people are able to combat exclusion through politicized collectives and cooperatives. Similar to people of African descent, many Indigenous communities' native to the Americas had a history of engaging in cooperative practices (Curl 2012). The practice of the social economy formally re-emerged in Mexico after the economy crashed in the 1980s, which forced millions of Mexican Indigenous farmers off their communal lands. Many southern Mexico communities were forced to migrate to northern Mexico to work in the factories, or to go further north to farms in the United States as undocumented workers (Lopez 2012; Góngora Almeida and Ramos Caizaluisa 2013).

The Indigenous Mexican communities highlighted in this chapter's two case studies drew on their cultural heritage of the social economy to survive exclusion upon arrival into racialized local enclaves in Perth Amboy, N.J. and Staten Island, N.Y. The social economy, illustrated here through Tandas and cooperatives, was a mechanism of economic survival, giving these migrants the opportunity to engage with agency in the economic sustenance of their families. The two case studies describe how two different groups of poorly resourced Mexican immigrants tapped into their cultural heritage of social economies to develop practices of social economy.

La Colmena: A worker-led cooperative in Staten Island, N.Y.

María was eight years old when she witnessed her grandmother organize an entire small village in Tamaulipas (Morelos, Mexico) to lead the effort to physically move their home from their employer's land onto their own small plot of land a few miles away. Strong men held parts of their house, while others held smaller items, a band played in the background, and the rest of the townspeople accompanied them with an improvised caravan celebrating the move. More than 50 years later, in a similar way to her grandmother, María became a community leader among immigrant workers in Staten Island as the founding member of the "Love and Learn Childcare Co-operative," incubated at La Colmena Community Job Center. This cooperative, along with many other similar initiatives, was created with economic development funding from the Worker Co-operative Business Development Initiative (WCBDI), a project established by New York City's Mayor Bill de Blasio in 2015. The initiative is part of the so-called solidarity economic model championed by urban planner and political scientist J. Philip Thompson, appointed by Mayor de Blasio as Deputy Mayor for Strategic Policy Initiatives for the City of New York. Thompson has also written and worked extensively on community health planning, race and community development, and the politics of Black economic advancement (Saegert et al. 2005).

The solidarity economy is a global movement that seeks to create a just and sustainable economy. In "Solidarity Economy: Building an Economy for People and the Planet," Emily Kawano et al. (2009) offer a pathway for transforming our economy from one that focuses on private profits to one that serves the people. She argues that socioeconomy practices like worker-owned cooperatives bring the commitment of common good in society to the workplace, calling the cooperative network the "civic infrastructure" of the social economy. Furthermore, as a policy practitioner, Thompson argues that cooperatives are a way of encouraging the working poor to engage as economic actors and to empower each other to demand rights, education, and investment in their community.

Established in 2015, the WCBDI issued $8 million in grants to eleven organizations to identify poor and immigrant communities willing to develop proposals for worker-owned businesses also known as cooperatives. Through popular education models, the incubator organization would lead workshops to teach interested immigrant worker circles basic professional and business skills so that they could run their own business. They would also come together to socialize, learn, and create a cooperative culture among themselves that would support the future sustainability of the worker-owned cooperative. Thompson saw the incubation process as having two distinct categories of organizing: a bottom-up model and a top-down model.

The former is a cooperative that is self-initiated by a self-organized community of interest. The top-down is a cooperative initiated by a cooperative development agency or not-for-profit community organization that identifies a potential group of workers and encourages them to form a cooperative (Gordon Nembhard et al. 2011).

From the start, the New York WCBDI became a top-down model. The original incubator organizations who received the city grants identified immigrant rights' worker centers with already active immigrant networks. Leaders of La Colmena, an immigrant worker rights center, welcomed the idea of worker-owned cooperative efforts as an opportunity to empower and organize excluded workers into a small economic bargaining unit that could create good paying jobs for themselves. La Colmena provides labor rights education and a variety of other services for excluded undocumented immigrants in the New York City area. Because most of the leaders were familiar with the practice of cooperativas in Latin America, they immediately recognize the practice as a tool with the potential to give low-wage immigrant workers a sense of ownership and agency in their everyday work arrangements. Many of the immigrants connected to La Colmena had informal work arrangements that gave them little security because they were employed in industries excluded from labor rights protectionism, such as domestic work as cleaners, child-caregivers, and elder home caretakers.

Interested in the promise of developing worker agency and economic sustainability for domestic workers, La Colmena worker center joined the incubation program financed by the WCBDI. The leaders of the worker center approached "María" to lead the effort because they saw her as a good community organizer who could identify other potential friends and co-workers interested in forming a cooperativa of domestic-workers. Back in Tamaulipas, the village where she grew up, "María" never used the word cooperative to describe her mother's mutual aid circles. She just remembered that from an early age, her mother participated actively in mutual aid circles, Tandas, to help her friends afford their basic family necessities. This practice of communal living had been ingrained in her mother's community since ancestral times and was part of their cultural traditions.

Together with the leaders of La Colmena, "María" began to organize some of her friends who were also domestic workers, most of whom were also from Mexico and in some cases from her hometown. Once a likely group of women was committed to come together to create a cleaning cooperative, they organized an Open House with the incubator organization to explain the requirements of becoming a cooperative and to learn how to begin to recruit other workers willing to become part of the project. Many workers became interested and they all agreed to attend a year-long cooperative training academy to learn basic business skills and governing rules of the cooperative model, with the goal of launching a worker-owned cleaning cooperative after one year of training. In addition to business training, members also scheduled professional classes to become certified child-care workers and learn safety skills for industrial home cleaning services. Using this top-down approach model, many of the workers who attended the training became skilled worker–owners of the seven different cooperatives: Love and Learn Childcare Co-operative, Brightly Port Richmond Cleaning Co-operative, Brightly Red Hook, Brightly Harlem Co-op, Palante, and Nanny Bee Childcare Co-operative.

The majority of the workers who joined the cooperative movement at La Colmena were women workers who were attracted to the idea of social circles fashioned after those they grew up with in Mexico. They also believed in the idea of independence and agency in their work arrangements. The idea of being owners and becoming their own boss was empowering. They were especially excited to have the flexibility of choosing the hours they worked because they often carried all the labor of raising their children, cleaning, cooking, and organizing their homes. They also felt supported by being able to negotiate a contract with a client, specifically stating their wages for each assignment and spelling out their rights as workers and owners. One of the worker owners, "Marcela," stated in an interview, "From the beginning, our goal was that women like me, immigrant women with kids, could join, and we could have a job that allows us to raise their kids and have a better wage."

"Marcela," another worker–owner and a founding member, described the transformative power of belonging to a co-op and owning her own business. She stated that even though as a worker on her own she had steady hours of work, she always kept her head down in front of any employer's demands and had wages stolen by employers who refused to pay her after she cleaned their homes. As a lone worker, "Marcela" did not know how to speak up and demand a contract and conditions prior to doing the work. After two years as a worker–owner in the cleaning cooperative, she felt a whole new world of personal and communal growth had opened up. She mastered new cleaning routines, created a cleaning manual, and became a trainer of other cleaners and domestic workers. Another worker–owner, "Carmen," talked about the family feeling the cooperative provided for her, which gave her a sense of community and of belonging to something bigger than herself. For instance, she shared that when she got ill and needed medical care, the co-op lent her money for her medical treatment and her fellow co-owners made sure she was taken care of, bringing warm meals to her family and even visiting her at the hospital.

"Rosana," another worker–owner of the cooperative, reflected on how the cooperative felt like family because members understood the struggles they faced as undocumented immigrant workers in New York City. During the interview, she stated the cooperative made her feel safe talking about her problems:

> There are things that are happening now that I could not have imagined before. I am living in a country where intolerance has reached its limit. The separation of families is a very important issue that concerns everyone here. In my case, my family and I are going through a deportation process that has been affecting us for six years. One morning I received a call informing me that my son had been arrested. From that moment, my mind and heart were in hell. Not only me, but my daughter and my husband also sank into sadness. For two months we were the living dead until we were finally given the news that he would be free.

The network of support and personal relationships built among the women was exalted as the most cherished benefit of being a member of the cooperatives. Belonging to a community of support, the social capital was always described by the members as their most important gain of belonging to the cooperative. This experience of belonging to a group who cared about their everyday lives transcended purely economic interest.

Impact of COVID-19 on the members of the Cooperatives at La Colmena

Around March 7, 2020, "María" got an employer's text canceling her contract, and others followed one by one. When the COVID-19 pandemic hit New York City, the state of New York imposed a quarantine on the city, including Staten Island. All contract work at "María's" cleaning cooperative were canceled, and within days all members of the cooperative were out of work. Although the cooperative was a legal entity and filing taxes, with "María" herself paying income taxes to the U.S. government for her previous 17 years of work, her lack of legal immigration status made her ineligible for the unemployment benefits or pandemic relief support provided to private business entities like the cleaning cooperative she had built with her friends at La Colmena.

Realizing they needed to fend for themselves, "María" and the other members of the cleaning cooperative decided to change their business model. Rather than seeking cleaning contracts, they turned their cooperative into a factory to make and sew face masks to sell to essential workers in New York City. With the help of La Colmena, they secured equipment and used their capital to find materials to start making and selling face masks to anyone who would give them a contract. Rather than waiting for the pandemic to end to seek new cleaning contracts, they had the courage, based on the culture of cooperation and entrepreneurship they had built with each other, to approach a new business. The members came together to address a need in the city and in the process to figure out together a new business model that could help them survive economically during the initial months of the pandemic crisis.

In the cooperative model, the women found the flexibility to address the immediate needs of their members. In addition to coming together to sew masks, the women built mutual aid circles to help members who became ill and needed help providing food to their children or taking care of a sick family member. They also began to organize daily Zoom meetings to check in on the health or needs of other domestic workers not joining in the new enterprise. They shared advice and safety tips on how to stay healthy while their fellow members reconnected with former employers to figure out how to renew contracts in the industrial cleaning business. Not all the members had sewing skills and therefore were not contributing or earning enough to stay members of the cooperative. Those who stayed employed continued to support each other during the quarantine through the mutual aid circles, adapting and helping all members survive the economic crisis.

The worker-owned cooperatives at La Colmena are formal examples of the solidarity economy that uses cultural traditions of mutual aid to uplift the agency and dignity of racialized people in capitalist societies like the United States. This particular cooperative model has been successful because it provides the members a communal way of surviving economic limitations. However, this model is only a harm reduction practice, not a systemic solution for the exclusionary practices of the legal system of immigration law and economic activity in the United States.

The WCBDI model thus provided a top-down approach that incubated the workers' ability to engage in the social economy. However, the worker-owned cooperatives still functioned with limited resources. Meanwhile, millions of dollars in funding go to mostly white-led incubator non-profits that so far have failed to trickle down any resources to the mostly Indigenous-led organizations like La Colmena that play a critical initial role in organizing the workers to start the incubation and later continue to support them long after the incubation period ends. Critics of the model argue that the power dynamics in the incubator white-led non-profits need to be addressed to make funding more equitable for the host organization, which must use its own resources and unpaid labor to support the workers who join the incubation process. Some workers–owners report that incubating and the extra time it takes for the leaders to start and run the cooperative takes an average of 12 hours of unpaid labor per week that do not get counted or remunerated anywhere in the arrangement with the formal non-profit that the city designates as the incubators.

Critics of the New York City cooperative model argue that despite the positive aspects of a supporting agency among the poor, this cooperative model does not change market dynamics because worker–owners must still compete for contracts with other low-wage workers. The current political anti-immigrant climate in the United States has increased the level of discrimination against immigrants and Indigenous people, making these workers' efforts an uphill battle. Given the pandemic and the ongoing economic downturn, the evaluation of the success of the model is yet to be completed. But one thing is certain: the women worker–owners of these cooperatives in Staten Island used their traditions of the social economy to come together and build a model of worker-owned cooperative that helps them adapt and meet their economic needs during a moment of global crisis.

Tandas as economic support in Perth Amboy, N.J.

This case study focuses on Tandas, a non-interest credit system with a focus on savings, used by Mexican immigrant women in Perth Amboy, New Jersey. Indigenous immigrants from Mexico have an ancestral tradition of communal living; they often share ownership of land with the tribe or in small villages with distant relatives and generations of the same family. They carry these cultural practices and belief systems with them into the new society they enter in the United States, and rely on extended family and village networks to survive their arrival and integration. According to Campos (1998) in her study on Mexican Tandas, their reliance on cultural practices also includes a mistrust of formal banks, which they feel excluded them from accessing capital and finance opportunities offered to white Mexicans.

In Mexico, financial institutions are usually located away from remote Indigenous communities. In response to this form of exclusion, Mexican Indigenous populations have a history of forming local lending circles, Tandas, to facilitate large investments or purchases in a time of need. Financial exclusion by the formal banks in Mexico conditions Indigenous people to mistrust banks in a new society like the United States. Hence, in response to the exclusion from the formal economy as undocumented immigrants, they find themselves returning to the practice of Tandas to save or avoid interactions with formal banks.

Anthropologist Carlos Vélez-Ibáñez (2010) shows that Mexican immigrants trust each other in the Tanda system because they have a tradition of focusing on the collective success of their tribe, not on the individual success of one member. Mexican migrants use Tandas not only as a response to financial exclusion, but also as a social connection to others like them who can alleviate the isolation of a new life in a totally new society and culture (Vélez-Ibáñez 2010). Tandas rely on the social dynamics and trust of group members to succeed. According to a report by the Mission Assets Funds, an organization that has formalized the practice of the social economy in the United States, 80 percent of immigrants who participate in the Tanda system actually make payments on time. Hossein (2016) makes an important observation about Tandas that applies across all cultures that participate in it: this informal lending system is female dominated. In her study of Black Canadian and Caribbean women, she found that women who started Tandas did so because they learned the practice from the women who raised them. She argues that this tradition of the social economy sees it passed down through generations as a way for women to support each other and create solidarity support networks. Along with the socialization that goes along with participating in a Tanda, women learn to manage their resources to meet their monthly commitments to each other. In this way, they gain social capital by increasing their trustworthiness and, in turn, their human capital as worthy members of an economic social lending circle.

This same experience is true for the Mexican women who immigrated to Perth Amboy, N.J. As Vélez-Ibáñez highlights, women can only participate in a Tanda when another member uses her social collateral to testify to the worthiness of their character. Therefore, the social capital an individual creates upon arriving in the new community becomes the economic collateral for joining a lending circle in a Tanda.

In the interviews, a woman called "Maribel," who has resided in Perth Amboy for 20 years, stated that the only person she knew when she immigrated from Mexico was her husband. Because she was undocumented, she wasn't able to find work, and so she felt isolated from the rest of the community. All that changed when she joined a local lending circle through a family friend who recommended her. With the funds she could access via the Tanda, she bought supplies to start making and selling homemade food and gelatins to other compatriots. The income she earned through her small food business increased her ability to contribute to her household budget and increase the family's standard of living. As "Maribel" states,

> In Mexico it was very common for us women to save our own money to buy our *vitrina* (a special cabinet), which is a must-have in all nice Mexican homes but it is not cheap. Men do not worry about house stuff. It is up to women to make the house look nice and we have to save by ourselves to make it happen. (Perth Amboy, NJ, 2019)

Another participant, "Maria," stated that since arriving in the United States in the 1990s, she tried to work multiple jobs, mostly in the restaurant industry, but she never had enough money to do nice things for herself or to send extra money back to her family in Mexico. She decided to start a Tanda to get enough money to send to her children in Mexico to pay for school tuition. She noted that it is common for the person who starts a Tanda to get the first pot of the money: "empeze la tanda y tome el primer numero. De ahi cegui el circulo." (Translation: I began the Tanda and I took the first number.) When asked if she was afraid people would not pay and leave her with all the liability, she stated that people not paying is a risk she takes because she knows most of the folks who join the Tanda and it is very rare that someone makes you *quedarte mal* (look bad) or disappears without paying their share. However, she notes, unlike 20 years ago, people save less than before because most of her neighbors are not earning enough to make ends meet.

Learning from the experience of other women she knows, "Maria" developed a system that would give her a sense of security, something similar to a regular bank credit rating system like proof of a job or a personal reference of good character from others already in the Tanda. As the Tanda grew larger, she accepted new people only when backed by someone already in the Tanda who promised to pay in case the person recommended was unable to meets its monthly contribution on time. For the most part, due to the personal relationships with folks who helped her expand the lending circle, the Tanda remains successful and is helping many families meet their financial obligations. After 20 years of living in the United States, "Maria" stated she has never opened a bank account in Perth Amboy: "I don't open an account because I am afraid that if I get deported it might be hard for me to get my money back. In Mexico, that happens a lot. If someone dies, the government keeps your money. Well, that is what I heard and what I believe" (Perth Amboy, NJ, 2019).

She states that she knows that it is hard for members in her community to get a loan in a bank because they have no formal job or any collateral to start a credit history with a bank. Therefore, like her, her neighbors keep relying on Tandas to find a way to *acomodarse* (to make do); that is, they can meet their family's basic needs and also afford a few luxuries, such as nice furniture for their homes or to pay for an important birthday celebration for their children.

4.7 Conclusion: Tandas for Social Integration of Indigenous Mexican Immigrants in the United States

The two empirical cases in this chapter illustrate how immigrants in two communities are using their cultural understanding and practices of the social economy to thrive and survive exclusion as undocumented migrants. Both of these strategies of economic activity—forming a domestic workers' cooperative and forming a Tanda—give the undocumented workers a sense of agency in their own struggle to integrate into the new society. Their illegal status as immigrants means that they must develop informal networks of economic support that includes not only their immediate family, but also their former village, tribe, and other compatriots. The social economy aids in their immediate economic survival and eventually helps them integrate into local economies.

As described in this chapter, the experience of integration for excluded undocumented Indigenous Mexicans reveals what is called a topology of vulnerability, covering four domains of analysis: the first is the context of their arrival predetermined by the immigration policies outside of the migrants' control; the second is the prejudices of the receiving society that values whiteness; the third is the conditions of the local economy upon arrival; and the fourth is the level of resources of the co-ethnic community that receives them (Portes and Rambaut 1990). Poorly resourced communities of undocumented migrants from Mexico, who lack access to formal jobs and the financial system, engage in mutual aid, Tandas, and in some cases pull resources together to form worker-owned cooperatives. These models of the social economy follow on the Mexican Indigenous tradition of community self-support: applying the social economy to fight against the exclusion they face as undocumented immigrants.

The current pandemic has demonstrated that in times of economic crisis, the social economy becomes a lifeline. The news stories during the pandemic reported examples of how vulnerable populations in communities across the United States began lending circles to support each other through job loss, aiding in the ability of immigrant women to stay afloat and avoid debt. The pandemic also brought attention to the social economy by the African American community in the suburbs, who went back to their cultural practice of mutual aid and created community lending circles to survive the lack of employment during the pandemic.

The success of Tandas and cooperatives as socioeconomic models in the United States cannot be evaluated using the metrics of traditional capitalist economics. They can only be evaluated by the sense of community, the experience of support and satisfaction the members get from helping each other while meeting their personal goals. Ultimately, the success of any one group of immigrants in the United States is measured not just by their survival, but by the many ways they overcome exclusion and build a stable financial support system to allow their children to one day demand a path to inclusion.

As political scientists evaluate how poorly resourced undocumented immigrants from the Global South survive in a racialized America, they need to focus more on the many ways these immigrants use their cultural ancestral capital in the social economy to build a life of opportunity, denied to them since the founding of the U.S. experiment as a model of capitalist enterprise. Exclusion is part of these Indigenous immigrants' American experience. However, their survival as a group is engrained in their tapping into ancestral cultural knowledge to create a sense of community and belonging in American society. Both exclusion and inclusion are therefore part of their American experience.

Works Cited

Borowiak, C. 2010. "Solidarity Economy Movements: Anti-Politics and the Crisis of Capitalism," paper given at the U.S. Social Forum, Detroit, Michigan (June 20). (Not published).

Bosniak, L. 2006. *The Citizen and the Alien: Dilemmas of Contemporary Membership*. Princeton: Princeton University Press.

Campos, P. 1998. "Las Tandas in Mexico, un enfoque de accion colectiva." *Sociologia* 13(37): 189–212.

Casas, A. and D. Boer. 2020. "Coronavirus Economy: The Banker Ladies Saving Friends from Debt." BBC News, September 21. https://www.bbc.com/news/world-us-canada-54035099. Accessed April 7, 2021.

Clarke, J., K. Coll, E. Dagnino, and C. Neveu. 2014. *Disputing Citizenship*. Bristol: Bristol University Press.

Cole, P. 2000. *Philosophies of Exclusion: Liberal Political Theory and Immigration*. Edinburgh: Edinburgh University Press.

Creswell, J. W. 2013. *Qualitative Inquiry and Research Design*. Los Angeles: Sage Press.

Curl, J. 2012. *For All the People: Uncovering the Hidden History of Co-operation, Co-operative Movements, and Communalism in America*, 2nd edn. Oakland: PM Press.

Góngora Almeida, S. O. and C. J. Ramos Caizaluisa. 2013. "Analisis Critico de la Economia Solidaria en Ecuador." *Revista Politecnica* 32(2): 127–133.

Gordon Nembhard, J. 2014. "The Benefits and Impacts of Co-operatives." *Grassroots Economic Organizing*, May 1. https://geo.co-op/story/benefits-and-impacts-co-operatives. Accessed April 7, 2021.

Gordon Nembhard, J., M. Johnson, J. Johnson, L. Krimerman, and A. N. Ifateyo. 2011. "Worker Co-operative Development Models and Approaches: A Brief Overview." *Grassroots Economic Organizing*, April 19. http://geo.co-op/node/627. Accessed February 9, 2014.

Hossein, C. S. 2016. *Politicized Microfinance: Money, Power and Violence in the Black Americas*. Toronto: University of Toronto Press.

Hossein, C. S. 2018. *The Black Social Economy in the Americas: Exploring Diverse Community Based Markets*. New York: Palgrave MacMillan.

Jenkins, D. and L. Justin. 2021. *Histories of Racial Capitalism*. New York City: Columbia University Press.

Kawano, E., T. N. Masterson, and J. Teller-Elsberg (eds.) 2009. *Solidarity Economy I: Building Alternatives for People and Planet*. Amherst: Center for Popular Economics.

Lopez, C. T. 2012. "Tianguis Indigena; The Solidarity Economy and Indigenous Women in Mexico." *Development* 55: 393–6.

Menjivar, C. 2000. *Fragmented Ties: Salvadoran Immigrant Networks in America*. Los Angeles: University of California Press.

Migration Policy Institute (MPI). 2021. "Unauthorized Immigrant Population Profiles." https://www.migrationpolicy.org/programs/us-immigration-policy-program-data-hub/unauthorized-immigrant-population-profiles. Accessed April 7, 2021.

Nichols, W. J. 2013. *The DREAMers: How the Undocumented Youth Movement Transformed the Immigrant Rights Debate*. Stanford: Stanford University Press.

Pauls, E. P. n.d. "Tribal Nomenclature: American Indian, Native American and First Nation." *Encyclopedia Britannica*. https://www.britannica.com/topic/Tribal-Nomenclature-American-Indian-Native-American-and-First-Nation-1386025. Accessed July 4, 2021.

Portes, A. and R. G. Rumbaut. 1990. *Immigrant America: A Portrait*. Los Angeles/Berkeley: University of California Press.

Robinson, C. 1983. *Black Marxism: The Making of the Black Radical Tradition*. Chapel Hill: University of North Carolina Press.

Saegert, S., J. P. Thompson, and M. R. Warren. 2005. *Social Capital and Poor Communities*. Ford Foundation Series on Asset Building. New York: Russell Sage Foundation.

Safri, M. 2015. "Mapping Noncapitalist Supply Chains: Toward an Alternate Conception of Value Creation and Distribution." *Organization* 22(6): 924–41.

Safri, M. 2021. "Mapping the U.S. Solidarity City: Spatializing Diversity, Difference and Social Justice." Liviana Conference for the Community Economies Research Network. https://www.youtube.com/watch?v=07KR7Zh9Zsk. Accessed November 11, 2021.

Vélez-Ibáñez, C. G. 2000. *An Impossible Living in a Transborder World: Culture, Confianza and Economy of Mexican Origin Populations*. Tucson: The University of Arizona Press.

Vélez-Ibáñez, C. G. 2010. *Tandas and Cundinas*. School of Transborder Studies and School of Human Evolution and Social Change. Tucson: University of Arizona Press.

Worker Co-operative Business Development Initiative (WCBDI). 2018. "Working Together: A Report on the Four Years of the WCBDI." Small Business Services, City of New York. https://www1.nyc.gov/assets/sbs/downloads/pdf/about/reports/worker_co-op_report_fy18.pdf. Accessed April 7, 2021.

5

Routes out of Racial Capitalism

Black Cooperatives in the United States

Adotey Bing-Pappoe and Amina Mama

5.1 Introduction

The hallmark of African people's collectivist or cooperative economic activity is often seen in the informal saving and lending schemes known as Susu or rotating and savings credit associations (ROSCAs). These arrangements are found in both the African continent and its diaspora (Ardener 1964). They have helped structurally excluded communities to mobilize their own financial resources. We know from Walter Rodney (1972) and Samir Amin (1974) that initially European imperialists/colonialists first captured African bodies, transported, and enslaved them, to produce wealth for Europe and its offshoots around the world. Then they restructured African production to suit the needs of European industrialization. In the United States, the social order was centered foundationally on the invention of "race" as a key trope in an imperialist, white supremacist ideology, known as manifest destiny. As Caroline Shenaz Hossein (2018) observes in her conceptualization of the Black social economy:

> Black scholars who write about the diaspora such as W.E.B. Du Bois, Marcus Garvey, and Jessica Gordon Nembhard (2014) have traced the African diaspora's community-focused economies back to the days of enslavement. They also note that Black people have taken great risks to develop new economies. Despite the terror Black people endured in the Americas and Europe, people found ways to create livable economies based on co-operation and collectivity through money pooling systems. (Hossein 2013)

In *The Black Social Economy*, Hossein (2018) also documents multiple instances in which people of African descent continue to use collective savings strategies, despite centuries of dislocation. African people therefore often deployed ROSCAs and similar initiatives to build safe havens from the rapacious racialized capitalism they had to endure at home and abroad. Sometimes these initiatives served as economic survival

Adotey Bing-Pappoe and Amina Mama, *Routes out of Racial Capitalism*. In: *Beyond Racial Capitalism*.
Edited by Caroline Shenaz Hossein, Sharon D. Wright Austin, and Kevin Edmonds, Oxford University Press.
 DOI: 10.1093/oso/9780192868336.003.0006

strategies that protected vulnerable groups from destitution. Others used cooperative strategies to consciously resist racial capitalism.

Often, cooperating was the only route through which African-descended families and communities could acquire the essential pre-requisites for the most basic levels of survival. Hossein (2018) details how in Toronto, Canada, the Banker Ladies were the ones who organized and administered these mutual aid financing schemes. The Banker Ladies in this study are racialized women, either Canadian or foreign-born, but all are Canadian citizens who find usefulness in collective organizing. In some places and times, Banker Ladies came to acquire positions of social leverage, able to influence the what, how, and why of the circulation of money within the economy. But over time, other more structured and systemic models of cooperative organizing were used to secure empowerment and agency.

This chapter explores three examples of cooperation—from resource pooling and lending to collective ownership of businesses. Cooperative initiatives often make use of three of the seven foundational principles of cooperative organizing: free and voluntary membership, economic participation, and democratic governance. We are interested in exploring what these three examples of cooperative organization offer in relation to the Black radical traditions of resistance and the theorization of "racial capitalism" advanced by U.S. Black radical thinkers. Our rationale is that our three examples are situated epistemologically and politically in the same national context: that of a United States in which white supremacy and Black poverty, accompanied by racialized mass incarceration and anti-Black violence, have persisted.

In considering the different kinds of cooperation in our case studies, we address both the existential–political and material aspects of organizing. We also found it productive to draw on the Marxist concept of alienation of Black labor in the U.S. context, given the particularly brutal form it has taken throughout its history. We find that the shifting discourses of Black liberation undergird the praxis of those involved in these more radical forms of cooperation in which both ownership and power are democratized and shared. We also find labor relations being redefined as a way of counteracting the alienation that characterizes U.S. capital–labor relations which remain extreme for Black workers because of the racialized variant of capitalism that continues to prevail in the United States.

To address our interest in the radical potential implicit in the transformation of labor relations into more cooperative and less alienating forms in the context of such a racialized form of capitalism, we identified three very different examples and carried out field visits to all three sites during the month of June 2019. The key question we were interested in exploring was to what extent does each cooperative offer the possibility of a radical haven from racial capitalism, which although still present, is being weakened through various struggles taking place within and across its interstices?

5.2 Methodology and Approaches

To address our interest in the radical potential implicit in cooperative organizing, we applied the theorization of racial capitalism that derives from Cedric Robinson's (1983) influential book *Black Marxism*. The three cases have been chosen to illustrate the diversity of scale and scope that characterizes Black resistance to racial capitalism in the United States, rather than for comparative analysis. The Federation of Southern Co-operatives (FSC), the Mandela Grocery, and Co-operation Jackson each offer a unique illustration of Black self-defence and survival in the face of the profound structuring of Black social and economic life by racism. To pursue our interest, we also examined their websites and materials, as well as the work of Black scholars such as Jessica Gordon Nembhard (2014) and Caroline Shenaz Hossein (2018), both experts on North American cooperatives.

In addition to touring and observing each site and considering the distinct historical and material conditions under which each was established, we carried out interviews with founders and other members of each cooperative. We were therefore able to gather qualitative information on the subjective experience of cooperative members and on how much their lives and economic circumstances were affected by their cooperative engagement. Following our initial outreach, our interviews were somewhat formal and by appointment. We presented ourselves through our declared interest in the liberatory power of cooperatives. We also openly identified ourselves as coming from the African continent (Ghana and Nigeria) and having a genuine interest in potential benefits of cooperative organizing for the development of Africans within the continent or abroad. With hindsight we consider this to have been a respectful and collegial approach that worked well, given the historic interest of African Americans on the "Mother Continent." In this respect, we positioned ourselves as colleagues who were in political and ideological solidarity with our interlocutors rather than attempting to simulate the alienating remoteness of certain kinds of scholarship. Our approach seems to have been very well received, judging from the quality of the discussions we were afforded.

Our approach was also in keeping with our desire to draw connections between the critical epistemology of Black radical scholarly discourse and the equally critical activism of those surviving and resisting the impact of racial capitalism through local organizing. This means U.S. Black studies and scholarship often had to respond to the same material and ideological conditions that faced those involved in Black cooperatives, particularly worker cooperatives which we regard as the most visionary and radical form among the wider range of economic strategies that Hossein conceptualizes as the "Black social economy." Many of these are about negotiating and surviving in contexts of racial capitalism or pooling resources to offset racialized economic vulnerability and insecurity.

Black cooperatives can be regarded as a form of Black social economy. However, cooperatives are not necessarily anti-capitalist but attempts to pool resources through joint procurement, selling, and/or savings to improve the lot of the Black underclass.

Such practices alleviate poverty but they do not eradicate the basis of poverty which in our view requires democratization of the ownership and governance of businesses. Worker cooperatives, which do just that, transform the capital–labor relationship into one where capital serves labor. Nevertheless, in choosing to investigate the three Black-owned cooperatives, (which were not all worker cooperatives), we intentionally privilege cooperatives that engage in efforts not just to increase wealth but also to secure some form of collective ownership and self-determination. In this way, they counter the racialized alienation to which the majority of African Americans are still subjected. We find that the alienation of Black communities in the United States informs the discourse of Black radical scholars as much as it informs the practices of Black-owned cooperatives at all three locations and over time. In other words, Black theory and practice are in the recursive (co-constitutive) relationship that contrasts with mainstream scholarly conventions of distance and "objectivity."

Our field visits and discussions also exposed us to the realities and legacies of U.S. racial capitalism. While one of us has resided in Alameda County, California, for the past ten years, neither of us had ever visited Mississippi or spent any significant time anywhere in the southern states. For example, we found to our surprise the absence of any legal framework to support or protect cooperative organizations, thereby obliging organizers in Mississippi to contort existing business forms to approximations of what they would have wished. In other words, our impressions are not those of locals but rather the product of our experiences of local places, of organizing sites and offices, and most of all with the people who generously participated in our investigation and shared their experiences. Overall, we interviewed fourteen people: six from the Federation of South Co-operatives, six from Co-operation Jackson, and two during our visit to the Mandela Food Co-operative. Most of our conversations lasted for several hours and were accompanied by tours of their facilities (the Appendix lists names and organizations).

5.3 Black Cooperative Praxis: Three Case Studies

Here we offer a brief synthesis of the results of our field visits to the FSC, Co-operation Jackson, and Mandela Grocery during the month of June 2019, before considering what insights the theoretical approach we proposed in Section 5.2 might generate.

The Federation of Southern Co-operatives (FSC)

Our interaction included conversational interviews with Ben Burkett, Myra Bryant, Wendell Paris, Hollis Jackson, Kimberly Crisler, and John Zippert. The FSC is the oldest and most established of the three examples considered here and is today a major player sustaining Black landholding in the United States. Indeed, the FSC could be considered the economic arm of the civil rights movement. Small farmers in general were not getting fair prices for their agricultural produce (e.g., sweet potatoes) in the capitalist marketplace, but it was the Black farmers who began pooling their crops for sale to overcome Jim Crow. They had little choice, given that they had been excluded from the farm support system built by the U.S. Department of Agriculture (USDA).

Discriminatory practices reigned. For example, state authorities were known to make Black, but not white, farmers, wait for up to 40 days to receive payment for their produce. The Southwest Alabama Co-operative Farmers Association was established in 1967 and headquartered on Black-owned farmland, where it played a significant role in the emergence of Black Power. When white people evicted them overnight for registering to vote, the organization built a vast tent city. Black farmers supported and protected the voting rights activists, including Stokely Carmichael, H. Rapp Brown, and others who were targets of white police forces and marauding white supremacists. Gerrymandering was so extensive in Tuskegee that it produced a voting region with 160 sides! The backbone of the civil rights movement grew among these Black landowning small farmers.

In South Central Alabama we were told how, in the 1960s, Black farmers had faced multiple efforts to cripple their business and had pushed back, over and over again. One example was the restriction of Black people's access to fertilizer to just three sources, so that white vendors could overcharge them. Black farmers responded by organizing to buy a train load of fertilizer and distributing it to their members. In another instance, Southwest Alabama farmers who grew high-quality pickling cucumbers and okra, and were being paid just 3 cents per pound (three dollars per 100 pounds) reached across the state line to sell in bulk for more than double the price—at eight dollars per 100 pounds. Governor George Wallace on one occasion personally intercepted their trucks using state troopers to detain them for as long as it took (72 hours) for the shipment to rot, leaving "Nothing but cucumber juice," according to Wendell Paris. All protestations were rebutted with the information that "the law states that state troopers can stop any vehicle for 72 hours without explanation. It's the Law."

FSC members understood that the authorities feared that cooperatives would enable local communities to negotiate from a position of greater market power. They situated their organizing under the historical conditions that have been elaborated previously by Black scholars, who have recounted them from memory. Cognisant that we were from continental Africa, they reminded us that in the United States, the enslavement of Africans ended in 1865 and that 35 years after slavery ended, at the beginning of the 1900s, African Americans owned as much as 20 million acres of land. Wendell Paris described how people began losing the land, especially after the depression of the 1920s, when the harsh conditions of the rural South led many to seek better prospects in the northern manufacturing industries. He estimated that by 1961, African American farmers owned only 16 million acres, and the loss of land has continued. Currently (2019), just 3 million acres of farmland are estimated to be owned by African Americans. This presents the real danger of Black rural people becoming a tenant class instead of landowning farmers. These figures indicating loss of land by Black farmers are mirrored by fluctuations in the number of Black farmers registered by the USDA. While there was an overall decline in the number of farmers in the USA from 1900 to 1997, Black farmers bore a disproportionate share of this: by 63 percent between 1900 and 1959, compared to 31 percent of white farmers, and then by 93 percent between 1959 and 1997 compared to 45 percent among white farmers. The situation in the South between 1900 and 1959 was 64 percent decline in Black famer numbers compared to 26 percent among white framers (Reynolds 2001).

Partially in response to this, the FSC was established in 1967. It was to serve as an umbrella organization that would connect and strengthen local cooperatives across state borders at a time when there was no state support for Black cooperatives. The early members set about educating themselves and training their members in cooperative organizing. The FSC operated in the Black Belt, the crescent of rich and fertile land running from North Carolina, through South Carolina, Georgia, Alabama, Mississippi, Louisiana, and Texas. This also happened to be Black in another sense, as it was where African American people were concentrated. As a result, the FSC faced constant efforts directed at removing it and its members.

White Americans wanted total control of the South, fearing that the large numbers of Black people living there would organize and take control. However, poor white farmers also joined Black-led cooperatives because of the benefits they could enjoy by doing so. Members came to appreciate that these cooperatives offered a collective ladder to individual advancement. The U.S. government systematically withheld support from Black cooperatives. Members recalled being shocked to discover that the U.S. government sponsored cooperative programs outside of the United States (specifically in Israel), while they refused to support the same among Black farmers at home. In any event, Black-owned cooperatives did not develop to much beyond procurement of input and the marketing of produce.

In the South the dispossession of Black farmers was executed by institutionalized, legal means. Among these was the practice of "Partition Sales" based on a rule that allowed any person who owned a portion of a plot of land to sell the whole plot, including the portion they did not own. Those who wished to challenge the growing strength of Black farmers only had to acquire a small portion of Black-owned land to be able to sell whole plots out from under them. "Adverse possession" was a practice that allowed a farmer who had improved land on the boundary with their neighbor to then encroach on it and eventually claim their neighbor's land as their own. Loans gave the lender a charge on the property of the person who had borrowed. Often, white lenders would simply refuse to acknowledge that a loan had been repaid in order to be able to take possession of Black land.

We were told that "there was a man in Alabama who wanted to borrow just 1,000 dollars to put on a tin roof, but he had to mortgage all 200 acres (valued at $300 per acre), and after he had repaid the loan and interest the bank refused to cancel the promissory note." We were also told of instances in which white farmers would call police to arrest Black farmers who were cutting wood on their own land. Another ruse used to prey on Black farmers involved identifying the weakest member of the family and then entrapping them in debt. Black people could hardly ever win a case in the Southern courts. However, Wendell Paris shared his personal experience of taking a case to the federal court to defend his land ownership. In a rare victory, he and his family "won" and were able to re-purchase their previously owned land back from a white farmer.

We were also told of how during slavery, all children of enslaved women were assigned the same ethnicity as their mother, irrespective of the ethnicity of the father. This practice increased the size of the enslaved population and allowed white men to impregnate the enslaved females on their farms while conserving their property, a practice that the Christian Church condoned. Despite some changes, land is still being lost to this day. Farmers are still having to mortgage land, and irrespective of the value of the mortgage, lenders still insist on mortgaging the entire property for even the smallest of loans. And even when loans are repaid, white lenders can still refuse to remove the promissory note from their books.

Individuals can become members of the FSC only by becoming a member of their regional body. The FSC has become as successful as it has by relying on the effectiveness of its regional offices. Some have argued that it has therefore not attracted the kind of opposition that it might otherwise have faced had it been more centralized. One challenge the FSC faces today is the difficulty in attracting the younger generation. Based on what we were told, the FSC sees its task today as being to maintain, sustain, and educate its current members and the wider Black community regarding the still untapped liberatory potential of cooperative organizing.[1]

Apart from these loftier strategic concerns the FSC is faced with maintaining its continued possession of its strategically located building, just one block away from the state capitol, which some would like to see them vacate.

Build and fight with Co-operation Jackson

Co-operation Jackson is an African American cooperative in Jackson, Mississippi. It began on May 1, 2014, and had its origins in the program to build a safe space for African people in the United States. The election of Chokwe Lumumba provided an opportunity for Kali Akuno, his partner Sacajawea Hall, and like-minded others to bring their history of radical activism to local struggles to transform social relations in workplaces. Their political orientation drew on the Jackson–Kush Plan

[1] We were also told of a new organization in the Mississippi area, Co-operation South, that lacks the history and land base of the FSC, but recognizes the viability of the model and is trying to influence Black people to buy land.

developed by the New Afrikan People's Organization (NAPO) and the Malcom X Grassroots Movement (MXGM) between 2004 and 2010. A crucial precondition for Co-operation Jackson was the accumulation of start-up capital. Akuno and others set about raising that capital from African Americans and liberal white supporters who wished to see Chokwe Lumumba succeed as mayor. Co-operation Jackson invested the funds raised to purchase property and so provide the owned base from which their operations could take place and generate the required revenues.

The model is based on what Co-operation Jackson calls "anchors." The first step of which is to use the seed capital to incubate a number of cooperatives. During this period, their paid members—the anchors—receive financial support from the central fund. When these initial cooperatives become successful, they are expected to make contributions into the central fund from which other incubating cooperatives will be supported.

At the time of the interview, there were three anchors: the Green Team, Freedom Farm, and the Community Production Centre. The Green Team engages in lawn cutting, trimming, mulching, and composting. All members were given training, and the anchors were provided with stipends and a start-up fund of $25,000. They made decisions around buying all their equipment, space, and infrastructure. In 2019, they paid about $100 a month into the Co-operation Jackson collective financial pool. The Freedom Farm focuses on growing a range of crops and exploring the use of hydroponic agriculture and aquaculture. At the time of the interviews (June 2019), it had just acquired an anchor, Imani, who had taken up the task of leading the project for the next year, which she did, and then remained thereafter. The Community Production Centre is a printing center using a range of modern techniques including 3-D printing. The anchors received two years' support for equipment and training. Membership of the community production center requires a contribution of $2500, but those who are accepted and do not have the funds to pay this fee are able to do so using a time-bank. At the time of the interview, the project had two anchors trained in electronic engineering.

Two other projects in the pipeline were a cooperative shopping center or mall and a housing construction project. Other possible cooperative ventures included a waste management business, recycling (sorting) and composting, a security service, arts and cultural production, construction, day-labor, solar insulation and green retrofitting, auto repair, food service and catering, healthcare, and childcare. In the medium term, the objective is to make the whole project self-sustaining and no longer in need of philanthropic funding. Among the challenges faced by Co-operation Jackson is that Mississippi law does not provide for workers' cooperatives. As a result, existing legal frameworks must be contorted to allow as much economic democracy as can be squeezed out of them.

The plan is that each of the cooperatives and Co-operation Jackson as a whole will operate along the International Co-operative Alliance's (ICA) seven cooperative principles. In addition to internal democracy the existing wage structure is the product of members' decisions. At the time of our visit all full-time members earned

$45,000 a year. The anchors of the Green Team and Freedom Farms earn $35,000. Money has been set aside for health insurance for anchors, but at the time of the interviews there was only one provider of Obamacare in Mississippi, and there was no Medicaid (insurance for those on low income) in the state. Training is continuous, and Co-operation Jackson is in the process of developing its own learning pack. Different individuals take the lead according to the subject of the training, but the training is done collectively.

During 2017 and 2018, Co-operation Jackson was involved in several initiatives involving the wider community. Peoples' Assemblies are meetings of the population of Jackson and intended as vehicles of Black self-determination. They are organized around specific proposals for discussion and determination. They can organize social projects and put pressure on the local government authorities to take or not take certain actions. Some of their sessions have dealt with specific topics, such as participatory budgeting. Conducting education programs in the surrounding community has been an important aspect of Co-operation Jackson's mobilization work.

Co-operation Jackson has made it a point to actively apply the ICA's cooperative principles about open membership. By insisting that all Black people are welcome irrespective of sexuality, for example, they have attracted hostility from certain sections of the "counter-movement" known as "Black Straight Pride." The personal testimonies of some people interviewed demonstrated the value to them of being part of a Black collective that seeks to be democratic and inclusive in its procedures.

Mandela Grocery in Oakland

Mandela Grocery is situated opposite the West Oakland Bay Area Transit Station, in Oakland, California. It's website reads: "Mandela is operated, centrally governed, and democratically controlled by our worker-owners. Our structure and operations are guided by cooperative principles and a strong community centered mission" (https://www.mandelagrocery.coop). This is a public commitment to worker cooperatives. But it did not start out as such. It was opened by a group of nine young people—seven African Americans, one LatinX, and one white—in 2009 as a non-profit community grocery store. Members told us that they did not initially invest in studying and learning the basics of cooperative organization.

An organization called Mandela MarketPlace provided grant writing services to raise the necessary start-up funds, and it was initially financed through loans and grants and by the City of Oakland. Interviewees told us that there was a public perception the store was run by the white executive director of Mandela MarketPlace rather than by the members, and that it was not patronized particularly by the local Black community. It was only after a couple of years that the business was turned into a cooperative. The members of Mandela Grocery celebrated its tenth anniversary in 2019, and it now operates on the basis of all seven ICA principles. Most importantly, it practices open, non-discriminatory ownership; economic participation through shared capital; and participatory-democratic decision-making. Today there are eight Black worker-owners, of whom three are men and five women, and the group is queer-inclusive.

The members hold weekly morning meetings (Mondays) and speak to a set agenda. The day-to-day operational issues are debated at these meetings, including, for example, whether to grant the request from this chapter's authors for an interview and who would speak on the group's behalf. There are also quarterly meetings where members discuss finances and issues such as training and the future, as well as more strategic issues. The default option is to achieve consensus, but there are instances when decisions have to be made by voting.

Similar to membership of the community production center in Co-operation Jackson, a would-be member of Mandela Grocery would have to pay a membership fee, in this case $2000 (previously $2500), which can be earned through a time-bank once they have been accepted as a member in principle. All the members are paid the same salary (at the time of the interview, this was $16 per hour, which we were told was under review) irrespective of the roles that they play. At one point, a manager was appointed (and paid $26 per hour), but for a number of reasons it did not work out and they left. The group has gone back to a flat organization and dispensed with a hierarchical general manager position.

Decisions made about how the profits should be allocated stipulate that in the first instance, 40 percent will be saved by the organization. The remainder is then divided up among the members based on hours worked. However, members receive only 30 percent of this amount in cash. The rest is retained by the cooperative and is treated as a debt of the cooperative to its members, similar in structure to the world famous Mondradon cooperative in Spain. This means that each year members are building up a fund that is held by the store. When members leave the cooperative, this fund is paid out to them. To date, only one member has left, which happened at the request of the rest of the group.

After ten years of business, the co-op is thinking of opening a second store in Oakland which they expect to have up and running in the next two years (as of June 2018). Among the lessons learnt were the importance of transparency and consensus and of providing training to prospective and existing members about the general demands of running a grocery business, as well as the special demands a cooperative business places on the shoulders of its members. The Arizmendi cooperative, a larger California-based organization, provides regular training sessions on cooperatives and cooperative businesses, which the members of Mandela Grocery have attended.

According to our interviewees, the business made a number of mistakes in its first five years, during which time the importance of training was highlighted by a high turnover. It was only in 2018 that the business became fully autonomous, no longer owing any money to any external agency or body. At this point, it became able to make strategic plans for its own future. Those we interviewed expressed a desire to promote their brand as an African American-owned cooperative business, although this is not made explicit on their website, which states a broader ethos, "We intentionally support businesses run by people of color because we are deeply committed to creating opportunity for interdependence in the food space, where POC entrepreneurs generate livable incomes." Mandela members are planning to introduce a kitchen project into the store so people can purchase cooked food as well as provisions. They want to use their purchasing power to bring other African American-owned businesses, particularly cooperatives, into their value chain. As part of that initiative, some public meetings have been held in the West Oakland area, leading to the formation of a West Oakland's Co-operative group, which meets on a regular basis. The testimonies of the interviewees provided numerous instances of the personal benefits they experience from being a member of a cooperative—and an all African American, queer-friendly one at that.

5.4 Theoretical Explorations: The U.S. Black Radical Tradition and Marxism

What can we learn from these three case studies, and to what extent and how is their practice informed by the ideas of the Black radical intellectual tradition? In all three examples, formation can be seen to depend on the concrete circumstances at the moment of their inception. The historical experiences of the members of the FSC were immediate and unfiltered. Structured and racialized capitalism threatened the lives and livelihoods of all Black people, especially those who sought to organize in any way and particularly in ways that did not appear to promote private enterprise. Their members were involved in a struggle for their very existence in the Jim Crow South of the 1960s. In the slightly different context of the twenty-first century today's Black community has had the benefit of post-segregation access to public education, and their struggles are as much existential as they are about resisting group exploitation. Members are conscious that unless they organize to resist prevailing conditions, these will continue to impoverish and alienate them, and self-determination will remain an elusive dream. Some members are acting out of a political motivation to see an end of systemic exploitation and see the current order as a racist one that impoverishes the majority by its very design. Co-operation Jackson was founded relatively recently, by activists from Oakland who moved to Jackson at a particular moment in Mississippi's history—following the first-ever election of former Black Nationalist Mayor Chokwe Lumumba in 2013. So, while it has local members and engages with local conditions, its founding members included Black activists from elsewhere in the United States, and Oakland in particular. In Oakland, California, members of the Mandela Grocery had less existentially hostile experiences, at least not ones that regularly involved direct confrontations with organized white supremacists.

The Black radical scholarly tradition associated with (among others) Cedric Robinson (1983), Robin G. Kelley (2002), and Angela Davis (1982, 2003, 2011) (all three of whom spent much of their careers in the University of California) articulates an anti-capitalist and anti-racist politics that was discernable among all three Black cooperative members. This led us to see Black cooperatives as an important part of the broader liberation project that is enunciated and affirmed by Black radical thinkers. To deepen our analysis, we therefore proceed to explore what a U.S. Black radical tradition that now includes Black feminist analyses and is queer-friendly further contributes to our analysis of the Black cooperative movement in the United States.

Noting the focus on the U.S. state, we found ourselves questioning whether it provides a methodology that adequately addresses the alienation created by everyday subjection to racism. Economic conditions of exploitation and marginalization are just one index of Black people's situation. To properly address this question, we begin by revisiting the historical conditions that situate both Black struggles and Black radical intellectual discourse in the United States. We found the collective alienation to include poverty and labor exploitation, facilitated by Black underemployment, but that the subjection to regular existential humiliation—such as fear of police violence and mass incarceration—dominated Black lives long before the Movement for Black Lives erupted.

Many of the Black movements in the United States have been neither revolutionary nor anti-capitalist, but they have generally been pro-Black and anti-imperialist. In the race-nationalist Garveyite movement, for example, capitalist and patriarchal ideas dominated. Black thought did, too, until continued failures led intellectuals to draw the connections between race and class, to develop the anti-capitalist thinking that has defined the Black radical tradition since Cedric Robinson's classic text *Black Marxism* was first published in 1983. Robinson and subsequent Black radical theorists unanimously place race front and center in the theorization of "racial capitalism," in which "race" predates and gives rise to class formation, not the other way around. In this respect, this work rejects earlier leftist theories of racism that locate it as an ideological construction that developed to justify the mass enslavement and exploitation of Africans that fueled capitalist expansion. In evidence, Robinson traces a history of racism all the way from ancient empires to the contemporary period of neoliberal capitalism (Robinson 1983).

The publication of Angela Davis' landmark text *Women, Race and Class* in 1981 (two years before Robinson's text) heralded the rise to prominence of Black feminist thought. Davis extends a Marxist critique of capitalism and imperialism not to afford precedence to race or class, but instead to demonstrate the inseparability of class, race, and sex/gender dynamics, referencing the systematic rape of Black women and the systematic lynching and castration of Black men by white men. In attending to the centrality of racialized sexual violence, Davis took Black radical and feminist thought to a new level of complexity. Black feminist analyses have acquired wider currency in the post-Black Power United States. The focus on the interconnections of gender, race, and sexuality has since been popularized through the term "intersectionality," coined by legal scholar Kimberly Crenshaw in a widely cited essay (Crenshaw 1989).

In the twenty-first century, this critical direction had developed into a more inclusive, queer-friendly, anti-capitalist discourse referred to as "women-of-color" feminism and was accompanied by a new articulation of abolitionist politics (Davis 2003, 2011). More recent work in the Black radical tradition emphasizes the historical links between the past enslavement and contemporary mass incarceration of Black people. Contemporary movements have been catalyzed by the ongoing extrajudicial murders of hundreds of Black citizens by the police (Ransby 2005, 2018). Historian Barbara Ransby (2018, 189) draws links between recent protests and broader class struggles:

> BLMM/M4BL (Movement for Black Lives) can be viewed as a Black-led class struggle—informed by, grounded in, and bolstered by Black feminist politics. This is evidenced by its links to the low-wage worker movement, through Alicia Garza's leadership of the National Domestic Workers Alliance, BYP100's collaborative efforts with the Fight for 15 and its "Agenda to Build Black Futures" economic justice campaign, and the Dream Defender's opposition to capitalism. Over and over, BLMM/M4BL leaders and organizers have insisted not only that racial justice must include economic justice and vice versa, but that the two are intimately connected.

We find the Black Youth Project 100's Agenda to Build Black Futures explicitly endorses Black cooperatives, as its website claims:

> Co-operative Enterprises (also known as co-ops) economically empower Black people and provide an alternative to top-down corporations within an exploitative, capitalist enterprise system. They promote shared decision-making power, shared ownership and shared profits. Co-operative ownership among Black people is not a novel idea, as market failures and economic racial discrimination have historically driven co-operative practice ... Several types of co-ops that could be started by young Black people right now to support Black communities include worker-owned business co-ops, producer-owned co-ops, housing co-ops, consumer co-ops. (BYP n.d., 38)

While M4BL was catalyzed by increasingly brutal police killings of Black people, it is also expressly anti-capitalist and directly informed by the prison abolition movement that preceded it. M4BL's decentralized, anti-hierarchical strategy and its public discourse and mass actions span class, gender, sexuality, ethnic, and other differences, reflecting the fact that it was started by three Black, queer feminists. The intersectional political analysis that M4BL embodies reiterates the core political ideas that we found in Co-operation Jackson just a year earlier. M4BL generated the most sustained protests by Black people in the history of the United States, attracting much wider support and participation than any previous movement. Black feminist theory has been an important influence on U.S. anti-capitalist thinking that continues to influence Black women globally.

5.5 Routes to Overcoming Alienation

In examining the circumstances of Black people, we found it helpful to press into service some ideas from Marxism, particularly on alienation. The idea of capital as alienated labor was a core idea that Karl Marx contributed to the analysis of political economy. Its foundation is the insight that, as a rule, workers in any social system produce surplus value. According to Marx's historiography, pre-capitalist laborers were not alienated from their product. They would have chosen to engage in its production, had their own means of production, would have determined how it was to be produced, and established social relations with those with whom they worked; perhaps most importantly from an economic perspective, the surplus generated during the course of production was theirs to determine how to use. Under capitalism, however, it is necessary to have a class of people who have been structurally separated from their own means of production. This separation is the foundation upon which the employment contract rests, and which while the worker toils under it, places them in a position similar to that of a slave. Workers agree to carry out work that has no meaning for them beyond fulfilment of the contract, and the employer determines whatever is produced and how. The labor performed has no special meaning for the workers, and with industrialization it became increasingly removed from any expression of their individuality or creativity. Finally, the terms of the capitalist employment contract stipulates that whatever the worker produces belongs to the employer. The fruit of their productive labor makes their employers more powerful and them relatively less so. It exemplifies the workers' lack of agency and their employers' growing agency and ability to exercise control over them, made possible by the workers' own labor, which has been alienated from them.

When Yugoslav theorist Jaroslav Vanek (1970) studied the cooperatives established in his own national context, he investigated their economic characteristics in a text entitled *The General Theory of Labour Managed Economies*. In the process, he became one of the first to show that an economy consisting mainly of democratically managed businesses could work effectively. Later he turned to their liberatory political, social, and psychological consequences for working and, also, colonized people. In *The Participatory Economy*, Vanek (1971) imagines a citizen of a colonized country. Here production is alienated, but in a somewhat different way from that under capitalist social relations. He examines this by examining labor-managed firms in the context of a country that has come out of colonialism which has chosen to make cooperative enterprise the dominant form of business organizing.

In Vanek's model the principle means of production are socialized—owned by the state. Workers would hire the means of production—specifically, the buildings and machines—from the state. This novel approach allows workers to retain their

Table 5.1 The political domain

		The Political Domain	
The Economic Domain		Internal	External
	Internal	Self-determination (Independent) Self-determination (Economic democracy)	No self-determination (Colonized) Self-determination (Economic democracy)
	External	Self-determination (Independent) Autocratic (Economic dictatorship)	No self-determination (Colonized) Autocratic (Economic dictatorship)

agency, even though they do not own the means of production. They are therefore able to avoid the loss of agency envisaged in Marx's theory of alienation. The employment contract would not be between the workers and an outside entity—the state or an individual or group of capitalists—but rather between the workers themselves. So, labor would be sharing with labor, while hiring capital rather than being employed by its owners. Vanek's work is relevant here because he explored how issues of national political and economic self-determination could be pursued by a group of people, and in particular how this could be achieved through a cooperative economy. As shown in Table 5.1, his framework identifies two domains: the political and the economic. According to his model, to be healthy, individuals and groups need to experience internal and external "self-determination" in both domains. On the one hand, external political self-determination involves the absence of limitations on group sovereignty while internal political self-determination involves individual rights and political democracy. On the other hand, external economic self-determination involves self-direction by the economic units while internal economic self-determination requires democratic decision-making by all members of the economic unit.

These ideas seem to us to be relevant to the struggles of African peoples, wherever they may be. Their focus in on the lived experience of ordinary people, an approach which in our view extends the Marxist concept of alienation in a manner that is useful for the analysis of Black liberation on both the political and economic fronts. He provides activist groups with a framework for assessing the degree to which they are achieving their political and economic objectives. We have extended this approach to a people subjected to a system of racial capitalism as a way of overcoming their alienation and regaining their self-determination. This approach helps us to explain our findings regarding the subjective benefits that members described in all three of the cooperatives studied here.

Indeed, in our view Vanek's focus on the practical pursuit of self-determination rather than the theorization of alienation has immediate relevance to Black radical theory and practice, or praxis. Since the days of the Garveyites, Black Americans have pursued freedom dreams that involved the acquisition of their own lands and control over their own labor, whether this required them to return to Africa or to establish Black-owned businesses as we found in the FSC, which set about seeking to protect Black land ownership. Black cooperative ownership is a key tenet of the Jackson–Kush Plan, which as noted earlier, informed the formation of Co-operation Jackson.

5.6 Conclusion: Historical Evolution of Radical Theory and Practice

The three Black cooperatives discussed in this chapter were clearly informed by the history and experience of earlier Black movements and the Black radical tradition. A small corpus of activist texts circulates among Black movements and community organizers, including the members of the three Black cooperative organizations: FSC, Mandela Grocery, and Co-operation Jackson. In examining the Black radical tradition and its engagement with Marxism, we discern three visions informing the Black freedom struggle: non-racial capitalism, racial capitalism, and non-racial anti-capitalism or socialism. We found we could productively apply these terms both to the theorists we referred to and to the three cooperatives. Our purpose in this section is to explore how they are interconnected and yet distinguishable.

Racial capitalism

In taking forward our discussion of Black cooperative praxis and the Black radical tradition in the contemporary United States, we are struck by the historical conditions that weave between U.S. Black struggles for freedom and self-determination and Black radical intellectual discourse, typified by the theory of racial capitalism. Black movements resisting white supremacy and racism have informed the Black radical tradition of scholarship, exemplified here by Cedric Robinson (1983), and pursued in the twenty-first-century writings of his former student Robin G. Kelly and the work of leading left Black feminists Angela Davis and Barbara Ransby (all cited earlier).

Not surprisingly, we find that reactions to white supremacy have been characterized by a race-nationalist discourse of resistance since the earliest years of the twentieth century. This began with millennial dreams of returning to an African Motherland (including returning en-masse to Africa), and the plans to create a separate Black nation in the Southern states. Either option offered freedom from the oppressiveness of the white supremacist power structure with its slave-based economy to people of African descent. For some, it freed Black people from the pain of having to encounter white people altogether. In the case of Black churches and mosques, there was the additional promise of spiritual freedom in a Black afterlife. The Garveyites, Ethiopianist churches, and the original Nation of Islam's plan for a Black capitalist state are all examples of Black nationalist dreams of freedom through separation from white America (Kelley 2002). So was the Jackson–Kush Plan that shaped Co-operation Jackson's formation, as Black radicals from California moved to seize the opportunity presented by the Black mayorship of Jackson in the southern state of Mississippi.

Non-racial capitalism to anti-racist socialism

Prior to any of these, the struggles of the Black farmers of the 1960s who formed the FSC were shaped by several coexisting systemic pressures, including the daily brutality of white capitalist racist supremacy. Their responses were a fusion of different readings and aspirations reflecting the range of formations that informed the struggle for civil rights. The broad movement was essentially for equality, for an end to racial discrimination that would enable "fair" treatment within the U.S. capitalist context, which we refer to as a "non-racial capitalism" (borrowing from the non-racial South Africa, and Mandela's idea of the "rainbow coalition"). But there were other forces at play as well. As the members of the FSC noted, a U.S. government that supported Israeli kibbutzim was determined not to support cooperative organizing in the United States, and especially not among Black people. All the cooperatives that were promoted by the U.S. Department of Agriculture were designed to support capitalist enterprise, and therefore did not accommodate worker ownership, which remains extra-legal in Mississippi to this day. Given the U.S. context, race consciousness is very salient in all three of the case studies. And yet the FSC told us they did not find it necessary to exclude the few white farmers who wished to join because it based its formation on the (non-racial) "common interests" of small farmers. Even as the FSC can be situated as the economic "wing" of the civil rights movement, it nonetheless accommodated among its fold members from many political perspectives.

At the present moment, highly visible, digitally empowered social media mobilizations are altering the political ecosystem within which Black people continue to struggle to overcome pervasive racism at multiple levels of their lives. Jessica Gordon Nembhard (2014, cited earlier) shows Black people continuing to pursue cooperative life strategies as a means of mutual protection against racist assaults and as an economic survival strategy against racist capitalist encroachment.

Applying Vanek's anti-colonial framework to the politics of Black cooperatives, we argue that Black farmers suffered from a double alienation—that is, a lack of both external (in relation to the wider political system) and internal (subjective insecurity and threats to their existence as Black people) self-determination, because the white-supremacist system excluded them from the political life of their country of birth. It seems fair to conclude that the repressive force of this capricious system meant that issues of individual personal "freedoms" and sexual "rights" were not foremost in their minds. In fact, these were entirely absent from our conversations with the older FSC representatives.

The influence of Black feminist and the Black LGBTQ politics that developed two decades later can be seen in the fact that Black women's equality and queer inclusivity were very much a part of the discourse of both Co-operation Jackson and Mandela Grocery. Once again using Vanek, we can argue that on the economic front, the southern Black farmers of the FSC were being denied external self-determination, since any interaction with their racist "neighbors" could result in economic expropriation of one kind or another. But within what were largely family-owned businesses, the issue of internal economic self-determination (economic democracy) was not of immediate concern to mostly male farmers who relied on the family labor of their wives and children. It is only the more recent Black organizers who insist on addressing both external and internal economic transformation, and therefore seek to democratize the very terms of the labor contract by embracing collective ownership and participatory decision-making, and to transform interpersonal relationships.

However, at the present time, the Black radical scholars we refer to here are just beginning to discuss the notion of cooperative organizing as offering economic alternatives to capitalism (Ransby 2018, cited earlier). For empirically demonstrable reasons, racist murders, extrajudicial killings, and mass incarceration have remained uppermost in U.S. Black consciousness, and as a result lend weight to pursue the new articulation of an abolitionist politics that seeks the abolition of the prison system en route to the abolition of racial capitalism. This is exemplified by the organization Critical Resistance, founded by Angela Davis, Ruth Wilson Gilmore, and Rose Braz in 1997. The more recent Movement for Black Lives (M4BL, https://m4bl.org/) also began with a focus on the racist state, having been catalyzed by mass outrage over the hundreds of previously undocumented extrajudicial murders by U.S. police forces. Thus, demands for "economic justice" initially took the form of vociferous demands to "defund the police." These have since coalesced with abolitionist politics in the COVID-inflamed months of continuing protests through 2020, as Black movements demand re-allocation of public resources away from coercive racist police forces and prisons and toward preventative social and economic programs. These are not referred to as socialist in the post-McCarthyite United States, but instead as "social and economic justice."

Anti-racist economic democracy

The Black-owned cooperatives discussed here have all attempted to overcome political and economic alienation that is central to the Black American experience. They also reflect the shifting focus of Black radical thought, insofar as all three are concerned to pursue freedom and self-determination through direct organizing of livelihoods for their members.

Most scholars of Black radical tradition do not (to our knowledge) provide any detail on the potential of cooperative economic organizing as a route to creating alternative ways of living, pending the overthrow of racial capitalism. Yet widespread concern with material conditions is reflected in the vehement demands for "economic justice" and the dismantling of the prison–industrial complex. From a historical viewpoint, today's expressions of anti-capitalism—to which we must add the anti-militarism and the demands to defund the police—reinstantiate an earlier (non-racial) Marxist focus on the collective interests of working people of all races. In this sense, theories of class oppression and alienation coalesce with Black and feminist theories to emphasize that freedom includes the "internal" transformation of self and community, and the quest for self-determination and autonomy. More complex theorizations of oppression have been assisted by the broader paradigm shift away from structuralist analysis and a much greater attention to shifting identities rooted in multiple oppressions (of race, ethnicity, gender, sexuality, and disability) in U.S. discourse.

Neither Co-operation Jackson nor Mandela Grocery have white members, though in the case of the latter it was not clear if this was by chance or design. Mandela Grocery may have become an all-Black cooperative, but their public interface does not indicate an intention to create a Black customer base. It does indicate their vision of partnering with other cooperative initiatives, which are not race-specific, and can be described as "non-racial" because they aspire to inclusivity. Mandela emerged out of a non-racial beginning that distinguishes it from the anti-racist roots of Co-operation Jackson in the Malcolm X Grassroots Movement in Oakland. The Black Democratic Party mayor, Chokwe Lumumba, had a personal history with the Black Nationalist Republic of New Afrika.

Both Co-operation Jackson and Mandela Grocery explicitly embrace feminist and queer-of-color politics, and speak about women, gay, and queer people of color as well as Black and African people. In this sense, they can be seen to have moved beyond hetero-patriarchal racial nationalism to a more inclusive leftist politics—more compatible with what we refer to as an anti-racist economic democracy that profoundly challenges racial capitalism. As such they are more revolutionary than the variations of Black capitalism (Garveyites, integrationist civil rights) because they have largely rejected the race essentialism and separatist politics of Black nationalism in favor of an inclusive anti-racist economic democracy.

At the political level, we did not find Black cooperatives pursuing a (nationalist) call for racial self-determination. The focus of action is to be within society, albeit not necessarily within white society as was the case in a civil rights movement that sought integration and an end to discrimination, and equal rights in education, politics, wages, and so on.

Anti-racist anti-capitalism and self-determination were articulated as early as the 1970s by the Black Panther Party for Freedom and Self-defence, alongside other revolutionary movements of the times. They presented a real threat to a racial capitalism that works by dividing the citizenry into confrontational camps rather than as joint victims of a common oppressor. However, the Black Panther Party's demands were based on a more developed theoretical position vis-à-vis personal rights and freedoms and focused on the internal as well as external political self-determination. The examples of Mandela Grocery and Co-operation Jackson, and later articulations of the FSC, can be said to be operating in a framework that is anti-capitalist and anti-racist, led by Black radicals informed by the Black radical tradition of ideas. It is important to note that they are also survivors, in the sense that they are also informed by the violent way earlier revolutionary organizations were neutralized—in some cases eliminated by the U.S. government.

Finally, we conclude that Black worker cooperatives provide a unique means of constructing alternative social relations in the face of a capitalist system that otherwise seems overwhelming. They create real possibilities for mutual support, cooperation, and ownership that can offer members freedom from alienation and decent democratized livelihoods. Beyond the frontlines—and spurred by a heightening of structural racism under President Donald Trump and others like him—we would anticipate a growth in Black worker-owned cooperatives. The racial nature of U.S. capitalism continues to be evidenced by Black experience in the twenty-first century, which has seen an intensification of racialized socioeconomic inequality and injustice globally. Within the United States, the heightened visibility and accumulating evidence of continuing racist murders and police violence, along with the mass incarceration of Black citizens, are surely creating a greater will to resist racial injustice and the alienation associated with neoliberal capitalism and contemporary manifestations of a global empire.

APPENDIX

List of Interview Dates (An Approved Ethics Protocol was Issued)

Federation of Southern Co-operatives Place: FSC—Jackson Office

Myra Bryant, Director of Mississippi Center for Co-op Development, June 18, 2019
Wendell Paris, founding member FSC, June 18, 2019
Kimberly Crisler, Director of Finance, June 18, 2019
Ben Burkett, Mississippi State Coordinator, June 19, 2019
Hollis Jackson, founding member of FSC, June 20, 2019
John Zippert, researcher and activist, June 22, 2019—phone interview

Co-operation Jackson Balogun Center, Jackson, June 20 and 21, 2019

Kali Akuno
Sacajawea Hall
Kali Shambe
Elijah
Imani Bridgett
Gyasi Williams

Mandela Grocery, Mandela Parkway, Oakland, June 24, 2019

Jenebah Kilgore
Adriana Fike

Works Cited

Akuno, K., A. Nangwaya, and Co-operation Jackson (eds.) 2017. *Jackson Rising: The Struggle for Economic Democracy and Black Self-Determination in Jackson, Mississippi.* Montreal: Daraja Press.

Amin, S. 1974. *Imperialism and Unequal Development.* New York: Monthly Review Press.

Ardener, S. 1964. "The Comparative Study of Rotating Credit Associations." *Journal of the Royal Anthropological Institute of Great Britain and Ireland* 94(2): 201–29.

Black Youth Project 100. n.d. *Agenda to Build Black Futures.* https://www.agendatobuildBlackfutures.com/our-agenda

Crenshaw, K. 1989. "Demarginalizing the Intersection of Race and Sex: A Black Feminist Critique of Antidiscrimination Doctrine, Feminist Theory and Antiracist Politics." *University of Chicago Legal Forum* 1, article 8.

Davis, A. Y. 1982. *Women, Race and Class*. London: Women's Press.

Davis, A. Y. 2003. *Are Prisons Obsolete*? New York: Seven Stories Press.

Davis, A. Y. 2011. *Abolition Democracy: Beyond Empire, Prisons, and Torture*. New York: Seven Stories Press.

Gordon Nembhard, J. 2014. *Collective Courage: A History of African American Co-operative Economic Thought and Practice*. PA: Penn State University Press.

Hossein, C. S. 2013. "The Black Social Economy: Perseverance of Banker Ladies in the Slums." *Annals of Public and Co-operative Economics* 84(4): 423–42.

Hossein, C. S. 2018. *The Black Social Economy in the Americas: Exploring Diverse Community-Based Markets*. New York: Palgrave Macmillan.

Kelley, R. D. G. 2002. *Freedom Dreams: The Black Radical Imagination*. Boston: Penguin.

Ransby, B. 2005. *Ella Baker and the Black Freedom Movement: A Radical Democratic Vision*. Chapel Hill, NC: North Carolina University Press.

Ransby, B. 2018. *Making All Black Lives Matter: Reimagining Freedom in the Twenty-First Century*. Oakland: University of California Press.

Reynolds, B. J. 2001. Presentation to the National Meeting of the NCR on October 31.

Robinson, C. J. 1983. *Black Marxism: The Making of the Black Radical Tradition*. 2nd edn. London: Zed Press.

Rodney, W. 1972. H*ow Europe Underdeveloped Africa*. London: Bogle L'Ouverture.

Vanek, J. 1970. *The General Theory of Labour Managed Market Economies*. Ithaca, NY: Cornell University Press.

Vanek, J. 1971. *The Participatory Economy*. Ithaca, NY: Cornell University Press.

Case study cooperative and Black organization websites

Federation of Southern Co-operatives – https://www.federation.coop/
Mandela Grocery – https://www.mandelagrocery.coop/
Co-operation Jackson – https://cooperationjackson.org/
Critical Resistance – http://criticalresistance.org/
Movement for Black Lives – https://m4bl.org/
The WEB DuBois Centre – http://webduboiscentreaccra.ghana-net.com/
Black Youth Project 100 Agenda to Build Black Futures, available at: https://www.agendatobuildBlackfutures.com/view-agenda
Jackson-Kush Plan, Written by Kali Akuno For the Malcolm X Grassroots Movement & the New Afrikan People's Organization, available at: https://mronline.org/wp-content/uploads/2020/07/Jackson-KushPlan.pdf

PART II
REFLECTIONS
On Cooperation in the African Diaspora

6
Maroons, Rastas, and Ganja Cooperatives
The Building of a Black Social Economy in the Eastern Caribbean

Kevin Edmonds

6.1 Introduction

> Black slave resistance naturally evolved to marronage as the manifestation of the African's determination to disengage, to retreat from contact. To reconstitute the community, Black radicals took to the bush, to the mountains to the interior . . . Away from the plantations, in the security of mountain retreats, on the continent toward the up-country sources of the great rivers that emptied into the oceans at the coasts, Black communities could be re-established.
>
> Cedric Robinson, *Black Marxism* (2000, 310)

Building off Cedric Robinson's (2000) argument that marronage was central to the re-establishment of community, this chapter is an exploratory study of patterns. It examines the emergence of organic resistance to the neocolonial project from below, in which Maroons, Rastafari, and ganja farmers struggled to create breaches in the plantation system where independent production and trade as the basis of a Black social economy could take root in the Eastern Caribbean states of St. Lucia and St. Vincent and the Grenadines. This chapter argues that despite the criminalization of their independent cultivation across time, such activities proved necessary not only to individual and communal survival, but also coincidently to the economic well-being of the state. These activities of illicit cultivation have acted as the primary form of self-sufficiency and survival outside the plantation in both colonial and neocolonial eras, but have also represented a direct challenge to it. By taking a historical approach, I outline in two parts how the structural weaknesses of the Eastern Caribbean economies have engendered the creation of alternative, informal economies deemed "illicit" by the state in a process that goes back centuries. In this way, many of the defining characteristics of Caroline Shenaz Hossein's *The*

Kevin Edmonds, *Maroons, Rastas, and Ganja Cooperatives*. In: *Beyond Racial Capitalism*. Edited by Caroline Shenaz Hossein, Sharon D. Wright Austin, and Kevin Edmonds, Oxford University Press. © Oxford University Press (2023).
DOI: 10.1093/oso/9780192868336.003.0007

Black Social Economy in the Americas (2018) travel well to the ganja fields of the Eastern Caribbean, acting as a form of resistance/marronage that falls within Cedric Robinson's Black radical tradition (Robinson 2000).

The connection between illicit and social economies may not be intuitive at first, as we tend to think of illicit activities as a staging ground of anti-social behaviors; but when placed in both historical and moral context, the ganja economy of St. Vincent and St. Lucia fulfills many of the positive characteristics laid out by Hossein. Hossein (2018, 2) argues that "community-based economies, created by Black people who encounter stigmatization, are essential to their survival. These marginalized people often have no choice but to participate in internalized local economies." This is true in the Eastern Caribbean context. While the ganja economies of the Eastern Caribbean took off dramatically due to the economic hardships that came with the decline of the banana industry, they are part of a much longer history of cultivating crops that were deemed "illicit" in the region.

The history of St. Lucia and St. Vincent reveals that state criminalization of crop cultivation (e.g., sugarcane, provision ground items, or ganja) for personal use or sale is not new to the modern era, which has been largely defined by the "War on Drugs." Indeed, the Caribbean has a long and brutal tradition of this practice, as economic and social control in the colonial era was tied to the denial of self-determination of African and Indigenous peoples. The issue of land and land use was central to exercising power over them, so the growing of sugar and a variety of food crops off the plantation during the colonial era by peoples of African descent was strictly prohibited and made illegal on paper. However, this repression facilitated the creation of a wide network of domestic and regional illicit economies, rooted in the production and trade of illegal items—which worked to directly undermine the power of plantation slavery.

6.2 Racial Capitalism, Marronage, and the Building of Eastern Caribbean Black Social Economies

While critiqued within class-reductionist Marxist circles, Black and Caribbean scholars have long been crucial to (re)centering the connection between race and capitalism as a way to challenge racism in both theoretical and practical settings (Williams 1944 [2014]; Jones 1949; Robinson 2000; Cox and Barnes 2006; Hossein 2018). The development of racial capitalism does not reject the main tenets of Marxism, but rather refined it to have greater explanatory power to understand a wider context in which resistance to capitalism took place. As Cedric Robinson (2000) outlines in *Black Marxism: The Making of the Black Radical Tradition*, particularly the chapters on the Caribbean and in the conclusion, marronage, that is, the fleeing of the plantation, must be regarded as a central part of the Black radical tradition and a primary avenue in which Black social economies could emerge. Within these spaces of resistance to a multifaceted system of brutality, enslaved peoples made the choices to face death and punishment in order to build illicit systems in the hills which could sustain their flight from the plantations in both the short and long term. Hossein (2018, 1) outlines how "it is the backdrop of this brutal past that Indigenous and Black people have been forced to conjure up ways to survive in a hostile environment, as a result creating economies, oftentimes hidden ones, that were different from those they encountered. These economies that enslaved people were rooted in social service and community."

This linage of resistance from the Maroons to the Rastafari has also been explored within "The Social Economy in a Jamaican Perspective," by K'adamawe K'nife, Edward Dixon, and Michael Marshall (2018), a chapter within Hossein's *Black Social Economies in the Americas.* In this chapter, K'nife, Dixon, and Marshall trace the role of Maroons, free villages, and Rastafari within the Jamaican context. In this chapter, I will be examining a similar trajectory in the Eastern Caribbean, looking specifically at the historical context and contribution of Maroon social economies, the role of Rastafari as a modern-day embodiment of resistance, and the role that ganja farmers have played in opening up spaces for independent production to occur during dire economic times.

Despite their small size, the Eastern Caribbean islands proved to be important strategic military sites for competing British and French colonial powers, primarily as naval bases that could secure important trade routes (with a corresponding lack of investments in permanent garrisons or roads) and, secondly, as a site for sugar plantations. While the British and French colonial rivalry was fierce, the battles for colonial control over St. Vincent and St. Lucia were for the most part not fought on either island. Rather, alternating control of the islands was largely achieved as the result of treaties from other European conflicts (i.e., the 1763 Treaty of Paris, 1778 in the midst of the American War of Independence, and the 1793 Treaty of Versailles).

However, both St. Vincent and St. Lucia were home to significant anti-colonial, anti-slavery wars in the respective Carib (1769–73 and 1795–7) and Brigand Wars (1795–7).[1] While large-scale rebellions and revolts, such as the Haitian Revolution (1791–1804), have understandably captured most of the scholarly attention, similar successful, albeit smaller-scale rebellions in St. Lucia (Brigand's War) and St. Vincent (Carib/Garifuna Wars) demonstrated not only the weakness of the colonial administrations but also the determination, ingenuity, and courage of African and Indigenous peoples to take up arms against the world's most powerful militaries to regain their freedom and lands. Given that the most militant of the Brigand, Garifuna/Carib fighting forces were eventually deported, they no longer posed a serious internal threat to colonial rule. Therefore, instead of protracted conflict, these

[1] In both cases, the guerilla tactics of the Garifuna and the Brigands proved them to be formidable foes for the British, resulting in a military stalemate in St. Vincent and total loss in St. Lucia. However, rather than allow the Garifuna or Brigands to establish revolutionary self-government in either territory (as would happen in Haiti in 1804), the British regrouped and later returned to each island, using the tactics of deporting the fighting forces to foreign lands unwanted by the British (the Garifuna to Roatan and the Brigands to West Africa).

historical developments led to a more widespread, informal practice and tradition of resisting state authority by evading its territorial control on the plantations and fleeing to the mountains (referred to as marronage) as a way for people to negotiate their own survival and reproduction outside of the repressive plantation system (Robinson 2000; Roberts 2015).

Many of those who were not captured and deported fled into the mountains to establish self-sufficient, independent settlements away from the plantations and would eventually come to be tolerated by the colonial administrations due to their importance in keeping the economy afloat during times of economic decline (Marshall 1991; Sweeney 2007; Harmsen et al. 2012). As long as the profits made from these "internal economies" (which illegally operated alongside the formal economy) eventually circulated within the formal economy and contributed to the overall political stability of the colony, the planter class had little incentive to invest in and expand their means of coercion beyond the private militias who secured the individual plantations, creating an environment of disengagement.

St. Vincent and St. Lucia were considered "home-fed" colonies (Marshall 1991), meaning that the enslaved did not have to depend solely on imported rations, but cultivated their own plots (supplemented by weekly rations of salted meats). The provision grounds in the interior acted as the primary form of self-sufficiency and survival outside the total institution of the plantation, but also as a direct challenge to it. When investigated further, it becomes clear that the viability of these larger-scale aforementioned rebellions were made possible only by the everyday forms of resistance embodied in the establishment of complex underground systems of production, trade, and communication (Black markets), domestically and regionally, revealing both the limitations and contradictions of national sovereignty and legal authority in the Eastern Caribbean that remain to this day.

Despite the physical horrors the system of slavery imposed and its determination to control everything from a slave's labor, name, home, language, diet, religion, and life expectancy, there still existed important spaces of resistance in the peripheries of these societies. The Maroon communities that would emerge throughout the Caribbean have been noted for their sophistication and self-sufficiency—important qualities, considering these communities were nearly always on the run and under threat. The most established Maroon communities existed in well-concealed places that were largely inaccessible to the state and their forces of slave catchers, and they were protected by a variety of traps and false paths that were useful for carrying out ambushes upon intruders. In periods outside of outright rebellion or revolution, the people of St. Lucia and St. Vincent resisted primarily by restructuring their relationships to the land and economic system.

The rugged, mountainous interior of these two islands has always been a place in which those seeking to escape from the horrors of the plantation or state persecution could find refuge. Central to the survival of the communities of Maroon runaways that would eventually form in the forested highlands were the provision grounds, which were plots on poor quality, stony, or mountainous land that were tended to in secret by the enslaved peoples. Before going forward, it is important to distinguish between the illicit network of provision grounds that existed off the plantation (often in the distant hills and mountains) and the smaller "kitchen" gardens that were approved by the planters for slaves to grow their own food on plantations adjacent to their homes (as it logically reduced the planter's food costs).[2]

The clandestine cultivation of the provision grounds resulted in independent surplus production that took place in the mountains away from the surveillance of the planters. The produce grown in the mountains and forests served a dual purpose: sustaining the runaway Maroon communities and producing a surplus that generated income that would in turn circulate throughout the colonial economy. While the work the enslaved did for the plantation accounted for most of their labor time, independent production in these clandestine sites acted as the foundation upon which viable, free communities would be able to emerge away from the horrors of the plantation. The phenomenon of these independent economic activities existing outside of the plantation as a form of resistance has been termed the "peasant breach" by Tadeusz Lèpkowski (1968), and popularized by Sidney Mintz (1977). Mintz (1977, 269) highlighted the overlapping nature of the different systems of production, arguing that in "every socio-economic formation, the dominant mode of production co-exists with others," in turn demonstrating the tendency for enslaved peoples to not only envision alternative economic systems that were fairer but also the struggle to bring them into reality.

In these early Black markets, items such as fruits, vegetables, poultry, livestock, and sugarcane were cultivated and sold illegally off the plantation (often in the forested highlands), and these illicit trading networks became important sources of income. In addition to being a source of food, the provision grounds also acted as an important way to improve Maroons' standard of living, as surplus produce was often sold or traded to access goods such as tools or clothing. In the instances where Maroons needed tools and weapons (e.g., machetes and rifles), they depended largely upon securing supplies from plantations via the establishment of clandestine networks of theft, smuggling, and trade with those who remained (Richardson 1992). Figueredo and Argote-Freyre have also noted the surprising reach and complexity of Maroon communities, as they occasionally engaged in trade with pirates and buccaneers to gain access to necessities and weapons (Figueredo and Argote-Freyre 2008, 69).

However, the initial threat posed by the independent production and trading that emerged from the provision grounds would eventually become outlawed by both British and French colonial administrations throughout much of the region. Colonial authorities attempted to control labor and force people back onto the plantations,

[2] The provision grounds were much larger in scale than the kitchen gardens but were much further away, harder to tend to on a regular basis, and most importantly existed outside the control of the planters (Brierley 1985). The majority of the illicit provision grounds were cultivated during periods of "petit marronage" or short-term escapes from the plantation, which could happen on a regular basis (often under the cover of darkness) or through longer escapes that consisted of days or weeks away from the plantation (Thompson 2006).

bringing them back to the system of stable, secure enclave settlements in valleys and towns that were easier to control (Thomas 1988). Clive Thomas (1988, 120) highlights the history of the destruction of self-sufficiency in the process of Caribbean state-making, arguing that it was "a common occurrence for military and paramilitary expeditions to be launched to destroy crops that were not grown on plantation-controlled lands, to prohibit plantation workers from rearing cows, pigs and the like and seize animals reared without permission." Many provision grounds were destroyed by the colonial administration to limit self-sufficiency and also to make any sustained rebellion much more difficult. This was, of course, in contrast to policies of accommodation and encouragement adopted in the "settler" colonies such as the United States, Canada, Australia, and New Zealand.

In *Provision Ground and Plantation Labour in Four Windward Islands: Competition for Resources during Slavery*, Woodville K. Marshall documents the influence that illicit trade networks had on the overall economic stability of St. Vincent and St. Lucia. Because of their small size, outward orientation, and weakness, the colony had to accommodate what it considered to be widespread "illegal activity" and was eventually forced to change the laws to accept it. A clear outcome was the emergence of market days; the transition from illicit networks of trade and production to an accepted part of everyday life (what Mintz (1955) terms the internal marketing system) in the Eastern Caribbean was complete. Marshall (1991, 56) traces the determination of the enslaved to continually push back against restrictions on their economic activity, as well as the influence they had on eventually overturning law and policy, remarking:

> By the end of slavery this "breach" in the slave system was virtually complete: while the restriction on the trade in plantation produce was retained, slave participation in the internal markets was officially recognized by the formal concession of the slaves' right to attend market on a designated day, and slaves were openly protesting the choice of market day and the organization of markets. Customary arrangements had overturned legal restrictions, and what had grown outside the law had become recognized in law.

Aside from having a monopoly on violence in one's territory, another element of sovereign power is the ability to make and enforce laws. In the cases of St. Vincent and St. Lucia, the colonial state created the laws but lacked the ability to consistently enforce them. Nevertheless, while planters and colonial administrators encouraged the destruction of communities engaging in independent cultivation, they also often developed contradictory and pragmatic relationships with the Maroon communities and those engaged in independent production. This was due to the inherent weakness of the state, which made sustained patrols financially draining, demoralizing, and impractical. By tolerating the emergence of independent, albeit illegal, production of foodstuffs and the clandestine trading networks, the state-planter apparatus was able to bring about relative political and economic stability (Marshall 1991).

While the emergence of these Black markets helped to increase the standard of living for the participants, their families, and urban residents (both African and European), this also acted to reduce the import cost of foodstuffs from the perspective of the planters. No formal documentation tracked the size of these alternative economies, but testimony from planters during the colonial era estimate that roughly half the gross domestic product (GDP) of the Windward Islands in the 1790s was in the hands of the enslaved as a result of illicit networks of trade and production (Marshall 1991). The additional circulation of income within the colonial economies helped to strengthen the merchants in the towns due to an expanded market, since "surplus produce was exchanged for dietary supplements, for 'finery' and for the 'little articles' like candles, soap and tobacco; small stock and poultry were marketed for cash which was saved or employed in the purchase of small luxuries" (Marshall 1991, 59).

Along with the economic motivations for these markets, they acted as important spaces for public conversation and the exchange of information outside of the strict surveillance of the plantation. They also provided an important space in which the enslaved could reassert their humanity and build community (Hossein 2018). As a stark alternative to the totalitarian nature of the plantation, this alternative production allowed for an important degree of self-determination, since cultivation and trade occurred outside the supervision of their owners, and they worked as family or community groups. While originally illegal, these activities, and the income and the increased standard of living they provided, had important psychological effects that would alter the nature and durability of the plantation itself, to the disadvantage of the planter–state apparatus (Berlin and Morgan 2016).[3]

6.3 The Social and Political History of Ganja, State Persecution, and Social Exclusion of Rastafari

Similar to other Caribbean islands, in St. Vincent and St. Lucia the origins of ganja cultivation are widely believed to have come directly with the indentured Indian laborers. Although St. Vincent and the Grenadines have several communities populated by East Indian descendants,[4] there is some debate as to whether indentured

[3] A final, important point to make is that the plantation gardens and the clandestine networks also gave rise to the emergence of early, albeit legal, rights and collective resistance against the planters that would result in significant political changes. In the case of property rights, from the 1780s onward not only were the enslaved providing most of their own subsistence, but they had also challenged the legal premises that as chattel property they could not own property or possess money themselves (Craton 1994).

[4] In total, 8 ships transported 2,474 Indians to St. Vincent and the Grenadines between 1861 and 1880 (Stone 1973)—and make up an estimated 6 percent of the country's population today. A number of Vincentians of Indian descent still live in the community of Rose Hall, not too far from several communities that are very well known for their ganja cultivation, and they mentioned that ganja was something in their grandparents' homes. In the case of St. Lucia, between 1859 and 1893 13 ships carried a total of 4,427 Indians, many of whom still live in communities like Jacmel, Forestiere, and Richfond (Harmsen et al. 2012, 212).

laborers or colonial officials brought ganja to the Caribbean (Campbell 1980; Besson 2010). According to Trinidadian historian Gerry Besson (2010), Bhang (a ganja-infused drink, often made with milk) was routinely used by the Indian laborers "to relax at the end of the day; to relieve fatigue; to obtain a sense of well-being; to stimulate appetite; and to enable them to bear more cheerfully the strain and monotony of . . . daily routines." Fraser (1974), Hamid (2002), and Besson (2010) have argued that the colonial authorities were the ones who allowed ganja to be sold under licence in the stores on the sugarcane estates as a way of discouraging the men from drinking the incredibly potent rum that was easily accessible. It was only when ganja turned from a sedative/analgesic (a naturally occurring plant taken for pain relief) connected to plantation laborers to a symbol of anti-colonial resistance in the early 1900s that it became outlawed (Bernard 2007).

Given the close proximity of Indian and African communities, it did not take long before the cultural practice of ganja consumption crossed over (Mansingh and Mansingh 1989). In *The Material Roots of Rastafarian Marijuana Symbolism*, Akeia A. Bernard (2007, 95) argues that "it is likely that Indian labourers acquainted Black Jamaicans with the practices and Hindu symbolism surrounding ganja . . . the labour conditions and the resulting 'points of contact' encouraged the exchange of ritualized marijuana use." This cultural diffusion is not surprising, as the first model Rastafari community was that of Pinnacle, located just outside Sligoville, in St. Catherine, Jamaica. Pinnacle was established in 1940 by Percival Leonard Howell and was also the parish with the majority of Jamaica's indentured Indian laborers (Lee 2003; Dunkley 2013; Chevannes 2015). Howell was initially a street preacher, but was the founder of Rastafari, creating a spiritual practice that offered a clear alternative to Christianity and other Eurocentric teachings, and hoped to open up a cooperative enterprise at Pinnacle. Rastafari ideology is predominantly one of self-sufficiency, self-reliance, anti-capitalism, and direct opposition to the white supremacist cultural/religious legacy and the socioeconomic structure left behind by colonialism (Campbell 1980; Dunkley 2013).

As a result, local ganja economies existed in St. Lucia and St. Vincent prior to the formal recognition of Rastafari in the Eastern Caribbean; as during the days of sugar plantation labor, ganja was regarded as an essential part of working-class life, to the point that William F. Lewis (1993, 60) argued that across much of the Caribbean, "the first taking of the spliff was a sign that a youth was ready to start his life's work in the cane fields." Aside from recreational use, ganja was also widely regarded amongst peasant communities as having a wide array of medicinal properties, acting as a panacea within traditional folk healing (Chevannes 2015). Taken as a tea or tonic or steeped with other herbs in a bottle of strong rum, it became a remedy for everything from coughs and colds to asthma and glaucoma. As a result, ganja became part of the peasant economy of the Eastern Caribbean—growing in the crevices of their societies and laying the foundation of a sophisticated and widespread underground economy that helped to sustain many poor and marginalized communities. Because of ganja's use as a folk medicine, as well as its ability to help those deal with the stresses

Fig. 6.1 Ganja field and growing shanty, St. Vincent
(Photo credit: Kevin Edmonds.)

associated with a life of hard, manual labor, it became rooted firmly in the culture and economy of peasant communities across the Caribbean.

With the passage of time, ganja became associated with schizophrenia, criminality, and social disorder, not due to any evidence, but rather due to convenience. Ganja was blamed as the cause of these maladies rather than as a symptom of a colonial society's oppression, which made ganja a necessary coping mechanism for the poor and marginalized. Similar dynamics could be witnessed across the Caribbean starting in the 1950s, as the anti-capitalist, anti-colonial Black liberation ideology of many Rastafari communities frightened political leaders in St. Vincent and St. Lucia. Regarding this movement as a subversive counterculture, political leaders used the repressive apparatus of the state against it.[5] This state repression pushed the Rastafari into the hills, and largely ostracized them from the wider society, motivating them to develop their own Black social economy, rooted in self-determination, self-sufficiency, and cooperative work practices and the sharing of resources (Fig. 6.1).

[5] Klein (2004, 27) argues, "Cannabis, celebrated as part of Jamaica's non-European heritage, was instrumentalized—not only by Rastafarians—during the independence struggle as a repudiation of white supremacy. In the hands of dreadlocked Black men ganja becomes a proxy call for political independence and cultural autonomy."

While the Rastafari communities in St. Vincent and St. Lucia do not have an extensively documented history like those in Jamaica, it was generally agreed in the course of my fieldwork interviews that Rastafari ideology came to the Eastern Caribbean in the 1960s via students returning from the University of the West Indies Mona Campus in Jamaica and the transmission of reggae music in popular culture (Bousquet 2019). As Howell's countercultural movement spread across the Caribbean, a number of Rastafari settlements sprang up in the hills in rural St. Lucian communities such as Fond St. Jacques and the Dennery/Mabouya Valley and Greggs in St. Vincent, as well as within the capital cities.

Some of these communities (such as the Roots Co-operative in St. Lucia's Mabouya Valley, established in 1983) traced their roots and economic practices back to the independent Maroon villages that existed in the largely inaccessible, forested peripheries that deliberately sought to distance themselves from traditional plantation agriculture. As K'nife et al. (2018, 66) argue, "this philosophy of self-reliance and collective security implies establishing an alternative economy in ownership but converging with the formal economy in practice." These self-reliant enterprises were largely connected to agriculture, cooking/serving vital foods to the wider public, the creation of artisanal goods (woodworking, painting, printing, and knitting), cultural industries, and the cultivation of ganja—which is used as a religious sacrament. With these self-reliant enterprises as the economic motor of the Rastafari community, they in turn act as forms of a solidarity economy, defined as "self-organized relationships of care, co-operation, and community," creating "democratic and liberatory means of meeting their needs" in the face of market and state failures (Miller in Hossein 2018, xi).

However, the criminalization of the use of ganja under the Dangerous Drugs Acts in St. Lucia and St. Vincent provided a convenient excuse for the widespread persecution, arrests, and murder of many Rastafarians across the region, leading to further social exclusion and marginalization (Campbell 1980; K'nife et al. 2018). A common occurrence was for police forces in St. Lucia and St. Vincent to arrest Rastas on the suspicion of cultivating, consuming, or possessing ganja and violently cut off their dreadlocks during arrest or while imprisoned (Campbell 1985).[6] While the 1963 Coral Gardens attack in Jamaica is regarded as one of the most brutal attacks against the Rastafari in the Caribbean, the Eastern Caribbean has its own share of horrors.[7] In St. Lucia, the 1981 Mount Gimie raids saw the paramilitary Special Service Unit of the Royal St. Lucian Police Force massacre the majority of the peaceful Rasta community

[6] In St. Lucia, the Iyanola Rasta Improvement Association became the largest organization representing Rastafari and the downtrodden. The association established its own newspaper, *Calling Rastafari*, and engaged in "radical journalism" for its critique of St. Lucia politics that went beyond the traditional bourgeois concerns and have been the longest and most consistent in their call for the legalization of cannabis/ganja.

[7] In Dominica, the Prohibited and Unlawful Societies and Associations Act, or the Dread Act, was signed into law by Prime Minister Patrick John in 1974, after Desmond Trotter was accused of murdering a white tourist. This act allowed for citizens and police to attack or murder any Rasta or dreadlocked person without consequence (Murrell et al. 1998).

(numbered in the dozens) and assault and imprison the rest (Stanislas and Sadique 2019).

The 1970s also saw a shift toward ganja cultivation to finance the activities of radical political organizations in St. Vincent in particular, centered on growing Black Power consciousness and Marxism (Cottle Interview 2014; Rose Interview 2014). As a result, the increased demand for ganja led more farmers into the hills to produce for a more and more diverse group of consumers, domestically and regionally. From these humble origins rooted in the peasantry's desire to escape the harsh realities of the plantation, in combination with the decline of the banana trade, ganja cultivation has arguably become one of the largest economic sectors in St. Vincent and St. Lucia—becoming the modern equivalent of the colonial era's illicit provision ground on which slaves grew food for survival and resisted colonial rule.

6.4 Methods and Approaches

Drawing from the scholarly literature and my previous scholarship on the Eastern Caribbean, I developed a number of working hypotheses that guided my preliminary research design for this chapter. The research question that informs this project is the following: Would the legalization of ganja in the Eastern Caribbean be an economically viable replacement for bananas? And my two sub-questions were: What are the power dynamics of the illegal ganja trade? What is the current contribution of the ganja trade to the economies of St. Vincent and St. Lucia?

In order to answer these questions, I interviewed a total of ninety-two people in the latter half of 2014—split between St. Vincent and St. Lucia (a breakdown is provided in Table 6.1). I spent a total of seven months between St. Vincent and St. Lucia using a multi-method approach, combining comparative historical analysis, fieldwork (ethnographic research, participant observation, and interviews), archival research at police stations and agricultural extension offices, and analysis of

Table 6.1 Breakdown of types of interview by country

Country	Civil society/ Public sector	Government/ Police	Trafficker	Cultivator	Community insiders*	Banana farmers
St. Vincent	11	4	12	23	6	4
St. Lucia	7	3	7	8	5	5
Total sample size						95

* Community insiders are individuals who did not disclose any specific affiliation to the ganja trade but provided important context and insight into how things operated in the community.

secondary sources including local newspapers and national, regional, and intergovernmental documents.

Spending time socializing on the street corners and yards, waiting at bus stops, taking long walks, sitting in rum shops, and being invited to the hills exposed me to a number of ganja farmers, traffickers, and individuals in close proximity to the ganja trade. Exposure to not just conversations but cultural cues and practices that became more apparent as participants became more comfortable with me—inviting me into their homes or up to their ganja fields—provided me with a perspective that could not be attained through reading secondary literature. In each country, I conducted in-depth informal ethnographic interviews with those who openly identified as ganja cultivators (n = 31), low- and high-level traffickers (n = 19), and "community insiders" (n = 11), who consisted of individuals who did not disclose their association with the ganja economy but who were knowledgeable about what was happening in their community.

Being able to rely on knowledge and contacts beyond academics proved to be very helpful in my gaining the trust of many of the growers and traffickers and helped to convince people that I was not a police officer or a totally naïve academic. Aside from personal and family connections in St. Lucia, another important way trust and relationships were developed was through a deliberate effort to reach out beyond civil society and public sector organizations in order to speak with the cultivators and traffickers themselves—with Rastafari organizations and community political organizations playing an important role in facilitating this. Being honest about my own "radical" politics and appreciation of the work, method, and legacy of well-known Caribbean radical figures like Walter Rodney, as well as demonstrating an understanding of local, regional, and global struggles for liberation, provided key connections with these groups and helped to open doors.

This was particularly the case in St. Vincent where I did not have family relations to fall back on. Being a Marxist and discussing my research as a commitment to political work rather than just as objective research for my own curiosity endeared me to many key contacts. It was because of this connection and spirit of solidarity that important figures in the Black Power Movement, such as Junior "Spirit" Cottle and Conley Rose, went above and beyond in terms of the help offered by organizing several important meetings at their homes where "groundings" on ganja could take place with cultivators and traffickers in Kingstown, as well as facilitating introductions across the island. It was within these spaces that this historical lineage between Maroons, Rastafari, and ganja farmers was made clear.

In addition to qualitative research, this study has aggregated ganja seizure data across St. Vincent and St. Lucia in a single place for the first time, creating a baseline for future studies. The data clearly show that ganja has been much more valuable to the Eastern Caribbean than bananas. However, a fundamental limitation of quantitative studies is that they are totally dependent on access to a large pool of accurate, "apolitical" statistical data. Reliance on quantitative data even for nations in the

Eastern Caribbean, which are considered stable middle-income countries, can often be problematic.

Lastly, statistics can be distorted for political purposes, as lack of data and scholarly work can help people carry on with their non-state illicit activities. While the DEA has often exaggerated numbers (Andreas 2011), Caribbean governments minimize reporting for their own domestic security and stability. It is also important to note that the governments of St. Lucia and St. Vincent have a political motivation to ensure that the statistics concerning drug production in their countries remain low. If global powers such as the United States determine that they are not doing enough to combat the drug trade, they risk a myriad of economic sanctions. There is also a domestic component, as the local population may feel that the government is not doing enough to combat the drug trade and the criminal activities associated with it.

6.5 Findings: The Economic Importance of Ganja and the Role of the Cooperative Model in the Eastern Caribbean

Periods of devastating economic collapse are not new to St. Lucia and St. Vincent. Moreover, they have historically triggered the islands' inhabitants to turn to everyday forms of resistance through the Black market in order to survive. Following the boom-and-bust cycle of cash crops outlined in plantation economy theory, these periods of widespread economic hardship have led to the emergence of illicit commodity production and corresponding clandestine networks of trade. This is as true for the outlawing of off-plantation sugar and other food crop cultivation during the colonial era as it is for the contemporary cultivation of ganja with the collapse of the banana trade.

While often overlooked in political economy and development studies, this historic tendency to revert to Black market activity accounts for a significant amount of the Eastern Caribbean economy. Quan (2017) reminds us that Robinson argued that marronage was the underlying consciousness of Black radical thought because people refused to be enslaved, that they had their own ideas of self-sufficiency. As Hossein (2018, 5) writes in *The Black Social Economy*, "People who endure isolation and exclusion from mainstream society are forced to think of new economies and so create businesses that are embedded in the communities in which they live." In this case, cooperative models (or what they referred to as teams) by Rastas who form their own Black social economy may be the antidote needed to make trade and production networks that think about the producers. Focusing on community would mean breaking out of the structural weaknesses of the economic and political status quo and serve as a catalyst upon which we cannot just imagine but also see the possibilities of a bottom-up alternative that puts the poor and marginalized first (Robinson 2000). In the words of one young Vincentian ganja farmer, "Bongo,"

> Alluh'we need fi separate ganja from di drug trade . . . It a unfairly attacked because a wha has been colonially cultured in di mind. Ganja 'as helped so many people, sent thousands a children a school, pay for operations and bought plane tickets for people to go a foreign [overseas] and better 'demselves. (North Leeward, St. Vincent, 2014)

Just as bananas once provided a way for the poor to achieve some degree of social mobility during the era of "Green Gold," the income and employment generated from the illicit ganja economy is now largely responsible for putting food on tables, constructing houses, sending children to school, and providing incomes that circulate in the wider domestic and regional economy. In the hills of St. Vincent and St. Lucia, I had the opportunity to get to know long-time Rasta cultivators like Ras Kofi, Kalonji, Tiny, and Yacob (among many others) who had initially only cultivated ganja for religious/cultural purposes but have since overseen the transition whereby ganja has turned into a regional cash crop. In the traditional model of ganja farming (independent production), it was not uncommon for a single individual to maintain a small crop a short distance from their home that was used for recreational, medicinal, and cultural use.

By selling or bartering ganja in their North Leeward (St. Vincent) and Fond St. Jacques (St. Lucia) communities (see Fig. 6.2), these initial ganja farmers were able to have the means to access consumer goods or services that were not available despite their best efforts at being self-sufficient in the hills. This initial peasant-based model of the ganja economy was small scale and served local demand. Early ganja farmers worked primarily as self-sufficient individuals on small isolated plots, or as cooperative teams/groups of three to five people up in the hills who would share democratically in the labor, risk, and reward come harvest time. While never formally referred to as cooperatives, the team model was described to me as one in which decisions about planting, harvesting, scheduling, and routines were made based upon the collective will, rather than having a top-down hierarchy. The labor to tend to the crops was also collectively shared, with rotations in and out, as well as a shared responsibility to take turns sleeping in the fields overnight to protect the crops from theft.

Furthermore, the agricultural know-how of former farmers and laborers on banana-growing islands has carried over into the ganja industry, allowing them to survive in the hills by intercropping with food plants. During one of my visits to the hills, "Ras Kofi" invited me up to his shanty to show me where he often slept while out on the ganja field, a surprisingly sturdy structure made out of various sizes of lumber and tarpaulins. Once inside, it became clear that it was not easy living, as there was little more than a piece of foam for a mattress, a radio, a portable gas stove, a chair, some dishes, a large water bucket, and several kerosene lanterns and flashlights. Down another path behind the shanty, I was shown the small garden plot where he planted yams and other provisions: "We got mango, breadfruit, a lot of dasheen (a root crop) and plantain there, too," he said, pointing to a ridge in the distance.

Fig. 6.2 Author on ganja plantation, North Leeward, St. Vincent
(Photo credit: Kevin Edmonds.)

Once in the hills, farmers spoke about the sense of community that exists, knowing who is planting where, pointing to the shanties further up the hill. Speaking about community, "Junior" remarked, "We used help each other, look out for each other, clear land, share supplies during tough times. We are mostly all from the same small communities like Fitz Hughes, Chateau or Rose Hall. We know we are all poor, but trying to make something good happen. We had no reason to quarrel with anyone. But now that is changing."

As revealed by Table 6.2, the ganja economies of St. Vincent and St. Lucia have helped to incorporate otherwise economically marginalized rural communities, which had been traditionally shut out of foreign and/or public investment, into important sites of employment and income generation that benefit the entire economy. As such, these economies offer a sophisticated alternative agricultural industry that represents an enormous portion of economic activity that brings millions of dollars into the economies of St. Vincent and St. Lucia.

"Ras Kofi," a veteran of the ganja trade, and someone who stated he had many connections to traffickers in St. Lucia, told me that after splitting with his team, "The most I ever made in a season (after expenses) was $10,000 [Eastern Caribbean dollars—just over $3,700 U.S. dollars]." With St. Vincent's GDP per capita standing at US$6,656 in 2014, cultivators like "Ras Kofi" are not living lives of luxury; rather, they are

Table 6.2 Value of banana exports vs. ganja seizures in St. Lucia and St. Vincent (1992–2012)

	Value of banana exports ($USD)	Value of remittances ($USD)	Value of ganja seizures ($USD)
St. Lucia	$639,131,000	$508,749,375	$1,670,862,270
St. Vincent	$283,022,212	$445,720,932	$5,118,409,991
Total	$922,153,212	$954,470,307	$6,789,272,261

Source: From Edmonds' field work and compiled in 2020/1

scratching out an income that puts them on par with those individuals who are able to get one of the increasingly rare jobs in the formal economy.

Even though the individual farmer does not make much income from cultivating ganja, the ganja economy has a multiplier effect that has an important impact in supporting the local economy and in spurring the emergence of related economic activities. This "multiplier effect" can be thought of as the amount of local economic activity that is triggered by the purchase of any one item. The more/faster a dollar circulates within a community or country, the more income and jobs will be created (Girvan and Beckford 1989, 252). For example, when a young man buys a gram of ganja from a low-level trafficker, the couple of dollars spent becomes part of a chain that links the mid-level trafficker to a ganja farmer like Kalonji, who spent his income on fixing his home, buying food, and buying his children school supplies, which in turn supported the hardware and grocery stores in town, the minibus driver, and so on.

In terms of the economic impact on the community, it is clear that the income from the ganja economy has spurred the creation of supplementary small businesses and services in ganja-growing communities, especially in St. Vincent. The income from the ganja economy helps to mitigate the formal financial discrimination that the poor face in the Eastern Caribbean. Poor people without collateral—but also small farmers—have historically been denied loans from banks in St. Lucia and St. Vincent for fear of default; they also face barriers due to literacy and class discrimination (Grossman 1998; Moberg 2008). Because unemployed young men cannot easily deposit large amounts of cash into their bank accounts without raising suspicion, Pasa noted that a common solution against robbery has been for them to invest in the construction/improvement of their residence and to establish legal businesses in their own names or those of their families and partners.[8]

[8] One of the most visible impacts has been the small, though sophisticated, outdoor kitchens scattered throughout the hills, where women cook hot meals to sell to the individuals staying on the farms to guard the crops. These popular kitchens offer tasty options to ganja farmers who have grown tired of eating canned goods such as tuna, corned beef, Vienna sausages, and roast breadfruit every day. The women maintain a regular schedule and menu, and some even go so far as to offer delivery of daytime meals to plots that are relatively close to their place of work. Additionally, small shops serving the needs of ganja farmers have sprung up.

Yet, the most significant change that Ras Kofi, Kalonji, and Yacob have seen in their decades of experience has been the shift from cultivation for the domestic market to becoming a regional exporter, as the intensity, competition, scale, and complexity of the industry have changed dramatically. When people traditionally think about ganja farmers and the ganja economy, an idealized image of the independent Rasta comes to mind. But the realities of capitalism's destructive tendencies across the Caribbean have led to another, more common type of cultivator: the impoverished young person (often male and landless), driven by economic necessity, who is trying to cash in. Many Rasta growers I had the opportunity to speak with were of the opinion that things were better before the "baldheads" started going up in the hills.

"Ras Kofi" spoke about the longstanding community that exists up in the hills but is now under threat, stating, "Up in the hills is like a village, the shanties are setup nice, almost like home. Back in the days when people were sick up in the hills, or had sick family, and had to leave, they would get taken care of and still get their cut—but now it is changing." As a result of the decades' long decline in economic growth, the traditional model of cooperative ganja cultivation embodied by the Rastas and other independent cultivators is being challenged and squeezed out by a new model of more efficient competition akin to sharecropping. While sharecropping is defined traditionally as an arrangement in which the owner of land allows a tenant farmer to cultivate the land in return for a percentage of the final harvest, the situation in St. Lucia and St. Vincent is slightly different due to the fact that the cultivation takes place predominantly on Crown Land. While the land is technically free for anybody to cultivate, it does require an initial financial investment to hire labor to engage in clearing the land, sowing, harvesting, and protecting it and purchasing necessary supplies such as food, water, fertilizer, and building materials to construct temporary shelters.

The growth of this sharecropping model is problematic because it capitalizes on longstanding social and economic inequalities within the wider society in order to provide cheap labor to those with capital. The tendency within the ganja economy to move from a community-based, cooperative venture to an industry rooted in exploitation is unfortunate but also not surprising given its unregulated nature and the need for the state to placate the demands of the elite for economic opportunities.

6.6 Conclusion

While the ganja economy offers many important lessons that can be transferred to other sectors, it remains an imperfect model with notable drawbacks, as its unregulated nature places it at the very real risk of being hijacked by local/domestic elites as a vehicle for capital accumulation. If left unchecked because of state inaction and a decline in on-the-ground organizing to ensure the cooperative model persists, this can lead to a situation in which the influence of domestic capital changes a sector dominated by independent producers and cooperatives into a system akin to sharecropping, reinforcing the racial and class dynamics that remain legacies of the plantation (Robinson 2000).

The ganja industry has taken on greater importance because the state has failed to fashion an economic development project/strategy able to deliver employment to the islands' poor and peasantry and to break out of the orbit of the plantation economy. Based on a qualitative and quantitative analysis, this chapter has argued that the illicit cultivation and trafficking of ganja has contributed more to the economies of St. Vincent and St. Lucia than during the glory days of the banana trade, as well as remittances from overseas combined. As a result, the illicit ganja economy has been crucial to each island's economy, even by conservative estimation methods, acting in a similar way to the provision grounds that sustained the majority of the population who were shut out of the formal economy during slavery and colonialism. However, it appears that the enactment of ganja reform policies reinstitute many of the most harmful biases and patterns of the plantation economy, as the significant economic benefits that traditionally flowed to small farmers (in terms of income and employment) are now in danger of being captured by the domestic elite and foreign investors.

If the ganja reforms enacted by the Vincentian government in 2018 are going to have a chance of protecting the traditional ganja growers, such as those rooted in the Rastafari communities, attention must be paid to the necessity of not only preserving but building upon the important elements of the Black social economy (Hossein 2018). Interviews and fieldwork point to a strong history of resistance and the immense, as well as everyday, lessons from the Maroons, Rastafari, and ganja farmers that should be taken into account as evidence of an alternative path of political and economic development for the Caribbean. Their pragmatic, often clandestine, but effective lessons concerning cooperation, production, trade, and justice demonstrate how Caribbean peoples have not only the desire but the capacity to construct and bring to life alternative systems despite having to fight against oppressive conditions and poverty at the local and global levels.

APPENDIX

Interviews

All interviews took place in 2014, and pseudonyms are given to protect the identities of cultivators and traffickers.

"Bongo"	Kingstown	October 14
Conley "Chivambo" Rose	Kingstown	December 3, 7
Junior "Spirit" Cottle	Kingstown	October 12, 15, 22, November 19, 26
"Junior"	North Leeward	October 22
"Kalonji"	North Leeward	October 23 & 24
"Ras Kofi"	North Leeward	October 23 & 24
Renwick Rose	Calder	December 1
"Tiny"	Soufrière Quarter	August 14
"Yacob"	North Leeward	November 20 & 21

Works Cited

Andreas, P. 2011. "Illicit Globalization: Myths, Misconceptions, and Historical Lessons." *Political Science Quarterly* 126(3): 403–25.

Beckford, G. and K. Levitt. 2000. *The George Beckford Papers*. Kingston: Canoe Press.

Benard, A. A. 2007. "The Material Roots of Rastafarian Marijuana Symbolism." *History and Anthropology* 18(1): 89–99.

Berlin, I. and P. D. Morgan. 2016. *The Slaves' Economy: Independent Production by Slaves in the Americas*. London: Routledge.

Besson, G. 2010. "History of Ganja Use in Trinidad." *Trinidad and Tobago Express*, November 9. https://trinidadexpress.com/news/local/history-of-ganja-use-in-trinidad/article_6b65fd0c-6e5c-54dc-b312-19a4e0141791.html. Accessed March 19, 2021.

Bishop, M. L. 2013. *The Political Economy of Caribbean Development*. London: Palgrave MacMillan.

Bousquet, E. 2019. "Borders and Marxist Politics in the Caribbean: An Interview with Earl Bousquet on the Workers Revolutionary Movement in St. Lucia." *ACME: An International Journal for Critical Geographies* 18(1): 246–64.

Brierley, J. S. 1985. "West Indian Kitchen Gardens: A Historical Perspective with Current Insights from Grenada." *Food and Nutrition Bulletin* 7(3): 1–10.

Campbell, H. 1980. "The Rastafarians in the Eastern Caribbean." *Caribbean Quarterly* 26(4): 42–61.

Campbell, H. 1985. *Rasta and Resistance: From Marcus Garvey to Walter Rodney*. Trenton: Africa World Press.

Chevannes, B. 2015. *Rastafari: Roots and Ideology*. Syracuse: Syracuse University Press.

Cox, O. and H. Barnes. 2006. *The Foundations of Capitalism*. New Smyrna Beach, FL: Oliver Cromwell Cox Institute.

Craton, M. J. 1994. "Reshuffling the Pack: The Transition from Slavery to Other Forms of Labour in the British Caribbean, ca. 1790–1890." *New West Indian Guide/Nieuwe West-Indische Gids* 68(1–2): 23–75.

Dunkley, D. 2013. "The Suppression of Leonard Howell in Late Colonial Jamaica, 1932–1954." *New West Indian Guide* 87(1–2): 62–93.

Edmonds, K. 2020. *Legalize It? A Comparative Study of Cannabis Economies in St. Vincent and St. Lucia*. PhD Thesis, University of Toronto.

Figueredo, D. H. and F. Argote-Freyre. 2008. *A Brief History of the Caribbean*. New York: Infobase Publishing.

Fineman, B. 2000. "Seeds of Distress in St Vincent." *Baltimore Sun*, January 28. https://www.baltimoresun.com/news/bs-xpm-2000-01-28-0001280218-story.html. Accessed June 18, 2020.

Fraser, H. A. 1974. "The Law and Cannabis in the West Indies." *Social and Economic Studies* 23(3): 361–85.

Gibbings, W. 1999. "Marijuana Report Wins Applause." IPS News, May 24. http://www.ipsnews.net/1999/03/narcotics-caribbean-marijuana-report-wins-applause/. Accessed February 17, 2021.

Girvan, N. and G. Beckford. 1989. *Development in Suspense*. Kingston: Friedrich Ebert Foundation.

Grossman, L. 1998. *The Political Ecology of Bananas*. Chapel Hill: University of North Carolina Press.

Hamid, A. 2002. *The Ganja Complex*. Lanham: Lexington Books.

Harmsen, J., G. Ellis, and R. Deveaux. 2012. *A History of St. Lucia*. Place Moule a Chique, Vieux Fort, St. Lucia: Lighthouse Road Publications.

Hossein, C. S. 2018. *The Black Social Economy in the Americas: Exploring Diverse Community-Based Alternative Markets*. New York: Palgrave Macmillan.

Jones, C. 1949. "We Seek Full Equality for Women." *Daily Worker*. September 4.

Klein, A. 2004. "The Search for a New Drug Policy Framework: From the Barbados Plan of Action to the Ganja Commission." In Axel Klein, Marcus Day, and Anthony Harriott (eds.), *Caribbean Drugs: From Criminalization to Harm Reduction*. London: Zed Books.

K'nife, K., E. Dixon, and M. Marshall. 2018. "The Social Economy in a Jamaican Perspective." In Caroline Shenaz Hossein (ed.), *The Black Social Economy in the Americas*, 59–78. New York: Palgrave Macmillan.

Lee, H. 2003. *The First Rasta: Leonard Howell and the Rise of Rastafarianism*. Chicago: Chicago Review Press.

Lèpkowski, T. 1968. "Haití, Tomo I, Havana," *Edición Casa de las Américas:* 59–60.

Lewis, W. F. 1993. *Soul Rebels: The Rastafari*. Long Grove, IL: Waveland Press.

Mansingh, A. and L. Mansingh. 1989. "The Impact of East Indians on Jamaican Religious Thoughts and Expressions." *Caribbean Journal of Religious Studies* 10(1): 36–52.

Marshall, W. K. 1991. "Provision Ground and Plantation Labour in Four Windward Islands: Competition for Resources during Slavery." *Slavery and Abolition* 12(1): 48–67.

Mintz, S. W. 1955. "The Jamaican Internal Marketing Pattern: Some Notes and Hypotheses". *Social and Economic Studies* 4(1): 95–103.

Mintz, S. W. 1977. "The So-Called World System: Local Initiative and Local Response." *Dialectical Anthropology* 2(1–4): 253–70.

Moberg, M. 2008. *Slipping Away: Banana Politics and Fair Trade in the Eastern Caribbean*. New York: Berghahn Books.

Morgan, I. B. and D. Philip. 1995. *The Slaves' Economy: Independent Production by Slaves in the Americas*. Milton Park: Routledge Press.

Murrell, N. S., W. D. Spencer, and A. A. McFarlane (eds.) 1998. *Chanting down Babylon: The Rastafari Reader*. Philadelphia, PA: Temple University Press.

Quan, H. L. T. 2017. "It's Hard to Stop Rebels That Time Travel." In Gaye Theresa Johnson and Alex Lubin (eds.), *Futures of Black Radicalism*, 173–93. Brooklyn: Verso.

Richardson, B. C. 1992. *The Caribbean in the Wider World, 1492–1992: A Regional Geography*. Cambridge, UK: Cambridge University Press.

Roberts, N. 2015. *Freedom as Marronage*. Chicago: University of Chicago Press.

Robinson, C. J. 2000. *Black Marxism: The Making of the Black Radical Tradition*. Chapel Hill: University of North Carolina Press.

Stanislas, P. and K. Sadique. 2019. "International Attitudes to Teaching Religion and Faith and the Policing of Minority Communities." In J. F. Albrecht, G. den Heyer, and P. Stanislas (eds.), *Policing and Minority Communities*, 11–27. Cham: Springer.

Stone, L. S. 1973. "East Indian Adaptations on St. Vincent: Richland Park." *Windward Road: Contributions to the Anthropology of Saint Vincent*, Research Report 12: 148–55. https://scholarworks.umass.edu/anthro_res_rpt12/17

Sweeney, J. L. 2007. "Caribs, Maroons, Jacobins, Brigands, and Sugar Barons: The Last Stand of the Black Caribs on St. Vincent." *African Diaspora Archaeology Newsletter* 10(1): 7.

Thomas, C. Y. 1988. *The Poor and the Powerless: Economic Policy and Change in the Caribbean*. New York: New York University Press.

Thompson, A. O. 2006. *Flight to Freedom: African Runaways and Maroons in the Americas*. Kingston, Jamaica: University of the West Indies Press.

Williams, E. 1944 [2014]. *Capitalism and Slavery*. Chapel Hill: University of North Carolina Press.

7

Fighting to Preserve Black Life and Land Rights

A Study of Quilombolas in the State of São Paulo, Brazil

Silvane Silva

7.1 Introduction

One of the first historians to study contemporary quilombo communities was Afro-Brazilian activist and author Maria Beatriz do Nascimento (Nascimento 2018). She stressed the importance of studying their experiences. Much could be learned from their successful rebellion against the slave system and their accomplishments in later years. In addition, they mobilized Black Brazilians, both politically and socially, for decades after the formal abolition of slavery. Professor Nascimento's research discusses the "quilombola peace" period when they were not fighting to defend themselves from attacks and, therefore, could organize and develop socially and economically (Smith 2016). Tragically, Professor Nascimento was murdered on January 28, 1995.

Although she had not completed her research at the time of her death, Professor Nascimento left records about the activities of contemporary quilombo communities and defines them in the following manner:

> Quilombo, I want to emphasize here again, is nowadays much more an ideological instrument for the struggle of the Black people than an instrument, as it was in the past, of rebellion. It is an instrument of self-affirmation, an instrument of understanding that you, that the Black man, is a capable man like any man, that he formed quilombos not only because of the corporal punishments. He ran away, he killed masters, he committed suicide, women aborted babies, there were several forms of resistance, but the Quilombo organization, which has an African root in the sense that means unity, unity of those who are equal, so the Quilombo still exists today and it is the organization which will give us all the possibilities to reclaim our role within the history of Brazil, as men capable of being free and who really fought for our freedom with all possible means through rebellions and through political struggle, fighting for abolition of slavery. (Nascimento 2018, 131)

Silvane Silva, *Fighting to Preserve Black Life and Land Rights*. In: *Beyond Racial Capitalism*. Edited by Caroline Shenaz Hossein, Sharon D. Wright Austin, and Kevin Edmonds, Oxford University Press.
DOI: 10.1093/oso/9780192868336.003.0008

Since their inception, quilombo communities have emphasized democratic and cooperative systems of mutual aid (Ferreira 2021). Just as Nascimento (2018) explained the importance of a quilombo as a Black organization for collective political and social development, Hossein (2018, 4) asserts that "no matter how relentlessly colonizers tried to make Black people conform to the masters' norms, the Black diaspora has held onto its African traditions. These traditions of living in society and making a living unfold in myriad ways—and much of what they do is grounded in co-operation."

This chapter discusses the leadership of the Black Brazilian female organizers of quilombos (who I will refer to subsequently as quilombolas). I analyze these women from a Black social economy lens to understand the racial capitalism affecting their lives. In addition, I refer to the influence of ubuntu African philosophies and buen vivir philosophies of the Indigenous Andean peoples on their struggles for land rights and self-sufficiency. These women have challenged many barriers designed to deprive them of land ownership. I discuss the importance of land rights for them in the oppressive capitalist society they reside in. Their battles and strong sense of solidarity provide us with many important lessons about cooperation, leadership, respect for the land and environment, the disadvantages associated with urbanization, and the never-ending efforts Black women engage in to demand that their communities are respected.

7.2 Methods and Approaches

There is no consensus on the exact number of quilombola communities in Brazil. The first census that estimated the quilombola population was in 2020. It discovered the existence of more than 6,000 communities. Of these, 80 are located in the state of São Paulo. The quilombola communities visited for this research include André Lopes, Bairro Galvão, Bombas, Brotas, Caçandoca, Cafundó, Cangume, Picinguaba Farm, Ivaporunduva, Jaó, Pedro Cubas de Cima, Nhunguara I and II, Sapatú, and São Pedro (see Figure 7.1).

I carried out semi-structured interviews and round table talks in sixteen communities. Black women leadership was especially apparent in seven of these communities, four were located in the Ribeira Valley (São Pedro, Sapatú, Pedro Cubas, Ribeirão Grande/Terra Seca), and two were on the north coast of São Paulo state (Quilombo da Fazenda e Caçandoca). Finally, two were in the countryside of the São Paulo state (Cafundó e Quilombo Brotas). The conversations were recorded and two were transcribed in full.

Using the methodologies of oral history, I think of these women as sources for their own history. Oral histories are a useful tool in investigating complex social dynamics because they involve a dialogue between two people. One of these persons reflects on their recollections of past events. We can then learn and understand things that we may not have learned from written scholarly narratives. For Malian historian Amadou Hampâté Bâ (1980), societies of oral tradition have an enormous accuracy.

Fig. 7.1 Quilombo Ivaporunduva
(Photo credit: Silva Silvane.)

From these oral testimonies that detail the individual and collective memory of quilombola women, it is possible to understand these women's struggles. From the accounts of São Paulo's quilombola women, I attempt to explain both their way of life and the solidarity in their struggles for civil and economic rights. The oral accounts from quilombolas will forever educate us about their experiences in Brazil.

7.3 The Origin and Evolution of Quilombos in Brazil

In Brazil, quilombo communities (also called mocambos in colonial Brazil) were first developed in the mid-1500s. At that time, African refugees escaped from the bondage of slavery, settled in these isolated areas, and valiantly fought to resist recapture. It can be argued that this was one of the first collective solidarity enterprises that, through farming and supporting each other, avoided being captured. However, these communities survived in the post-slavery period.

Quilombos are ethnic-racial groups with a long tradition of resistance to historical oppression. In these communities, the fight for land rights and territory concerns not only the right to own the land, but also to control its use (Ferreira 2021). In addition, these communities share common trajectories because of their cultural tradition of respecting their ancestors as well as their common identity and history

(Gomes 2012, 8). The occupation of Brazilian lands took place in a violent way. First came the expulsion and killing of Indigenous peoples when Europeans invaded America in the sixteenth century and divided the territory into large tracts of land called *sesmarias*. This gave rise to the slaveholding *latifúndios* (plantations). Then, the Land Law of 1850 mandated that the acquisition of land would only occur through purchase and sale, ignoring previous possessions, regulations, and the rights of Indigenous peoples. Over time, oppression at the hands of land-thieving elites strengthened the movements for access to land, such as those of the Indigenous, the quilombolas, and landless rural workers. The history of the quilombos is immersed in the processes of resistance to appropriation and expropriation of the land. Because of this history, quilombolas are aware that they must fight to maintain their territories as part of a larger rural social movement (Gomes 2012).

Since the 1960s and 1970s, an acceleration of the urbanization process has occurred in Brazil. Both landowners and tenants have been violently deprived of their land. I use the term "traditional communities" as defined by Convention 169 of the International Labour Organization (ILO) on Indigenous and Tribal Peoples. That is, traditional peoples are culturally differentiated groups that recognize themselves as such, possessing their own forms of social organization, uses of knowledge, innovations, and practices generated and transmitted by tradition. They are occupants and users of territories and natural resources as a condition for their cultural, ancestral, economic, social, and religious reproduction. The members of these traditional communities normally own the land, but not its title.

Black people, who were forcibly expelled from the countryside, moved to the cities where they still experienced prejudices. First, they were unfairly driven from their homes. Second, city dwellers, who perceived themselves as being culturally superior to rural people, discriminated against them. In addition, their jobs have been menial and the lowest paid.

The biases associated with racial capitalism are obvious when observing the plight of Afro-Brazilian people. Cedrick Robinson argues, "Race became largely the rationalization for the domination, exploitation, and/or extermination of non-'Europeans'" (Robinson 1983, 27). In Brazil, the capitalist system, and the intense forms of racism associated with it, negatively impacts the lives of Black people. Racism in Brazil is present in all spheres of life—whether it be in institutions, the family, or social, political, and economic relations (Almeida 2019).

Traditional quilombola and Indigenous communities are persecuted and threatened in Brazilian cities for these reasons. However, if they remain in the countryside and earn a livelihood, they would not need to flee to the cities and join the queue of unemployed and underpaid workers. The quilombola ways of being and successful utilization of solidarity economics directly threaten the capitalist system (Silva 2019, 67). Denildo, national coordinator of Coordenação Nacional de Articulação das Comunidades Negras Rurais Quilombolas (CONAQ), describes the threat quilombola communities pose to the capitalist system as follows:

> In the Quilombola and Indigenous struggle, these territories are outside of the land sales market, so there is a great confrontation of some sectors of society so that the Quilombola and Indigenous agenda does not advance. Today, we understand that Quilombola lands are the lands that are preventing agribusiness and capitalism from settling once and for all in the Brazilian countryside. Why? Because these areas have specific laws, both Indigenous and Quilombola, that prevent agribusiness from pressing on them and at the same time "strengthen up" the peasant movement, because there are several instruments, international treaties, such as ILO Convention 169, and Decree 4887/03 that protect our lands. Communities are strategic lands, where there is a lot of water, there is a lot of forest and there is a lot of ore. In Brazil, we had some borders to be overcome by capital: the first frontier was the Amazon, and the forest code was made more flexible so that capital could enter the Amazon and legalize common land, another sector of difficulty for capitalism is the Quilombola and Indigenous lands. In the matter of ore, they are already making the legislation more flexible in order to enter our territories. So, we are the frontier for this advance, we are in our lands and we are an obstacle for them. (Silva 2019, 67)

Quilombola and Indigenous communities also disagree with the idea that urbanization is always beneficial to society. In the capitalist way of life, land and natural resources are intended to be extracted in the service of profits and infinite pro-growth development. In Brazil, national and state parks are the only "oases" left unaffected by growing urbanization. In many places, such as the North Coast (Ubatuba) and the Vale do Ribeira (Jacupiranga, Eldorado, Iporanga), these parks are located in quilombola and Indigenous communities (see Fig. 7.2).

Harmful environmental laws have been imposed on communities established in these territories long before the parks existed, with some having lived in these territories for over 300 years. Conservation units in these traditional communities are based on the idea that nature can only be preserved without the presence of human beings. In drafting and applying such environmental legislation, governments have at no time been interested in respecting or protecting traditional local populations (Nascimento 2006). Instead, these populations are affected by what scholars are calling environmental racism. Environmental preservation laws emerged in Brazil around the 1950s. More and more traditional populations—such as Indigenous, *caiçaras* (sea coast people), riverside, and quilombolas—oppose the prohibitions imposed by these laws. They not only change their way of life, but inevitably make it impossible to survive in the lands where they have always lived.

Many Black Brazilian women in the state of São Paulo have worked collectively to acquire land, attain fundamental human rights, and achieve economic gain. Quilombola women have worked collaboratively for several years, but especially since the 1988 constitution, to enact public policies that guarantee equity in land ownership. Article 68 of the Transitional Constitutional Provisions legally reorganized the remaining quilombola communities and acknowledged their ownership

Fig. 7.2 Ribeira Valley
(Photo credit: Silva Silvane.)

of land. However, the constitutional text alone did not guarantee access to these rights. The rural and urban Black movements fought to attain what the law affirmed. The right to land is at the center of quilombola women's struggles and has been one of the dominant issues discussed at quilombola women's meetings in Vale do Ribeira. Without land and territory, there is no quilombola. Based on the definition of quilombo in the National Guidelines for Quilombola School Education, we can see decisively that the quilombola identity is entirely linked to the land and the uses of it.

7.4 Knowing the Context: "Buen Vivir" Meets the Black Social Economy

Black Brazilian women have always been in the struggle for their communities, whether from the terreiros (Afro-Brazilian religions: Candomblé, Umbanda), samba, or quilombos. They have fought for their individual and community lives within a hegemonically capitalist society (Bohn and Grossi 2018; Ferreira 2021). The concept of "buen vivir" (good living) of the Indigenous populations of Latin America means being aware that everything is connected and interrelated (land, water, mountains). The buen vivir of the Indigenous peoples is similar to the ubuntu concept of the Bantu

Xhosa and Zulu peoples whose motto is "*umuntu ngumuntu nagabantu*" ("a person is a person through other people"). This motto describes their emphasis on living and existing to enhance other people in the community, rather than just themselves as individuals. In 2015, buen vivir was the motto of the March of Black Women in Brazil. It refers to a community worldview in which the community is everything. Therefore, the emphasis is not just on individuals but focused on the collective. As their motto of buen vivir indicates, Black women promote collectives in their society and oppose individualism and profit at the expense of communal life. Mogobe B. Ramose (2010) has written about one of the basic values of ubuntu—"*feta kgomo tshware motho*"- which means "If and when a person has to face a decisive choice between wealth and preserving the life of another human being, you should always choose to preserve life" (Ramose 2010, 175). In quilombola communities, this is a dominant view. It is very common to hear from quilombolas, "Here in the quilombo, there is no self. There is us." Care for the other is constant, as is the respect for all elements of nature, similar to the concept of buen vivir. It is not only the human being that matters, but also rivers, plants, and land.

It is essential to highlight that these two concepts are related to the economical and social concept of Black social economy. One of the editors in this book, Caroline Shenaz Hossein (2018, 8) defines it as follows:

> The Black Social Economy in the Americas is applied in its material, drawing on ideas from Black thinkers to show that community-based markets are many and that Black people have been at community building for a long time. Many of the economic projects undertaken by Black people are born in part out of crisis and exclusion in efforts to civilize the world's economy. Understanding business exclusion means drawing on literature by and for the African diaspora that speaks to collective economic projects that Black people have had to develop to live well.

Agriculture is also an important pillar in quilombola communities. They produced everything they consumed until the 1960s and preserved the Atlantic Forest in which they lived. They have already demonstrated throughout their history that they utilize the proper practices of food production in harmony with nature. Quilombolas only stop planting when they are banned in some way, either by environmental laws (communities within state parks, for example) or by lack of land; in the case of urban communities, whose territory has already been incorporated by the cities, there is no space for food production.

It is important to emphasize that quilombola communities are not expected to remain frozen in time. I recognize the need to incorporate new techniques. However, the disrespect for the worldview of traditional peoples in the name of progress or development violates the human rights of these communities. Technological advances are included in the buen vivir concept, but only if they further the idea of a harmonious world (Acosta 2013).

I now will refer more specifically to the oral accounts. For Nilce Pontes Pereira, from Quilombo Ribeirão Silveira, recognizing and respecting the ancestral knowledge that shapes quilombola identity should be of the utmost importance.

> Our products are all organic, because we don't use any of these pesticides, our food serves as food and as medicine. We also have a healer and an herbal handler, because if you don't have it, although you have the herb you don't know the dosage, you don't know how to use it. So, you have to have these two things in the community. (Nilce, Ribeirão Grande/Terra Seca, 2017)

Nilce also says that in their community they work with the agroforestry system:

> In my community there are 77 families. We work with family farming, agricultural production, and we also have livestock. Our community is self-sustainable. The means of production are agroforestry. We have a traditional production method and, at the same time, agroforestry technologies. We do not have confrontation within the community, territorial conflict or an environmental conflict. (Nilce, Ribeirão Grande/Terra Seca, 2017)

It is important to note that Nilce's community uses traditional methods, as her parents and grandparents did, but also incorporates new technologies from agroforestry. The community does not deny the new knowledge acquired in the work carried out with organizations that support them and through the technical courses they attend. Nilce's statements reinforce the idea that new learning, provided it is built together with the community, is not incompatible with the community's philosophy of life.

Recent studies show that large commercial forms of agribusiness production are unsustainable. In a few years, there will not be enough food to feed the world's population if the big producers continue to act in a predatory way, worrying only about profits. The excessive production of some items (soy, for example) at the expense of others—only aiming at the market price—and the unrestricted use of poison in the crop impoverish the soil and pollute rivers and springs. Since 2008, Brazil has been ranked first among those countries in the world that most use pesticides. There are many experiences here of producing organic food in a sustainable way, without poison or pollution, but unfortunately it is not the model followed by big landowners, nor is it encouraged by the public authorities (Silva 2019, 77).

On September 29, 2018, the traditional agricultural system of the Vale do Ribeira Communities was recognized by the National Historical and Artistic Heritage Institute (IPHAN) as an intangible cultural heritage of Brazil. The coivara plantation, about which Heloísa spoke, is a traditional planting technique that maintains soil fertility, preserves the diversity of cultivated species and the environment, and guarantees the community's livelihood. Research studies have proven what quilombolas have known for centuries.

Traditional populations have never lost the dimension of the land as culture. Quilombola farmers already carry the idea of sustainability within themselves and are environmentalists by tradition. Any activity on the land that does not respect these principles is not agriculture; it is agribusiness. From my interviews, I discovered that the quilombola women who took part in this research are farmers. They emphasized in their interviews that they build their lives from the land, through the "pure" food that nourishes and brings health, as they say. It is also in this same land that "the navels of their ancestors" are buried. For this reason, garden making in quilombola communities is a cultural heritage. The garden is survival and at the same time freedom, as Nilce pointed out: she may not have money, but in the community she has everything she needs to live.

7.5 Environmental Issues and the Forms of Economic Organization of Quilombola Women

All the reports of older residents are similar. They tell us that until approximately 1960, communities produced everything they consumed: they planted, raised chickens and pigs, fished, and hunted. They only purchased or traded for clothing fabric, salt, phosphorus, and kerosene for lamps in the local cities. Everything else was produced in the community. Today, the reality is quite different. Newly created environmental laws often disregard the ways of life of traditional populations. They were dispossessed of their lands, taken by large entrepreneurs in the mining sector or by entrepreneurs interested in building hotels and condominiums. They faced the construction of roads and encroachment of cities. As a result of all this, quilombolas were forced to reduce their productive activities: mainly the production of food for their own consumption, making life much more difficult.

Currently, a large number of the quilombolas live with few resources and are forced to work outside the community, in the fields of other producers or in the cities, in domestic jobs for family houses, and in other urban services. Some also receive retirement payments or Bolsa Família (Family Welfare) from federal programs. Unfortunately, the quilombolas and Indigenous people who were responsible for the preservation of a huge area of Atlantic Forest existing in the Vale do Ribeira and on the north coast of São Paulo (Ubatuba) are now disadvantaged by environmental legislation. This legislation created parks and areas of environmental preservation within the quilombola territories and banned activities carried out for centuries by these communities, such as maintaining the fields and hunting for their own consumption. Inland communities, such as Cafundó and Brotas, were "swallowed up" by the city in an accelerated urbanization process, and today they live in a much smaller space than they were originally entitled to. This is because they are in a region in which real estate speculation is rampant due to the high value of land in the region of Sorocaba (Cafundó) and Itatiba (Brotas).

Traditional populations, representatives of governments, non-governmental organizations, and other interested parties have been debating the relevant environmental legislation that removes the rights acquired in Convention 169 of the International Labour Organization on Indigenous and Tribal Peoples. Many traditional groups have heralded the acute environmental racism that riverside, quilombola, and Indigenous populations experience, arguing that those communities who preserved the land for centuries now cannot enjoy and benefit from what they have cared for for generations.

Some communities, especially those that have already been certified and have their land titled, live mainly off the banana and palm heart plantations. This is the case for certain communities in the Vale do Ribeira. Almost all of them raise chickens and pigs (in small numbers) for their own consumption, and they manufacture, in a traditional way, products such as manioc flour, banana, papaya and orange sweets, breads, and cakes, as well as banana fiber crafts.

The communities have also been organizing themselves for ethnic-cultural tourism, of which the Ivaporunduva community is an example. It owns an inn and receives groups of tourists and visitors (mostly teachers and students from basic education and universities). The community holds thematic workshops on the history of quilombola communities. Monitored visits take place in almost all communities, at which time their members perform dances (e.g., Nhá Maruca and Mão Esquerda), viola jams, and "storytelling." Some young people from the communities surrounding the municipality of Eldorado work as environmental monitors in the varied natural attractions of the region, such as the Devil's Cavern and the many waterfalls that exist there. These examples show the attempts of some communities to adapt their economic activities to the new environmental regulations.

Many of these Quilombo communities are located in regions that are difficult to access, far from urban centers, since they historically were strategically organized areas that guaranteed security from slavers. This characteristic is often used by the government as an excuse to remain absent from quilombola territories, denying them basic health and education services: for example, health posts are rare in areas close to quilombolas, revealing the lack of care in relation to health rights. Quilombolas also have great difficulty accessing health care and hospitals in the cities.

It is necessary to highlight the strong presence of women in the struggles for rights in their communities. Quilombola women have established networks of trust when creating residents' associations (the first step to seek land title) and incentives that will ensure a quality education for their children. There are many reports about the participation of women in the search for piped water, the construction of schools and health centers, and maintaining customs (e.g., prayers, midwifery, and storytelling). Thus, through their solidarity, these women enhance both their lives and those of their families in quilombola territories.

In the women's meetings that took place in the 1990s in Vale do Ribeira, a region where most of the quilombola communities in the State of São Paulo are located, it was clear that new awareness among the women was already growing. In 1986, the so-called Irmãs Pastorinhas, from the catholic congregation Irmãs de Jesus Bom Pastor in the diocese of the municipality of Eldorado, started Bible studies meetings in the quilombola communities of that region. In these meetings, people talked about what needed to be improved in the lives of communities. Women raised issues related to basic sanitation, transportation, and health—that is, basic social rights. These demands were sent to the local government.

In 1992, motivated by the International Women's Day celebrations, women's groups from various Black neighborhoods in the Eldorado region met at the first women's meeting, which had the theme "The woman in the Bible," with the motto *Wake Up Women!* The Ecumenical Centre for Biblical Studies (CEBI) and members of Black Catholic movements in São Paulo participated in the organization. This meeting was attended by 270 women, members of other congregations, and representatives of entities linked to the fight against racism and male chauvinism in Brazilian society. In the years that followed, the themes included "Health: Women organize and fight"; "Rescuing culture through dance and typical foods: Women continue to fight"; and "Women's rights: Women know their rights and act."

In these meetings, women felt free to speak and express their ideas. In the conversation I had with Dona Esperança, from the Sapatu Quilombo, she spoke of the fundamental importance of these Bible study group meetings for women in consolidating the quilombola identity of their community and increasing their awareness of their own strength, motivating them to self-organize. An example of this was the creation of the collective garden, which guaranteed income for all. It enabled the founding of the residents' association and the formalization of their request for certification as a quilombola community from the Fundação Cultural Palmares.

> So, from this community here, the organization started after we, the woman group, began studying the Bible. We discovered the values of the women in the Bible; they had a lot of struggle to get their rights, so we studied, and that's where we started our women's organization. We started to work together, because if each one worked for each other, we got stronger. From that time to nowadays, we started to do a women's meeting in Eldorado to celebrate the 8th of March, which is the international day of woman . . . for a long time I have been coordinating things here within the community. I have coordinated a garden since 1994 to now; I have become coordinator of Pastoral da Criança (Children Pastoral); Sister Sueli, Sister Angela came to give us Bible Studies. I studied for five years, so I've already learned many things. The Residents' Association emerged when we worked with the vegetable garden group: we were a group of ten women who worked in the community vegetables garden, and then when I formed the Association, we were the first people to enter the Association to be able to register. Since then, the woman's group hasn't stopped. (Dona Esperança, Quilombo Sapatu, 2015)

Another interlocutor, Dona Jovita, from the Quilombo Bairro Galvão, also spoke of the importance of the women's meetings for herself and her community. Dona Jovita is a farmer who always liked to sing and write poetry. She told us that she carried a copybook to the farm, and when an idea came to her, she ran to write it down.

> I had a day with a hot sun like that, in a *corguinho* (stream), everything inside the Sertão, then I sat on the rocks to listen to that little noise of that water running, that I love. Then, I was so astonished that I started thinking to myself, "I could make a song for us '*muié*' (sista)". Right then I started to meditate, you know, but I hadn't taken the copybook, because when I carried my notebook, each verse that I thought, I had already written it down, not to forget it. (Dona Jovita, Quilombo Bairro Galvão, 2015)

One feature of the women's meetings was the possibility of producing songs and verses with the themes that involved the lives of these women. An example of this are the verses sung by the women against the construction of the dam on the Ribeira do Iguape River:

> Today I saw a group of women who went out in procession and I asked them where are all you going? Maria replied that they were going to the meeting to fight, so the people could scream again: "Earth Yes, Dam No!!!!" [against the construction of a dam that would flood their land] The women are brave enough to fight against such a dam . . . let's unite, hold hands . . . Because we have our reason . . . We are a Group of Women . . . that fight without stopping . . . May God give us much health . . . And courage to work! . . . . Oh! Friend, don't be sad . . . Because we are going to work . . . We must not be discouraged . . . Because Antonio Ermírio [a big Brazilian entrepreneur that wanted to build the dam] wants to rob us. We wish for women's groups . . . a good meeting . . . We need a lot of support . . . "EARTH YES, DAM NO!". (Silva 2019, 51)

It was during this period of women's meetings that the Movement of the People Threatened by Dams (MOAB) was created. Communities were threatened by the construction of dams on the Ribeira de Iguape River. The creation and importance of MOAB was prevalent in the interviews of the quilombolas who participated in the women's encounters between 1992 and 1995. MOAB is coordinated by the Articulation and Advisory Group for Black Communities (EAACONE). It was created to raise awareness, organize, train, and inform the population of Vale do Ribeira about dam construction projects on the Ribeira de Iguape River carried out by Brazilian Aluminum Company (CBA, owned by Antonio Ermírio de Moraes). The objective was to show the population that such projects prioritized not social and environmental issues, but rather the profit of the company. As Dona Jovita wrote, "Antonio Ermírio doesn't want us. He builds a dam, puts his foot in, and throws us away." The collective voices of these women build strength, courage, and great hope for the transformation of their realities and their communities.

Last but not least, it is important to note that the impact of the struggle for land has been an uphill battle. Few quilombola communities have been titled and few Indigenous reserves demarcated. This scenario, when taken in the context of the political coup that occurred in 2016 (the illegal impeachment of President Dilma Roussef), encouraged the actions of landowners and corporate raiders on lands who were still in the process of demarcation and titling. It also led to a wave of increased violence and murders of quilombola and Indigenous leaders. The agrarian issue still remains one of the greatest obstacles to the fight against structural racism in Brazilian society. Communities depend on the land for the production of food and the preservation of their knowledge.

In view of this situation, one of the paths found by CONAQ (quilombo central offices) was the elaboration of a report providing official data on the killings of quilombola leaders. The report was also a denouncement of the omission of this data by the state in the broad context of violence that affects quilombos in Brazil. The *Report on Racism and Violence against Quilombos in Brazil*, published November 21, 2018, asserts that in 2017, eighteen quilombola leaders were murdered. Anti-Black racism is behind this violence. The report emphasizes the responsibility of the Brazilian justice system for this widespread violation of civil rights. Racism, despite being the main element of social relations and power, continues to be denied systematically—at the same time that violence continues to rain down on the quilombola population.

The CONAQ Women's Collective collaborated directly in the preparation and publication of this report. According to Givânia Silva, one of the coordinators, documents from the CONAQ collection, newspapers, social networks, and other publications were used to produce the report's data. The report clearly shows the devaluing of Black lives, as many victims had been reported without first names, only by their surnames. For this reason, the testimonies of the families of the murdered people were the most important sources. "They are bodies and lives that have defended our territory and that's the reason they were murdered" (CONAQ 2018 188).

Regarding the struggle for civil rights, women appear as the pillars of their communities and they are still denouncing the fact that many people do not interpret the struggle of women as a political struggle. The titling of land, refusal to participate in the current economy has left those who belong to the quilombos vulnerable. These situations of violence and the subjugation of women, which are denounced by CONAQ, also tell stories of the heroism of these women, who often suffer violence precisely because they are exercising leadership or raising their voices against oppression. The quilombola communities are attacked because they organize their economy differently and oppose discrimination and sexism.

The state has responded with laws to limit the work of quilombolas because they feel threatened by the collectivity of Black Brazilians. As of 2017, a process of criminalizing social movements and government actions has targeted traditional communities. Family farms, quilombola communities and settlements, and Indigenous reserves have been blocked by the "ruralist bench" of the national congress.

Black populations and, more specifically quilombola communities, are now organizing to radicalize democracy and build collective power to address the ongoing injustices. They continue to struggle for the rights of Black populations. Dona Jovita, a veteran protagonist of this research, started participating in the women's meetings in the 1990s. She has led demonstrations against the construction of dams in the Vale do Ribeira, emphasizing her commitment to the struggle for land and social rights. "My name is Jovita Frutini França, I am a descendant of slaves, I do not run from shots . . . My brother was shot in the back by a jagunço (hitman) . . . You must know that God did not leave the land for businesses that sell land, eat and destroy land, and forget to produce food." Dona Jovita's message inspires us to build alternatives to combat racism and capitalism.

Through this research, I amplify the voices and struggles of quilombola women who generously offered their testimonies to enlighten and educate us about their work and experiences. Making the voices of quilombola women public helps them to have a political voice as well. In this chapter, I primarily want to demonstrate that their collective efforts are directed at the maintenance of life and the spreading of joy while resisting unfair and exclusionary systems.

7.6 Conclusion: Quilombola Women Draw on Politicized Action to Bring Social Change

Self-organization and cooperation are at the core of Quilombola communities. Black people have always trusted their own community as a way of guaranteeing their survival amid persistent racism and violence. The racial capitalist system wants to take away their lands and way of life rooted in the collective. The exclusionary economic and political system denies African-descended people in Brazil a chance to live freely and to thrive. This is why the quilombola communities persevere in today's modern world.

The very concepts of buen vivir and economic cooperation is threatening to the state so there is a hostile response by state actors towards quilombola communities. Forms of Black and Indigenous peoples' organization must be seen as authentic contributions to the knowledge-making of the political economy. To that end, the Black social economy is a space of politicization and the collective self-determination for African peoples, including those in the diaspora.

The quilombola women from Vale do Ribeira have organized themselves to collectively produce organic food for their communities and to fight against displacement and the construction of dams. The courage shown by Dona Jovita to face all forms of violence to remain on the land that is rightfully hers and the resolution shown by Quilombola Nilce are deeply connected to the ancestral knowledge of the quilombola identity—to fight for Black liberation at all costs. As activist leader Nascimento rightly noted, the quilombo was an important site because it was the basis for political and social organization for Black people, and mostly Black women, in Brazil.

Simply put, quilombola communities want to live moments of "quilombola peace" so they can produce food, Black culture, and joy. For them, that is the very essence of life.

Works Cited

Acosta, A. 2013. *El Buen Vivir. Sumak kawsay, una oportunidade para imaginar otros mundos*. Barcelona: Icaria Editorial.

Almeida, S. 2019. *Racismo Estrutural*. São Paulo: Pólen.

Bohn, S. and P. K. Grossi. 2018. "The Quilombolas' Refuge in Brazil: The Social Economy, Communal Space and Shared Identity." In C. S. Hossein (ed.), *The Black Social Economy in the Americas: Exploring Diverse Community-Based Alternative Markets*, 161–86. New York: Palgrave Macmillan.

Coordenação Nacional de Articulação das Comunidades Negras Rurais Quilombolas (CONAQ). 2018. *Racismo e violência contra quilombos no Brasil*. Curitiba: Terra de Direitos.

Ferreira, P. 2021. "Racial Capitalism and Epistemic Injustice: Blindspots in Theory and Practice of Solidarity Economy in Brazil." *Geoforum* 132: 229–37.

Gomes, N. L. 2012. "Resolução no 8, de 20 de novembro de 2012." *Define Diretrizes Curriculares Nacionais para a Educação Escolar Quilombola na Educação Básica*, Seção 1, p. 26. Brasília: Diário Oficial da União.

Hampaté Bâ, Hamadou. 1980. "A tradição viva." In Joseph Ki-Zerbo (ed.), *História Geral da África I. Metodologia e pré-história da África*, 181–218. São Paulo: Ed. Ática/UNESCO.

Hossein, C. S. (ed.) 2018. *The Black Social Economy in the Americas: Exploring Diverse Community-Based Alternative Markets*. New York: Palgrave Macmillan.

Nascimento, B. 2018. *Quilombola e Intelectual: Possibilidade nos dias de destruição*: Diáspora Africana: Filhos da África.

Nascimento, L. K. do. 2006. *Identidade e territorialidade: os quilombos e a educação escolar no Vale do Ribeira. Dissertação (Mestrado em Geografia)*. Universidade de São Paulo, São Paulo.

Ramose, M. B. 2010. "Globalização e Ubuntu." In Boaventura de Souza Santos and Maria Paula Meneses (eds.), *Epistemologias do Sul*, 175–220. São Paulo: Cortez.

Robinson, C. J. 1983. 2000. *Black Marxism: The Making of the Black Radical Tradition*. 2nd edition. London: Zed Press.

Silva, S. A. da. 2019. *O Protagonismo das Mulheres quilombolas nas lutas por direitos nas comunidades do Estado de São Paulo (1988–2018)*. Tese de doutoramento: Pontifícia Universidade Católica de São Paulo.

Smith, C. A. 2016. "Towards a Black Feminist Model of Black Atlantic Liberation: Remembering Beatriz Nascimento." *Meridians: Feminisms, Race and Transnationalism* 14(2): 71–87.

8

Black Irish Women and Esusu

The Case of Self-Help among Nigerian Women in Dublin, Ireland

Ebun Joseph and Kesiena Mercy Ebenade

8.1 Introduction

In a complex and predominantly white Catholic society like Ireland, the Nigerian community, and especially women, have had to adapt to settle into Irish life. This chapter examines the use of rotating savings and credit associations (ROSCAs) by Nigerian Irish women in the Irish economy and society. This savings scheme, commonly called Esusu in Dublin, has strong origins in the African continent. In the western part of Nigeria among the Yoruba-speaking populations, these saving schemes are called Ajo, while they are referred to as Adashe in the northern regions (Hausas) and Esusu or the variant Osusu (Edo) in the eastern region (Igbos). Women from other parts of Nigeria who participate in the process generally call it one of these names.

This study builds on previous research on how Black workers in the diaspora (re)negotiate their career/economic pursuits toward what has been described as areas of least resistance and greater acceptance (Joseph 2019). One concept that is important to African Irish women in Dublin is the African philosophy of ubuntu, which rejects individualism and embraces cooperativism and is based on its understanding that we are truly human only in community with other persons (Lutz 2009). It underpins Africans' way/s of forming community economies (Graham-Gibson 2006), managing economic difference, making choices, and re/negotiating their career pursuits in their individual and collective economic lives.

The presence of African women in Ireland is interpreted within Afrophobic discourses that are used to justify harassment and abuse against them (Michaels 2015). The victimization of women and children provides a glimpse of a particularly Irish anxiety in the aforementioned 2015 report. Joseph (2019) similarly argues that Nigerian migrants in Ireland have limited recourse to state resources in the form of paid employment. He notes that the group experiences the most pejorative encounters in the labor market, going around in cycles despite having high levels of education. This is precisely what Robinson (1983) speaks of as racial capitalism, where Black people are exploited for their labor by the dominant group. It is the Black social economy

Ebun Joseph and Kesiena Mercy Ebenade, *Black Irish Women and Esusu*. In: *Beyond Racial Capitalism*. Edited by Caroline Shenaz Hossein, Sharon D. Wright Austin, and Kevin Edmonds, Oxford University Press.
DOI: 10.1093/oso/9780192868336.003.0009

(Hossein 2018) that gives a place of refuge for the African diaspora to cooperate with one another; and in this case study of Nigerian immigrants, we show how they make their own social economies.[1]

This chapter commences by discussing how Esusu operates in Dublin, Ireland. Next, we discuss how racialized and gendered experiences shape the economic lives of Black African migrant women. We look at issues of economic integration, or the lack thereof, that compel migrant families to seek alternative financial means—such as ROSCAs, which operate on their own terms. We also analyze the reasons Nigerian Irish women use Esusu despite access to modern commercial banks and a multitude of formalized credit systems, and we recognize that racial capitalism has relevance in the Irish context for Nigerian–Irish people. This community-building by Nigerian women is reliant on what they know from their homeland, and they count on people they know and trust to help each other as a way to diversify economies (Gibson-Graham 2006).

The exclusion of the African diaspora from business and society has been occurring in the Americas for centuries since the time of enslavement. African American scholar Cedric Robinson (1983) confronts the hostility to Black people in the capitalist system and calls it racial capitalism. Racial capitalism also occurs in the Irish context toward Black immigrants. Robinson (1983), however, misses the intersectional exclusions affecting women. Black women, being both Black and female, are affected not just by one axis but by multiple axes of oppression and by many identities that complicate life (Crenshaw 1994). We draw on the philosophy of ubuntu to shift attention away from gender inequality to the concept of being as "being-together," through which Gibson-Graham (2008) introduced a new language of economic diversity described as occurring notions of sociality and commerce. Nigerian women develop cooperatives known as Esusu to contribute to the Irish social economy through what is referred to as the Black social economy (Hossein 2018). The Black social economy is the space where people of African origins are able to connect both socially and economically to meet their needs—it is a politicized space in which they choose cooperation to counter the racism in a society. We thus aim to widen the scholarship by providing insight into how racialized migrant women in Ireland negotiate race and gender within a racist environment that is hostile to Black people from the Global South.

The empirical evidence in this study is collected through the narratives of ten women of Nigerian descent who have engaged in Esusu in an Irish context. It is grounded in the African concept of ubuntu, which centers on human-ness and interconnectedness. The African culture and the concept of ubuntu (which translates as "I am, because you are") literally means that a person is a person through other people. Kenyan theologian John Mbiti (1970, 141) described this sense of community

[1] On 14 July 2022 the Institute of Anti-racism and Black Studies invited Hossein to give a lecture on mutual aid financing to a large number of Black women in Ireland who attested to their own trauma and why they organize ROSCA systems (Maynooth University).

interconnectedness thus: "I am, because we are; and since we are, therefore I am." The philosophy of ubuntu emphasizes caring, sharing, reciprocity, cooperation, and compassion as key elements of how people should live with each other.

Ubuntu is not known to many people in the modern world, who typically see profit-driven institutions, such as banks, as the way to advance. However, ubuntu is a deeply ingrained African culture and tradition of common humanity, community, and oneness. Robinson (1983) recognized world history and lived in Zimbabwe, so he was able to appreciate varied living experiences. Despite the diversity in culture, dress, food, and language amongst the sub-Saharan Africa countries, their non-individualistic character is one practice they have in common. Even with modernity, this strong sense of community life is still the bedrock of society and how people organize. In other words, the community way of life is ingrained, as it has been argued that "an African is not just an individual, but a person within a community" (Lutz 2009, 1).

8.2 Understanding Esusu in Ireland

A ROSCA is "an association formed upon a core of participants who agree to make regular contributions to a fund which is given, in whole or in part, to each contributor in rotation" (Ardener 1964, 201). While a ROSCA fosters individual empowerment similar to peer-to-peer lending, it also brings people together in a group setting that cuts across different cultures. In the community economies sector, the work of Gibson-Graham (2006) refers to ROSCAs as a community of economy, whereby this economic diversity is used to negotiate interdependence with each other, humans and the environment. ROSCAs have indeed been extensively researched from different perspectives across the world. It has been argued that ROSCAs foster the mechanism for creating savings (Aliber 2001) and that the investment contribution can be managed through collective risk sharing by multiple people in the ROSCA group (Besley 1995). According to Besley et al. (1993), the informal means of saving, the economic impact, and the performance as a result of this coming together as a group cannot be discounted. The women members interviewed in Peterlechner's (2009) study of people's motivations for joining ROSCAs reported that their financial empowerment increased to some extent as a result of partaking in the ROSCA scheme.

On the surface, ROSCAs (from here on we use Esusu) can seem like an "alternative" way of accessing economic resources, especially for socioeconomically disadvantaged groups experiencing limited access to paid employment and collateral to secure loans from the traditional economies. It has, however, always been part of the financial devices people of African descent use to succeed in places inside and outside their native lands. Canadian scholar Caroline Shenaz Hossein (2018) describes how African people have held onto these ancient African systems of collectivity as a means of surviving in the Western world. While it is still surprising to some that

Esusu finds a home in Ireland, it should not be, particularly given the high unemployment rate of Black Africans in Europe, and specifically in Ireland. In order to settle in, Nigerian Irish women living in Dublin, Ireland, on the margins of the economy draw on familiar African money systems such as Esusu to meet their livelihood needs because of embedded business and social exclusion in the dominant white society. This exclusion of Black people from capitalist markets has led them to co-opt business and create their own community economies (Hossein 2018). It is important to note here that the practice of community economies is not a foreign or new ideology in Ireland. It has a long history in the credit societies from the West of Ireland, who sought to combat chronic rural indebtedness among small farmers through what is now known as the credit union. A history of cooperatives also exists through the Irish agricultural cooperative movement, which was based on the suggestion to the rich to help the poor by trading with them by means of cooperative stores (King and Kennedy 1994).

8.3 The Lived Experience of Nigerian Irish Women in Ireland

While migration affects all migrants, they are not all affected in the same way. In Ireland, the darker skinned people of African descent are worse off than their white European counterparts (Joseph 2018). This study insists it is because darker skin workers of Black African descent start from a disadvantaged position that is the result of the racial strata to which they are assigned on arrival in Ireland. The racialized, classed, and gendered experience of African women who immigrated to Ireland in the 2000s is not recognized. According to the country's 2011 census, 17,642 people of Nigerian descent resided in Ireland. This number appears to have decreased sharply by 25.8 percent to 13,079 based on records in the 2016 census. One feature of this group is the reversal of roles between men and women that many Nigerian Irish women encounter. In their traditional family structure and hierarchy, Nigerian males are seen as breadwinners and heads of the household. The reversal can be attributed to the unique migration of Nigerians to Ireland, which saw the arrival of the women before the men. As a result, many of the men were not granted residency rights to live in Ireland with their families. And of those who were, some opted not to relocate because of the poorer employment prospects in Ireland than they had in Nigeria.

Consequently, many Nigerian households in Ireland are led by single parents, with women as the head of the home (FRA 2017; Joseph 2020). According to the 2016 Census Statistics Office, this group also had the highest percentage of those whose main activity is within the home. What this means in Ireland is that they are primary home carers on very low income, with limited access to the loan system due to lack of collateral or full-time paid employment outside the home. It is important to state here that many of these Nigerian Irish women arrived in Ireland as graduates of tertiary institutions in Nigeria, with years of work experience in different sectors of banking, business, marketing, communications, law, and education.

Faced with the inaccessibility to paid employment and the challenges of raising young families without a network of support from family and long-standing friendships, many women found themselves as long-term unemployed over time. While it might appear that these women lacked the confidence to apply for the types of jobs they had in Nigeria, studies show that those who did and ventured into the labor market were disappointed because of the racial discrimination against Black African migrants and their credentials (Joseph 2019; Michael 2015). For those early arrivals in Ireland, the closure of the labor market to this group was mainly attributed to their lack of Irish work experience and education from outside Europe, while recruiters were reluctant to give them the opportunity to gain the required experience. The logical solution, which many of these women took, was to obtain Irish qualification by retraining and seeking voluntary work to boost their chances of getting into the Irish workforce.

However, this came with its own challenges, as the women caught in this cycle only had recourse to a weekly social welfare system that barely provided for the family's immediate needs. The situation was exacerbated because many of the women after retraining were still unable to gain access to paid employment. Many Nigerian Irish women were compelled to down-skill through vocational training to access health-care jobs while others fueled the Black economy in Ireland, drawing on skills such as hair plaiting, sewing, manicuring nails, doing makeup, tying head scarves and child minding in their homes to gain some economic autonomy. While this Black social economy (see Hossein 2018) often generated small sources of income for these women, it meant they had poor bank records, no collateral, and no legal proof of income. Hossein (2018), in the first ever in-depth exploration of the Black social economy (and coined the concept), explores the myriad ways persons of African heritage have built humane economic alternatives to the dominant commercialized economy that excludes certain groups and what they do is form their own alternative socioeconomic communities. In this study in Ireland, many of these women interviewed were in full-time professional roles before relocating to Ireland. This also suggests that many of the Black women immigrants would have come from a market system where banking was part of their everyday lives to a situation where they could not access some of the basic services in Ireland's banks.

8.4 Methods and Approaches

To fully understand Nigerian Irish women's self-help banking groups called Esusu in Ireland, we interviewed ten women. The selection criteria included that the women had a legal residency right to live and work in Ireland, were female and of Nigerian descent, and had completed at least one full cycle of Esusu while resident in Ireland. A WhatsApp text message requesting an interview about Esusu was sent to thirty Nigerian women living in Ireland. Out of eighteen respondents, ten participants between 36 and 49 years (with a mean age of 46 years) were selected based on the criteria stated above. The selected participants did not express any worry or risk about the study. We carried out semi-structured interviews over the phone between February and March 2019.

All interviews were conducted with the participants' permission, audio recorded, transcribed, and subsequently color-coded and thematically analyzed using a template of analysis. An interview tool consisting of five questions was developed to prompt the conversations. For the most part, the interviewees (whose names we anonymized to protect them as a vulnerable ethnic minority in a white society) were encouraged to discuss how they got involved in Esusu, the benefits, challenges of Esusu, and whether they would advise others to participate in Esusu. Since one of the authors had never participated in Esusu, we were particularly interested in understanding why people participate in this form of community banking. Thus, we specifically asked why they chose Esusu despite the presence of more structured banking systems in Dublin, Ireland.

8.5 Findings

In this section, we analyze the kinds of Esusu used in the Irish context and what we learned from the ten subjects. We found four formats of Esusu: continuous (which differs only based on its regularity, i.e., daily, weekly, and monthly); unstructured; intermittent; and blind. In all the cases, the members decide how the Esusu will be structured and a designated person called the collector receives the contributions for the stipulated time frame. Admittance into any of the cycles of contributors is usually through referrals by existing members or the group collector. Considering the small population of Nigerian Irish women resident in Dublin, we have represented the ten Nigerian Irish women participants with pseudonyms as Participant 1 to 10 (P1 to P10).

Building up democratic local systems in Esusu through continuous Esusu

The continuous Esusu is usually made up of a small and close-knit group of between five and fifteen members consisting of family or friends who share commonalities. The group is initiated with the primary goal of "mutual aid and self-help" (Hossein 2018) but it is sustained because of the social gathering and connectivity elements. The amount of money contributed in this cycle can range from €50 ($56) up to €500 ($560) monthly. We refer to this type of contribution as continuous because of its nature of having no real end date, as the process is tied to the reason for initiating the group (self-help, mutual aid, connectivity, and social gathering). This form of

Esusu is embedded in the same ideas of ubuntu that promote African communal cultural life, unifying and bringing people together regardless of their background or access to wealth (Sithole 2001). It becomes a way people can help others from their community in times of difficulty without incurring excessive personal risk. It is also an informal way people can loan each other money with limited risk of destroying friendships because the group seeks the payments rather than individuals, which can be conflictual.

The Black social economy acknowledges the trauma and complex environment in which the African diaspora live, and Esusu is a way of making a place of refuge so that people who have been harmed can organize collectively. Members in this type of Esusu often attribute a "saver" quality, as in rescuer, to Esusu. By this we mean it serves as a way for them to meet their key needs at crucial points, where group members, who are most often women, were without other options of intervention. Continuous Esusu was, for many of these women, a last resort to meet their particular needs—to pay, for example, for school fees, rent for housing or business, a new car, or to start a small business. The need was particularly strong for those with young children who could not entertain the idea of seeking a loan as they already pre-empted an unsuccessful outcome (as either they have been refused a loan or they have seen others from their community refused loans). Participating in Esusu thus comes at a time of key need for these women, so that it creates a good feeling—of gratitude, beating the system, and winning against all odds.

These associated benefits of Esusu make it almost addictive in nature. Many of our interviewees continued with the process long after those initial emergency needs had been met. A second-generation Esusu participant, who we call P4 here, not only saw her mother participate but also helped her in processing the payments. She describes her mother's continuous participation in Esusu for over 40 years:

> Whether there is a benefit or it has just become a habit that she is involved in. People don't need it but continue to do it. My mother doesn't need it but she continues to do it. It starts to work in their minds as if, if you don't do it, you will not be able to meet up. Hers is like a habit. She looks forward to the interaction and conversation with the collector. Like someone gets used to talking to the counsellor or looking forward to meeting them. (P4 female, HR Personnel, mother of four)

This form of Esusu helps these women build their own systems parallel to mainstream banking and social networking systems where they are in charge of how it operates, who it allows in, and who they help.

Flexible and unstructured Esusu as a loan system

The unstructured Esusu is common among business people who need capital to invest in small business ventures. Esusu in this format gives money to a member for a specific time, who then agrees to repay from 0 percent to a fixed 1–5 percent interest of the amount received. The borrower in this case signs a written document as part of the process. This type of unstructured loan comes with many challenges, as there can be great loss in some cases. At the agreed time, the borrower returns the full amount borrowed. In some cases, the borrower returns the money in twelve monthly installments, depending on what the lender decides and what suits the business venture of the borrower.

Robinson (1983) notes that Black people in a white environment have a hard time accessing goods and resources. Esusu responds because equity and inclusion are built into its system. Providing these unstructured loans to Esusu participants benefits the lenders through the interest paid by the borrowers. It also particularly suits people who do not have full-time paid employment and as a result lack good credit standing with the banks. Unstructured Esusu also reflects the African culture of ubuntu of helping family and friends when they are in need. It provides a safety net and a binding process, making it a formal loan with relaxed rules rather than a friendly loan, which is much easier to abuse.

Social lives and intermittent banking

The intermittent informal banking method of Esusu is linked to people's social lives. Many life experiences that require spending happen at certain times of the calendar year: for example, before Christmas, during the summer holiday season, or in the month of August when parents in Ireland face back-to-school expenses for their children. Nigerian Irish women organize Esusu to ease the financial burden during these cost intensive periods—when they have to pay for school fees, plan holiday trips or birthdays for young children, or purchase Christmas gifts. These life events are often given lower priority, particularly in financially strenuous times.

These women reorganize money to suit their social lives by giving their individually agreed amount towards a particular social event. The collector receives the money (which can be different amounts for different members) at the start of the year. This means members can only receive the total amount they have individually contributed. As such, issues of members defaulting do not arise in this case, as contributors receive only what they have individually contributed. This type of Esusu is also very popular because of the flexibility it offers for each individual to decide their contribution and its link to specific life events.

The concept of blind shareholders in Esusu

In the blind shareholders Esusu that we discovered through our field work, the collector brought nine women together to form a contribution group for a monthly amount of €100 ($113). The group was set up in 2009 with the singular purpose of eliminating the credit card debt of members. On successfully achieving this goal, the collector, a finance student, refocused the group and began a strategic investment for members. We call it the blind shareholder Esusu because members here have never met each other—it is not a requirement for them to know each other personally. This is unlike other forms of Esusu, where knowledge and trust of group members is vital and membership is usually a close-knit group. This system also uses the formal banking system, as the monthly contribution is carried out through bank transfers. Some unique features include the order in which the contributed funds are assigned at the end of each collection month. For example, members do not have to receive their funds at the end of the cycle if they have no pressing purchases or spending needs. In addition, members only receive 90 percent of the contributed monies while the coordinator invests the 10 percent balance in purchasing shares for that group member. This is a more sophisticated system, where the group advances the Esusu collection into a wealth-building investment system. It also uses many of the mainstream banking systems.

8.6 Discussion

Black women lead social finance

It can be a stressful process for women anywhere to access money, and this is even more so if they are Black in a predominantly white country like Ireland. This is evident in the high unemployment rate of Black Africans in Ireland, where, despite their high levels of education, Blacks still experience five to eight times the unemployment rate of Western Europeans (Irish Central Statistics Office 2016; Joseph 2019). For many Nigerian Irish women, participating in Esusu is one way they can mobilize money as a group. While the process involves saving on a regular basis, the group recognizes its usefulness for entrepreneurial ventures. This is because Esusu, as practiced in Ireland by our participants, is typically tied to an existing or projected need. One participant, P2, a mother of two and law graduate intern, stated, "I needed to rent a house and starting Esusu enabled me to cover the cost and expense." What we found is that ROSCAs are appealing to racialized people with limited or no access to the formal banking system. Banks operate complex systems, and people from marginalized groups are often excluded from accessing loans because of bad or biased credit ratings and precarious employment. In Dublin, Esusu is one way for women to counteract this exclusion and access financial resources, as P5 stated:

> Before I became a qualified accountant, I needed money for various personal and family needs. Even now, I have bills and things I need to pay for. The contribution gave me bulk cash without having to submit loads of documents to the bank or lenders. (P5: 42 years old, female, accountant in Dublin)

Some participants saw Esusu as a way of having their own autonomy in a society where Blacks are engaged in menial work, undervalued, and still viewed as strange. It was an opportunity for the women to be in charge of one aspect of their lives. The financial enablement afforded them by Esusu was empowering, particularly for those in unequal relationships at home or in society:

> For me, the contribution was great. It helped me start a small business when I was in school. I didn't stop there as I saved a percentage of the profit through Esusu. It just meant that I had my own money that I was saving. I didn't need to borrow or ask my parents or anyone. When I needed it, it was there. (P4: mother of four, HR personnel)

Many of the women we interviewed were introduced to the concept of ROSCA from their homeland of Nigeria where they would see market women (traders) use Esusu to buy goods and invest in growing their businesses. The Esusu system turns many women in the diaspora who use it into money managers of a new kind, as they bring a home-grown African money system to help them in their new country of residence.

Black Irish women are focused on equity and inclusion

The story of how Black Irish women are leading financial inclusion is not well known in Ireland. But Nigerian Irish women are bringing Esusu from their native homelands and they are using it in Dublin to uplift their lives. The main commercial banks in Ireland, such as the Allied Irish Bank, the Bank of Ireland, and the Permanent TSB, operate through a private transaction system in ways that make the women we met feel invisible and excluded from financial services. In fact, Audrey Deane (2018), an author on money matters, writes in an opinion piece that one is invisible without money in modern Ireland. She maintains that the "unbanked" are financially excluded because they have problems accessing mainstream, affordable financial products, such as current and savings accounts, credit, and insurance. They end up excluded from basic everyday transactions, such as bill payments, money transmission (direct debits, standing orders), and housing. They in fact end up paying more for services, often as an added charge on each financial transaction, when they engage with the banking system.

Esusu, as practiced by these women, treats people in an equitable way, adhering to the ubuntu philosophy of treating others as connected communities and supporting each other at different times when able. The operation of Esusu through group membership means that defaulting is public knowledge within the group. This serves to instil discipline in participants. But this is done in a supportive way and not as a humiliation of defaulters. The process compels members to meet their contributory obligation. Their awareness that the group cares about them fuels their effort to meet this obligation. P5, a 42-year-old female accountant and a mother of three who lives in Dublin, explained it succinctly:

> The thing is if you have to put it in a bank, nobody is actually forcing you to do that, you can decide that this month is tight for me [financial hardship], I don't want to contribute and repeat this two months in a row. The likelihood of skipping the next month is high. In this particular one [Esusu], you just have to put the money in, because one particular person is going to get the money. You can't do that [default] because when it comes to your turn, you do not want it to happen to you, so it is like it is a must that you have to do. At the back of your mind, you are spending money, you get your salary and you will put the money aside for this particular thing. You get your pay, you have to take this money out of it and what is left is for you. You don't want to ruin it. After a while you get used to it. (P5: 42 years old, female, accountant)

Two other participants also shared how participating in Esusu makes members disciplined about their spending:

> I had weekly income and I was not able to control my expenses. But when you are committed to Esusu, it makes you think and spend wisely. (P2: mother of two, law graduate intern in Dublin)
>
> Esusu helps you to cut down some expenses that are not necessary because you are thinking of the contribution you have to make at the end of the month. It enables you to manage and live within your means. (P1: 38 years old, female, healthcare assistant in Dublin)

For many members, saving alone did not enforce any discipline, despite potential bank penalties such as loss of interest on savings. Rather, commitment to others was the main reason many of the participants maintained their part of the contribution process, as accountability to others disciplined them. P5 said, "when you are committed to other people, it makes you disciplined." Another interviewee, P4, explained that having people believe in you can change your ways and be a motivator. She stated, "It instilled discipline: I always collected the contribution first, so once done, I have to keep contributing."

Part of making money inclusive is making systems inclusive. The women in our study revealed a lack of belief in the Irish banking system, and the perception of members is that what they have is not valued or seen as valuable. P4 explained:

> I observed my father who dealt with the bank constantly going to the bank and bank managers coming to him. I thought it was for people like my dad. I had no investment or regular income, I also knew banks didn't give much bank interest, so why put my money in the bank? My mother, on the other hand, has done Esusu

> for over 40 years, as she never dealt with the banks in her daily business in the open market, where she is a trader. (P4: mother of four, HR personnel)

The inclusive way women use money in Dublin makes many of them see Esusu as more than "taking" (meaning receiving the bulk funds contributed). They experienced Esusu as somehow *rescuing* them. This is because in addition to Esusu offering a form of loan without interest charges, it allows all groups and classes with low qualifying criteria to access this informal loan. Most of the groups mainly worked off the recommendation of a trusted group member, with none of the forms, credit checks, or work history checks one would encounter in mainstream banking systems.

> I found out that many of the members of our Esusu group will not be given loans even if they apply. We will not tick the boxes. They [banks] give you money when you don't need it. They are not there to save you on the rainy day [times of trouble]. In Esusu, so far as you can pay your contribution, we don't need to know your banking history. (P2: mother of two, law graduate intern in Dublin)

Building trust, solidarity, and friendships

The building of trust between Esusu group members and the collector, who is often the group leader, is a prerequisite for a successful Esusu cycle. Although none of the interviewees reported being explicitly told that they needed to be trusted, they all mentioned the need to trust each other and the organizer. This is evident in the fact that participants are usually known to each other. They might also be introduced by someone they know or who is part of a community of people with whom they already interact, like a faith community, a community group, or work colleagues.

> The person who introduced me to it [Esusu] is trustworthy . . . We are choosy about who we get involved in our group. If you join newly, there is a rule, you cannot collect first or second, you must be the last person to pack [given the bulk contribution]. I do not allow someone I do not trust in the group to collect first or second. They collect towards the end like the seventh month. (P5: 42 years old, female, accountant in Dublin)

The trust is two way. It is not only of the potential member, but members also have to trust the Esusu team to complete the contribution cycle and process all payments. The importance of trust in the process cannot be overstated. For example, when we asked the participants what makes a complete Esusu cycle go well, they all mentioned trust, previous experience of the process or the group, and repeat participation with groups with which they have successfully completed an Esusu cycle.

The narratives from interviews also indicate that the Esusu process as organized by the Nigerian Irish women in Dublin also builds, maintains, and strengthens relationships. Women who didn't all know each other were brought together in a system offering them a supportive network for each other, as they reported: "It brought closeness between the women in that after you've added yours [contribution], the women look out for each other to make sure they have it to give back when it's their turn . . . We had each other's back" (P1: 38 years old, female, healthcare assistant in Dublin). For some of the women, being part of the Esusu contribution group was a way to meet new people and develop relationships. This was particularly true for those who were new to Ireland, who were in hostel accommodation due to the asylum process, or who were without family members in Ireland. It allowed many to build collegiality and provided reciprocal childcare between new mothers who were retraining in the Irish education system or in low-waged employment. As P4 reported:

> When I first came to Ireland, I did Esusu with some Nigerian women who I didn't know, but it made us closer as I was constantly on the phone to these women asking if they had collected their share of the money. Making sure they had it. It lent itself to friendships, created additional support in terms of cheaper child minding. I was in college then. When they needed childcare, I provided the same. (P4: mother of four, HR personnel in Dublin)

When people move to a new country, they need comradery. We know from first-hand experience that having a local support system matters. The women see Esusu as a pathway to achieving a common goal and building close bonds:

> I was passionate about getting my people to get involved in our local community meeting and bring people together to become active members of the group. I found that some people who didn't want to be part of our native group meetings have become very interested in the meeting after we started Esusu . . . It is more a service that I will do for my people. (P3: 49 years old, female, customer service operative)

When we asked the participants if they would advise others to participate in Esusu, they mainly said, "it depends on the people you are doing it with." This suggests that despite caution and awareness of potential challenges with Esusu—for example, conflict due to its informal nature—the practice of Esusu is not very different from most group practices, where in-group favoritism sees most people gravitating toward those they are familiar with.

> The people I do this with are people from my mosque and family members and the relationships have been long. There is someone involved in my group, a man to be specific who now resides in London and he is still involved with us in the Ireland group. It depends on the group of people you are involved with. If you have developed relationships in the past with the people, that is good. You have to be

> very careful. I have been with this group for a long time. (P5: 42 years old, mother of three, accountant)

Some of the women saw Esusu as a way of supporting marginalized women and group members who were in challenging financial and emotional situations. This idea stems from the gender inequality they see between the sexes in patriarchal systems. One participant described some of these women as "hustlers." Another participant who gave an example of these kinds of situations stated:

> Their husbands are at home, doing nothing and so this helps the women. Some also use it [Esusu] as a way to hide money from their husbands. It also became their savings for future urgent purchases, particularly for those who cannot get loan or capital. (P6: single mother of four, community worker)

While the contributed amount generated was not always a strong incentive for all the participants in the study, they were still willing to be members of the groups because of the connection with others it offered, a quality that is absent in mainstream commercial banking. For example,

> It is not of any immediate benefit for me now because my financial needs are higher than what we are collecting, but I still want to be a member. I started it because I wanted something I could bring to my community, people from my state and tribe. (P3: 49 years old, female, customer service operative)

> I have seen it make an absolutely significant difference in the lives of the women. As the facilitator, what I hear is why women and people participate and why they sometimes want to collect early. A few people who need the money to pay their children's fees for those who still have family in Nigeria and they cannot access bank or student loans. Some use it to start businesses. It has absolutely been helpful to raise required capital while paying back in a small way. (P6: single mother of four, community worker)

Social finance and ubuntu in the West

The closeness of Esusu group members operates differently than mainstream business in the Western world. In the Esusu contribution system, the group is responsible for modifying the process to respond to their needs. For example, the women in the blind shareholders Esusu worked toward developing the core skills to enable them to improve the scheme. In one particular case, the initial aim of the group was to pay off their credit card debts. They responded to the 2007–8 economic recession in Ireland by building individual group members through their personal development. P7 described the process:

> We were taking some online courses on investment in stocks and shares and decided that since we have paid off our credit card debts, we should adapt the scheme as an investment scheme for ourselves. Having a form of investment in shares is good as I can also track how my shares are faring and it gives me a kind of assurance that I am putting something aside purposefully for me and my children. (P7: mother of three, business graduate)

The informal development of Esusu members is not often recognized or even acknowledged. It is also not the way mainstream banking operates. In this case, the participants in the scheme invest 10 percent of the contributed amounts to purchase shares and stocks. They develop appropriate new behaviors and ways of working in response to both internal and external changes. The skills group members acquire are beneficial, for example to their personal lives and future work, as P7 further stated:

> I was not very good in mathematics and this affected how I viewed issues around finance. But the Esusu scheme has enabled and empowered me to look at the area of financial literacy and how to use the skills I developed to make decisions about my money that will benefit me in the future. (P7: mother of three, business graduate)

These informal continuous learning opportunities are created in the group because group members are encouraged to seek and share learning opportunities that can facilitate the groups' development.

8.7 Conclusion: Nigerian Irish Immigrant Women Use Esusu as Self-Help

Nigerian Irish women have innovated and pioneered self-help banks called Esusu in Dublin, Ireland. These systems are by no means perfect for the new context, but the women are experimenting with flexible, blind, and continuous types of Esusu. The work of Gibson-Graham (2006) on community economies fits with how this concept can travel. Localized money systems that operate in Nigeria can find a home and be adapted when people move to the West. Nigerian Irish women—who are often excluded from jobs, careers, education, and opportunities—are using their own business ethics to recreate their economic lives. Esusu has served many Nigerian Irish women. The women we met show that it is one way to cope with the structural inequalities that have excluded them from access to resources through paid employment or bank credit. It is important to note the perception that Hossein (2018) highlighted in her study is still cognizant in our study: "Black social economy is about mutual aid and self-help that remains autonomous from the state and business sectors because in most cases it is fighting against these two sectors."

While we acknowledge that not all Nigerian Irish women in Dublin participate in Esusu, the meaning it brings to those who do is undeniable. There was a strong sense of group belonging among the women participants interviewed. Esusu also provided a means of generating capital (albeit in small amounts) for group members' immediate economic need/s when commercial banks turned their backs on these women and their dreams. The women were individually empowered in and by the process. For many, it offers them an opportunity for solidarity with each other, a structured way to help and support each other and build up other women, and, most importantly, a way to resist their marginalization. The ten women interviewed shed light on the phenomenon of Esusu in the Irish context—one that few would know about but that is a lifeline for these newcomers. The Black social economy has been noting these deliberate moves to create cooperatives among the Black diaspora using co-op systems people know from back home. The interviewees were Black women who were in financial difficulty and had an impending need. But the research also unveiled a story of preserving identity and culture and tapping into a money system that is flexible and inclusive.

Ubuntu can appear as an unclear concept to many, particularly in the West and among profit-driven institutions such as commercial banks. The concept of Ubuntu is, however, deeply ingrained in many African cultures and traditions where people understand the fundamentals of common humanity, community, and oneness. Esusu is literally a saving device, that reaches those who are the most alientated. The actual act of coming together helps women and saves them from racial capitalism. Esusu comes to their aid when they feel they are not able to provide for their families' needs—from deficits in small investments like back-to-school requirements at the beginning of each academic year, to large needs like paying the rent to keep a roof over their heads or starting a business. It saves them from credit card debt and the associated challenges of being a credit risk. On the social side, Esusu saves some from loneliness and isolation by providing a sense of belonging. Many who are in the diaspora without their family networks find that the common goal gives them a sense of belonging and common purpose.

Many Black women in Ireland endure the impacts of racial capitalism. This study shows how Esusu for Nigerian Irish women in Dublin provides a cooperative network, acting as a motivator and adviser when they are not able to qualify for state services or cannot afford private services. Esusu in Ireland contributes to cooperative development and the social economy but it remains largely unknown. This was evident in the narratives of Black women who would have spent their limited resources on items that were not a necessity but instead curtailed their excesses—mainly due to the collective monitoring that instils a sense of discipline and to not wanting to disappoint the others in the group. We can indeed see the African philosophy of Ubuntu in the saving quality of Esusu, which makes it addictive to many women—who after a while continue with the process not only for the financial needs it meets but also for the social needs.

Works Cited

Aliber, M. 2001. “Rotating Savings and Credit Associations and the Pursuit of Self-discipline: A Case Study in South Africa.” *African Review of Money Finance and Banking*: 51–73. https://www.jstor.org/stable/23026350#metadata_info_tab_contents

Ardener, S. 1964. “The Comparative Study of Rotating Credit Associations.” *Journal of the Royal Anthropological Institute of Great Britain and Ireland* 94(2): 201–29.

Besley, T. 1995. “Nonmarket Institutions for Credit and Risk Sharing in Low-Income Countries.” *Journal of Economic Perspectives* 9(3): 115–27.

Besley, T., S. Coate, and G. Loury. 1993. “The Economics of Rotating Savings and Credit Associations.” *American Economic Review* 83(4): 792–810.

Community Economies Collective and K. Gibson. 2009. “Building Community-based Social Enterprises in the Philippines: Diverse Development Pathways.” In Ash Amin (ed.), *Social Economy: International Perspectives on Economic Solidarity*. London: Zed Press.

Crenshaw. K. W. 1994. “Mapping the Margins: Intersectionality, Identity Politics, and Violence against Women of Color.” In Martha Albertson Fineman and Rixanne Mykitiuk (eds.), *The Public Nature of Private Violence*, 93–118. New York: Routledge.

Deane, A. 2018. “In Modern Ireland, You Are Invisible without Money.” *The Journal*, May 25. https://www.thejournal.ie/readme/opinion-in-modern-ireland-you-are-invisible-without-money-4030832-May2018/

FRA European Union Agency for Fundamental Rights. 2017. *Second European Union Minorities and Discrimination Survey*. Luxembourg: Publications Office of the European Union. http://fra.europa.eu/en/publication/2017/eumidis-ii-main-results

Gibson-Graham, J. K. 2006. *A Postcapitalist Politics*. Minneapolis: University of Minnesota Press.

Gibson-Graham, J. K. 2008. “Diverse Economies: Performative Practices for ‘Other Worlds.’” *Progress in Human Geography* 32(5): 613–32.

Hossein, C. S. 2018. *The Black Social Economy in the Americas: Exploring Diverse Community-Based Markets*. New York: Palgrave MacMillan.

Irish Central Statistics Office. 2016. http://www.cso.ie/en/. Accessed April 26, 2021.

Joseph, E. 2018. “Whiteness and Racism: Examining the Racial Order in Ireland.” *Irish Journal of Sociology* 26(1): 46–70.

Joseph, E. 2019. “Discrimination against Credentials in Black Bodies: Counter-Stories of the Characteristic Labour Market Experiences of Migrants in Ireland.” *British Journal of Guidance and Counselling* 47(4): 524–42.

Joseph, E. 2020. *Critical Race Theory and Inequality in the Labour Market: Racial Stratification in Ireland*. Manchester: Manchester University Press.

King, C. and L. Kennedy. 1994. “Irish Co-operatives from Creameries at the Crossroads to Multinationals.” *Contemporary History* 2(4). https://www.historyireland.com/irish-co-operatives-from-creameries-at-the-crossroads-to-multinationals-by-carla-king-liam-kennedy/

Lutz, D. W. 2009. "African Ubuntu Philosophy and Global Management." *Journal of Business Ethics* 84(S3): 313–28.

Mbiti, J. 1970. *African Religions and Philosophies*. New York: Doubleday.

Michael, L. 2015. *Afrophobia in Ireland: Racism against People of African Descent*. Dublin: European Network Against Racism ENAR.

Peterlechner, L. 2009. "ROSCAS in Uganda—Beyond Economic Rationality?" *African Review of Money Finance and Banking*, 23: 109–40.

Revans, R. 1980. *Action Learning: New Techniques for Management*. London: Blond & Briggs.

Robinson, C. 1983. *Black Marxism: The Making of the Black Radical Tradition*. Chapel Hill: University of North Carolina Press.

Sithole, J. 2001. "Africa Can Only Use Own Culture to Influence Globalization." *afrol News*, May 15.

9

Caribbean Banker Ladies Making Equitable Economies

An Empirical Study on Jamaica, Haiti, Guyana, Trinidad, and Grenada

Caroline Shenaz Hossein

Caribbean women create ROSCAs to take care of the needs of their community and to show that cooperatives have a place in society.[1] These women also push against commercial banks which fail to diversify lending and include certain groups, namely Black poor women. The argument here is that ROSCAs are an antidote to racial capitalism, and that these money groups do not depend on external subsidies to achieve financing for the community because Black women, usually from lower income areas, create ROSCAs to mobilize local resources. In this chapter, my empirical research reveals that the Caribbean Banker Ladies are acknowledged, without gratuity (no renumeration), for their self-help financial cooperatives and their contribution to equitable economies.

It is no secret across the Caribbean that Susus, Partners, and Sols have a lasting legacy in the Americas (Harrison 1988; St. Pierre 1999; Poto Mitan 2009). Back in the 1940s fieldwork by anthropologists Herskovits and Herskovits (1947) examined kinship among African descendants in Toco village and documented the use of Susus. People, even if they do not participate in ROSCAs themselves, are very much aware of them. The Banker Ladies dedicate plenty of their own time developing these groups, mentoring members, and employing their talents to uplift community and address inequities. Yet, they are not paid for these economic development efforts. The women understand this reality and continue doing their community work without requiring payment from the state or society.

During colonization and the complex period of post-colonization, self-employed women, known as higglers or hucksters, carried out co-op business which is a testimony to how far back these systems go (Katzin 1959; St. Pierre 1999).

[1] This chapter draws on my body of work over the years, including a major monograph under review. This chapter draws mostly on sections from my journal article (2016) titled "Money Pools in the Americas: The African Diaspora's Legacy in the Social Economy," published in the *Forum for Social Economics* 45(4): 309–28. Reprinted sections of the article by permission of Taylor & Francis Ltd. on behalf of *The Association for Social Economics*.

Caroline Shenaz Hossein, *Caribbean Banker Ladies Making Equitable Economies*. In: *Beyond Racial Capitalism*. Edited by Caroline Shenaz Hossein, Sharon D. Wright Austin, and Kevin Edmonds, Oxford University Press.
 DOI: 10.1093/oso/9780192868336.003.0010

Through the focus group discussions and one-on-one interviews I conducted, I saw that Caribbean women are in charge of co-op economies and are vested in friendships, but they also make sure that people who are excluded are being mentored. It is this economic cooperation towards creating an open economy that they do—ever so quietly—that receives praise from local elites, who remain distant from these very women.

This chapter examines five country cases—in Jamaica, Trinidad and Tobago, Grenada, Guyana, and Haiti—to show how Black women cooperators revamp colonial financial systems through African ideas of Kombit (collectivity). Elites who deprive many poor women of access to finance are the first ones to respect the ROSCAs called Susus, Partners, and Sols that these women organize (this is contrary to the Canadian Banker Ladies in Chapter 10). It may be that some of these elites—though not all—had mothers who relied on ROSCAs to pay for their schooling and family expenses. Some may even join a ROSCA because these systems are so culturally ingrained in the social life. Susus, Partners, and Boxhands are co-op systems being copied by commercial banks to roll out products such as “Mama Sol” or “Partner Plan” to attract new borrowers. Bankers in the islands know full well the appeal that these banking co-ops have to Caribbean women.

9.1 Beyond Racial Capitalism: Investing in Community

ROSCAs take care of people’s needs through collaboration and mutual aid. In proposing collective banking the women show that they are also addressing financial exclusion. Everywhere one goes ROSCAs are seen as a vital part of Caribbean life, especially among Black women. Much of it has to do with the intense forms of exclusion they experience. C. Y. Thomas’s (1974) convergence theory is boiled down to making self-sufficiency the economic concept that matters in terms of resisting exploitation by capitalist firms. The Banker Ladies converge local needs and productivity to do what is needed for those denied opportunities. Together with my political science colleague Kadasi Ceres (Hossein and Ceres 2022), we credit C. Y. Thomas’s convergence theory, which states that people focus on local production rather than goods for the export markets. The convergence theory of focusing on local economic development has been the basis for the community economic development principles in Canada but this is seldom noted as such.

African diaspora women proudly hold up and carry on an ancient African legacy of collectivity. I should note that the ways in which Black women in the diaspora outwardly show gratitude for ROSCAs depends on one’s context. None of the West Indian women I met with in the region feared reprisal or that what they do would be labeled “illegal” or likened to a corrupt Ponzi scheme. The work that comes naturally to them—such as caring for others, self-help, cooperating, and community business—may be actually influencing hardcore commercial bankers to think about the products they offer. It is not a far stretch to imagine the impact ROSCAs have had in the banking world (Bortei-Doku Aryeetey and Aryeetey 1996; Bhatt 2007; Devika and Thampi 2007; Christabell 2009; Kinyanjui 2019; Hossein and Christabell 2022). Where there is a level of trust for the state, citizens demand that the state actively involve informal collectives.

9.2 Inventorying Caribbean ROSCAs

Caribbean Indigenous banks—Susu, Partner, Meeting-turn, Boxhand, and Sol—are a longstanding ancient tradition that has taken historically—and still to this day, thanks to the women who organize these co-ops—a bold stand against unfair financial systems. Caribbean people's ancestors, like my own, African or Indian, came from various countries that practiced economic cooperation, and these systems traveled with them while they were in bondage. Those who came from West Africa draw on names like Susu and Asousou. Indians who came in as indentured servants after slavery was abolished and lived in the same logies as the African people went mostly to namely Guyana, Trinidad, and Jamaica, and their descendants also hold onto creolized versions of ROSCA systems too. Caribbean people, whether of African, Indian, or Dougla (mixed African and Indian) heritage, participate in ROSCAs because it is part of a cultural heritage and tradition.

No matter where one goes in the Caribbean, women speak affectionately about ROSCAs. They point to things they were able to buy, including their children's education, because of pooling money with other women—saving money in a safe way and borrowing lump sums when they needed it. ROSCAs are second nature to Caribbean people because they were raised with loved ones who were members: many of them remember running around, as children, making money deliveries to members. The work in ROSCAs in the Caribbean context is for the most part carried out by low-income women who depend on them for economic support and to push against exclusionary systems. This is not to say that other segments of the society do not use ROSCAs. One can find many office assistants and salaried workers organizing Susus for special events or to assist them with a capital inflow to help in their sideline businesses. Caribbean people, and primarily the women, know about and join ROSCAs because they find it to be an inevitable part of living life.

9.3 The Black Social Economy

Black diaspora women *politicize the solidarity economy* because of racial capitalism and violence they encounter in business and society. They use informalized cooperativism as a way to defeat commercialized markets.[2] This is what is at the

[2] See Curtis Haynes Jr. (2019) for his use of the term cooperativism.

very heart of theory making in the Black social economy. The work we see is not hearing Black women's voices and the efforts they do to fight for a safe economy. Nina Banks (2021) uncovered the work of economist Sadie Alexander, and endured a lot of criticism and tension as a result of doing this work. Much of the thinking on exclusionary capitalist systems do not invite Black women into the conversation about *how* capitalism can be transformed. The Black social economy aims to bring Black political economy and take note of the applied work being carried out by Black women in particular (e.g., through cooperatives) to stymie commercial harmful economies.

Black diaspora scholars have been writing on political economics in and outside of the academe for a very long time; yet what they have been saying has been largely sidelined (Wallerstein in Hunter 2000). American scholar Manning Marable's *How Capitalism Underdeveloped Black America* (1983 [2015]) was influenced by Walter Rodney's work (1982) on the power of extraction by European people, and he affirmed that the actual role Black people played in the capitalist economy would always be limited and that the root of capitalism is fundamentally flawed because of racism. Cedric Robinson's *Black Marxism* (1983) also echoes these findings of certain social forces being in charge and others enslaved. We now read it that marginalized Black people would lose out to an inherently racist capitalist system—an idea that was muted in socialist gatherings. America's capitalist system, like most Western business systems, was born out of bigotry and white supremacy, as the slave trade and enslavement bought profits to certain elite white folks.

It is Gargi Bhattacharyya (2018) who pushes us further to rethink racial capitalism as a mystery in and of itself, and that this capitalist system works to dispossess and divide certain people. Extreme forms of capitalism were never about trickle-down economics; they were about entrenching racial bias that would undercut the labor of people of color, especially Black people, and sabotage any idea of entrepreneurship and self-help (Marable 1983 [2015]). Unravelling the myth of markets, and its inclusion, is a key learning in Cedric Robinson's work (1983) and the concept of racial capitalism helps to trouble the idea that dividing people based on identities was deeply embedded in these capitalist structures from the very start. Knowing that neoliberal economic systems are set up this way also clarifies to those who are historically excluded that markets are not neutral, and the goods will never trickle down to help those less fortunate. The theory of racial capitalism anchors extreme forms of capitalism, which is that class and colored tiers exist to benefit privileged white men and women.

Knowing this history has led innovators like Jamaican-born social entrepreneur Marcus Mosiah Garvey to emerge in the 1920s as a powerful leader. Kelley (2002) notes that Garvey pioneered the largest member-owned organization, U.N.I.A., and organizations that prioritized Black life. After he traveled and worked around the world, it was while living in Harlem, NYC, that Garvey introduced a philosophy of racial self-reliance to counter mainstream business practices (K'adamwe et al. 2011).[3] This message, which he brought to his conferences with the Black diaspora, remains very relevant to the lives of Black people outside of Africa (Martin 1983; K'nife et al. 2011; Hossein 2016a, 2016b).

Garvey's own upbringing in colonial Jamaica and his lived experience as a migrant worker in Panama and Costa Rica no doubt made a mark on his teachings (Hill et al. 1987; Lewis 1987). Black people around the world have been deeply influenced by Garvey's teaching on Black empowerment in advancing notions of self-help. Many of the Banker Ladies I interviewed over the years have been inspired by the racial pride and the business ethics of Marcus Garvey. As all of these examples show, Black liberation theory is thus crucial in analyzing the social and solidarity economy of racialized peoples. The challenge for this work has been to move Black liberation theory along a feminist path so that we learn about Black diaspora women and their role in cooperative building too.

Africana feminist political economy

The work of Black diaspora theorists in politics and economics is in plain sight. But it is not being read into political science and economics as it should be. Feminists like bell hooks and Patricia Collins Hill (2000a, b) who examine such erasure in the academe speak to the importance of lived experience. In *aint I a woman: Black women and feminism*, hooks (1981 [2015]) demands a rightful place for reading Black women, arguing that their life struggle is a form of theorizing. This makes sense when we consider Black women whose contributions in the economy and society have been erased. It is not surprising that Black women are ignored in the social and solidarity economy. Take the extensive field work in South Africa by the American political scientist Tiffany Willoughby-Herard, who dares to push the political domain to include Black feminist thought and in her book *Waste of a White Skin: The Carnegie Corporation and the Racial Logic of White Vulnerability* (2015) questions the racism in white foundations under the pretext of "helping" Black folks. Aid and the social and solidarity economy institutions have built up resources under the banner that they do good.

Haitian American scholar Gina Ulysses in *Downtown Ladies: Informal Commercial Importers, A Haitian Anthropologist, and Self-making in Jamaica* (2007) included lived experience in her theorizing about the business lives of Jamaican higglers in the informal economy. In her book, the voices of the Banker Ladies, many of whom lived in or emigrated from the Caribbean region, are the living expression of what

[3] I presented a paper on Garvey as a social entrepreneur at the *Global Garveyism* symposium held in Richmond, Virginia on April 23, 2016. See Hossein (2017).

Ulysses (2007) captures. Despite the identity politics at play in these communities, these creative "Downtown Ladies" are taking care of their livelihoods on their own terms. The risk of doing business and organizing collectively seems worth it, as this way of working has helped certain groups for centuries. By claiming and co-opting resources, and experimenting how the market functions, Black people are, in essence, disrupting the racist business sector. We see this in the film *Poto Mitan* (2009), which U.S. scholar Gina Ulysses helped to curate, in which Black women are quitting firms that exploit their labor and leading the way with Sol.

African American economist Jessica Gordon Nembhard, who grew up in an intentional community, knew first hand what she was writing about in her book *Collective Courage*. In it, she documents cooperatives, arguing that Black people create "intentional communities" to form their own economic livelihoods in a racist society. The economic unfreedoms that people endure because of their cultural identity can be a life threat (Sen 2000). The concept of intentional communities is very relevant to the work that Black women do in the economy to help and support their members.

Black diaspora women's economic and political lives have often been ignored. Nina Banks (2020) argues that the community is an important site where racialized women are active and carry out nonmarket collectives to meet people's needs not met by the public and private sectors but this is often plainly missing. Banks (2005, 2008) documents the life of Sadie Tanner Mossell Alexander, who was the first African American to earn a PhD in economics and who retrained herself in law and fought for the human rights of Black Americans because economic departments would not hire her. Studying the intersection of community, race, and economics is theory-making of its own kind: to show that these actual experiences on the ground—trying to make politics and economics inclusive—is what many Black diaspora women do without any regard.

Fusing the practice and theory of Black activists and scholars engaged in politics and economics is a way of making theory and creating new knowledge. In Sharon D. Wright Austin's (2018) *The Caribbeanization of Black Politics* she surveyed 2,000 Black immigrants from Cape Verde, Haiti, and other Caribbean islands living in Boston, Chicago, Miami, and New York City—all U.S. cities that have major Black populations—and found that Black people have a strong sense of group consciousness when it comes to issues that matter to them. Black people coming together in economics is also true for political matters. By telling stories about how Black people, especially women, use economics and politics to transform a system through self-help from within their own communities and out of sight, we can show the world how to tie academic knowledge to what they are doing. Black political economy rooted in the lived experiences of women making community development possible is theory-making, or at least it should be considered as such.

The Black social economy with a strong feminist lens awakens our sense of what we already know and leads us to read widely. The Banker Ladies are a real-life action of what it takes to politicize and mobilize change from within. And we should be drawing on Africana women scholars who are thinking about lived experience and misogynoir (being Black and female). Solidarity, to make sense to excluded Black people, needs to deliberately co-opt goods and push for cooperation in order to make conflict and change meet. Caribbean Banker Ladies are drawing on ancestral philosophies of Ubuntu, "I am because you are," and Kombit (collectivity) knowhow to build their cooperative economies.[4]

9.4 Methods and Data Collection in Five Caribbean Countries

This study of the Caribbean Banker Ladies adopted multiple methods in researching the attitudes and motivations of lenders and borrowers in fourteen low-income communities across five countries. The work started during the latter years of my doctoral field work but continued afterward because it was the story that should have been told first. I held focus groups and interviews with 583 people in Jamaica, Guyana, Trinidad and Tobago, Haiti,[5] and Grenada, and also in Barbados, Panama, Canada, and the United States, from June 2007 to December 2013. As noted in Table 9.1, 298 Banker Ladies were interviewed in the Caribbean.

The research was conducted in Kingston, Jamaica, for most of 2009–10, which is the country that forms the main case. Interviews were held in mostly the south-west part of Kingston, called Downtown, south of Cross Roads, which includes the neighborhoods of Trench Town, Bennett's Land, Whitfield Town, Rosetown, Frog City, and the former prime minister's constituency of Denham Town and Tivoli Gardens.

In Haiti, I interviewed those living in the bidonvilles (low-income urban areas). These included Cité Soleil, Carrefour, Martissant, and La Saline, as well as Bel Air in Centre-Ville and Jalousie and Flipo in the hills of the chic suburb of Pétion-Ville. The

Table 9.1 Interviews with Banker Ladies in five countries

Method	Jamaica	Guyana	Grenada	Haiti	Trinidad	Total
Focus group sessions with ROSCA members, average 2–3 hours	57	5	0	74	0	136
Individual interviews, average 60 minutes	89	14	17	19	23	162
Total	146	19	17	93	23	298

Note: Author's own data collected from May 2007 to July 2015. The interviews and focus group with Banker Ladies in Ghana (2017) and Ethiopia (2018–19) are also not included in this table but I do draw insights from them in those focus groups

[4] Refer to Nussbaum (2003) and Kinyanjui (2019) for the use of Ubuntu by people of African descent.

[5] On January 12, 2010, Haiti experienced a 7.0 magnitude earthquake that left 300,000 persons dead and 1.5 million people displaced and living in tent cities and this affected data collection in the latter part of 2010 and 2011.

focus groups in Haiti were held in the poor areas of Bon Repos, Port-au-Prince. In 2008 and 2010, interviews were carried out in Albouystown in Georgetown, Guyana, which is ethnically diverse and has a large Afro-Guyanese and Dougla (mixed African and Indian) population, as well as East Indian, Portuguese, and Amerindian people. In 2013, I interviewed people in the Grand Anse valley; in the bus terminal and the central market in St. George, Grenada; and in Laventille, Beetham Gardens, and Sea Lots in east Port-of-Spain, Trinidad. The research intention was to design interview tools so that people could tell a story and, at times, engage in dialogue. Some of the questions we asked business people engaged in money pools included: (1) What kind of financial provider meets the needs of persons in poor communities? (2) With many banking options close by, why are ROSCAs prevalent? (3) Why do persons organize and join money pools? Interview tools were standardized as much as possible to enable comparison across the cases, and tools were adapted to fit the local, contextual realities, such as in Haiti to account for the post-earthquake priorities. Ten two-hour focus group meetings of six to eleven people were held at neutral locations, such as community centers or churches or bars, depending on the area.

9.5 ROSCAs as Equitable Economies

African-descended people have embraced informality. In Jamaica, Haiti, Trinidad, Grenada, and Guyana enslaved people have had to hide ROSCAs and pool goods as a way to rebel against the inhumanity. The Quilombola is one such example of resisting enslavement (Kelley 2002; Smith 2016; Bohn and Kreiger Grossi 2018). People still carry the historical legacy of ROSCAs around with them—most knowingly that enslaved people carried out market days and engaged in buying clubs because they imagined freedom (Herskovits and Herskovits 1947; Katzin 1959; Harrison 1988; Witter 1989; Wong 1996; N'Zengou-Tayo 1998; St. Pierre 1999; Kelley 2002). Caribbean people choose ROSCAs because members could ensure dividends are shared by the members. The Banker Ladies are ultimately rejecting commercialized models. They are conscientious and activist cooperators.

My great-grandmother, Maude Gittens, was a Grenadian-born migrant who migrated to Sangre Grande, Trinidad. She was a caterer and a well-respected leader in the community. She was a Susu banker for many decades. Her main role was to collect weekly deposits from the members and give a lump sum of cash to queueing members. The structure of Susus varies from community to community, and the rules are determined by members who discuss the fixed deposit to contribute every week. The Banker Lady usually has a business out of her home that allows members to pass by and drop off their deposits. The group decides how long they will do this, but a period of ten to twelve months is common. Once all the members agree on the rules and structure of the Susu, the Banker Lady launches the bank with the first in-take of deposits. Banker Ladies explain that they lend out the deposits to the members that very same day to avoid having a large sum of cash on their person. The system of rotation can take a number of forms, and again this will vary based on the group dynamics. Money can be allocated on a first-come-first-served basis, based on need, or by lottery or drawing names.

Coming together

Black people have always had to cooperate and to pool resources quickly to survive. ROSCAs embedded in their African origins are remade for those living in the Americas (Mayoukou 1994). European narratives do not acknowledge ROSCAs as cooperatives, and in white-dominated places ROSCAs are seemingly unknown or "never heard of" (this issue will be discussed in Chapter 10). Yet the Raifeissens banks or Rochdale weavers of the latter part of the 1800s (Guinnane 2001) or Quebec's Desjardins of the 1900s are frequently spoken about (Shragge et al. 2000; Mendell 2009). Yet Ethiopian scholar Mamo Tirfe (1999) held that Equub is an Indigenous co-op banking system that has been practiced by Ethiopians for centuries (see also Bekerie (no date)). Mary Njeri Kinyanjui (2019) has exposed the fact that Kenyan co-ops are local inventions, not Western imports. For so long Du Bois (1907) made this point that cooperatives inside and outside of Africa are the business model of African-descended people, often informally (Haynes 2019).

More than two decades ago, Ardener and Burman's (1996) *Money-Go-Rounds: The Importance of Rotating Savings and Credit Associations for Women* detailed ROSCAs as grassroot co-op banks used to socialize and address women's exclusion in banking. Yet, the origins of cooperatives seldom acknowledge the role of ROSCAs in co-op finance. It suits white scholars to start from what they deem "formal" cooperatives. Given that ROSCAs are cooperatives, the people who lead them are the pioneers of cooperative development and the solidarity economy.

This would bring ROSCAs to their rightful place in political economic history—that is, to the top. If we want to push the solidarity economy sector to radicalize and to open up economies, then including the narratives of the slaves' experience and their defiance to slavery is crucial. ROSCAs are part of that story. Pooling their earnings made from the Sunday market and gathering together to share the money in clubs without the masters' permission were acts of defiance, revealing that ROSCAs have a militant aspect to them.

ROSCAs have been purposefully informal. They save people, usually women from a tyrannical and unequal business life. ROSCAs appear harmless to the oppressor and, in this way, it allows women to carry on with their business lives. Feminist anthropologist Faye Harrison's work (1988) shows that since the times of slavery, and during colonization Jamaican higglers (traders) who struggled to make a livelihood used Partners to meet their economic needs. Even with the freedom to organize ROSCAs, these Caribbean Banker Ladies are not being hired for their experience in equitable development practice. We draw on their expertise, say thank you, and do not pay for these services.

9.6 Findings: Caribbean Women Lead Economic Development

Caribbean women have had a profound influence on economic development and they are acknowledged for this work but they have not been remunerated for their contribution to society. In *Outsider Within*, Harrison (2008) analyzes the case of Mrs Belulah Brown in Kingston, Jamaica, and how she contributes by helping her community despite the loss of her job. For many Black women burdened with making ends meet through precarious work, adjustment programs are a way of life. Black women also make sure there are enough provisions for those needing help in their communities but this work is never counted and valued as work (Banks 2020). The past colonization experience and the effects of racism within society have ensured that ROSCAs are not made redundant, even with more banking options in the region. Caribbean women continue to turn to ROSCAs because conventional banks are decidedly capitalist. This kind of living beyond fundamentalist capitalist systems to remake community economies is the kind of work that the African diaspora has been doing, according to scholar Beverely Mullings (2021). ROSCAs counter this by being built on trust and reciprocity, values that are important to historically marginalized people. Banker Ladies provide a safe place for people to come talk, to lodge their savings, and to draw on loans from people they know and trust.

ROSCAs are a meeting place to meet and socialize—to find a group of people they can relate to and talk with about the troubles in their lives. Community economy scholars Gibson-Graham, Cameron, and Healy (2013) show that people actively resist a corporate business model, and that their natural inclination is to engage with cooperative business anchored in the community. In the sections that follow, I list a number of key findings that show ROSCAs are social institutions, as well as economic ones, that are highly political and can arouse a sense of consciousness.

Banker Ladies in Trinidad and Guyana confront racial capitalism

African people held onto the Susu system because they knew it could help them be free one day (St. Pierre 1999). Indentured servants of East Indian background also held onto ROSCA systems. Both groups, colonized and treated without regard in the region, brought with them co-op banking systems because they did not want to live under domination and wanted to own their own lands. To counteract racial capitalism and exclusion, Caribbean people, especially women, have always pooled resources as it made sense for their local realities.

Formal bankers are culturally distinct from their borrowers in Jamaica, Trinidad, and Guyana because they differ in terms of class, culture, and sometimes gender (Hossein 2014a, 2014c, 2016a). In previous work, I have shown that these bankers use politics in a way that deforms and limits micro-banking, and they can do so because of their own personal prejudice. Class-based racism and partisan politics in Trinidad and Guyana have interfered with people's access to finance (see Hossein, 2014a, 2015). Until very recently, in both Trinidad and Tobago and Guyana, politics has been dominated by Indo-Caribbean political elites to the exclusion of persons of African descent. A pervasive cultural narrative disparages the business acumen of African descendants, and the commercial bankers, usually educated men of East Indian descent, are hesitant to make loans to poor Black people (Hossein 2014a, 2015). Even within professionalized finance programs, the "norms" found within the commercial banks have influenced economic development programs to discriminate against people of African heritage. A 28-year-old Guyanese hair and nail salon owner, "Nee," based in Albouystown (a low-income area in the capital city) advised that money pools have helped her and it is a cherished tradition:

> Box help me start my own business. Yuh get all di money from people who believe in me. This here Box is a norm passed down from generation to generation, grandmother's time and it helps me. (Interview, Georgetown, Guyana, May 11, 2010)

Empirical data has shown that at least 65 percent of the entrepreneurs interviewed in Allbouystown, Georgetown, claimed that they borrowed money from Boxhand because they could not access loans from a commercial bank or microfinance institution. The largest microfinance bank in Trinidad is the state-run National Entrepreneurship Development Corporation (NEDCO), which has a history of partisan-politics-influenced lending, with the result that 75 percent of its loan portfolio was in arrears as of July 2013 (field work 2013). Black entrepreneurial women, like the Banker Ladies in this study, cannot easily access loans because of identity and party politics in Trinidad and Guyana, so they inevitably turn to Boxhand and Susu (Hossein 2014c, 2015).

The fact that women are systemically excluded from formal finance provides the logic for aid agencies to make a major business out of development finance to "help" Black women. What these experts fail to mention is that the already-existing system of ROSCAs are vested in mutual aid that meets the economic needs of these women. ROSCAs are standing up to exclusions and racial capitalism that leaves many Black Caribbeans, especially women, left out of formal financial systems. The Banker Ladies have this lived experience of racial capitalism. And they have developed banking co-ops with this in mind, knowing what works and what doesn't in order to reach those denied access to finance. The Banker Ladies in Trinidad and Guyana who feel alienated from conventional business systems know that they have ROSCAs at their disposal. Susus and Boxhand are prevalent throughout these two countries because of the limitations of commercial banks to meet the demand. Banker Ladies fill this gap. And while they do their business in a modest way, the fact that ROSCAs help all citizens is common knowledge. The Banker Ladies have a deep knowledge about

ROSCAs that took me years to understand as a mere scholar. They speak about these systems with ease and authority. Even elite bankers who turn people away recognize that the Banker Ladies are providing financial access to those left out of the economy.

Jamaican Partner is inclusive finance

The Jamaican Partner is used by people from all socioeconomic classes. However, it is a lifeline for those who really have no other choice, like the women I met in downtown Kingston. Politics in Kingston's main urban center is marred at election time by violence, as local political elites, usually the ones who have power, make promises of money, lodgings, and jobs to very poor political activists in the downtown core (Sives 2010). If the activists fail to deliver the vote for their candidate, they lose the handouts. Academics have written extensively on this entrenched process of elites using uneducated masses in the downtown slums to carry out heinous crimes to assure votes and political victory in exchange for housing or other financial benefits (Rapley 2006; Tafari-Ama 2006; Sives 2010). Years of politicians and gangsters using poor residents to carry out their dirty work has led people to distrust the political and business elites (Hossein 2016a, b).

The Banker Ladies told me that people in garrisons do not want to be controlled by elites or gangsters. Partner banks run by women not trained in formal banking but who have acquired years of expertise as a cooperator are aware of the local politics that can intervene in business. Countless times the Banker Ladies let me know that they do not allow the politicking to come inside their Partner. According to Handa and Kirton (1999) they found, after surveying 1,000 Jamaicans in Kingston, that 75 percent of the Banker Ladies were women aged between 26 and 35 who ran the Partner for an average of nine years. In the interviews I carried out, all of the women lived in downtown tenement yards (corrugated metal tin roofs) and many of them did not have a formal bank account unless they had salaried employment and were required to do so. Not having a bank account made no difference to the women I interviewed, especially because they felt that they had a valid banking history with the Partner. One business woman who requested to stay nameless argued:

> Pardna is fi wi, and bank is fi di big man uptown'—that is, the partner bank is for the poor [us] and formal banks are for the rich. 'Yuh don't have to be rich or educated to throw Pardna. (Interview, Kingston, Jamaica, July 15, 2009)

A Partner is by far the leading choice of how to bank, and the women say that it is the trust element that they value most. Unlike commercial banks, a Partner is inclusive finance because the women who run them are reflective of the needs of people who use these Partner banks. The members trust and know them and want to contribute to collective banks like these because they respect the people who own them. Rickie, a 29-year-old bar owner, clarified the purpose of a Partner and why people are loyal to these informal Partner banks:

> Pardna. Live for dat ting. Most people here [in his low income community] don't have go to banks. Dem [the bankers] don't know what's going on here and wi na know what's going on in their banks. Downtown know Pardna . . . it is the one ting here for wi. (Interview, Kingston, Jamaica, July 9, 2009)

Partner banks offer people a place to save and borrow money. Women said they preferred the Partner banks because there was "no rigmarole" (paperwork). They also liked that the women who run Partners are trustworthy and that there are few fees and easy access. "Millicent," a 66-year-old clothes vendor in Woolmers arcade for 20 years, explained:

> Doin' business and sellin' is rough in the city but as a small business person you have to learn to take it. Partner softens it . . . Partner is discipline because we can trow money every week. Faster and its easy. A draw can help you in your business to thrive and to do X, Y, Z when no boady is there. (Interview, Kingston, March 30, 2009)

The Banker Ladies interviewed claim that repayment rates are high (usually 100 percent) because members trust these systems. Partner banks are deeply rooted in social relationships: they are there when nobody else is and are able to help people develop self-confidence and their communities. Everywhere else in society, these women are not viewed as "experts." But when these women run a Partner, they are the experts. They are the bosses of the agenda together, and they decide with group consensus who gets access to the lump sum of money first, and they assess the person's risks for defaulting, just as a trained loans officer would. The sustainability of these systems shows that they are viable.

Partner banks are made up of a group of people who know each other (sometimes they are related). Several variants of the Partner bank exist, and although all are saving plans, many are also lending plans (Klak et al. 1992; Handa et al. 1999). Each person's contribution to the Partner is called a "hand" and it is "thrown" (deposited) for a designated period of time; the pooled money is called a "draw." In some Partner banks, people draw lots to determine the order for obtaining a loan (interview with three Banker Ladies, Kingston, Jamaica, March to July 2009). One Banker Lady, named "Charmaine," was very proud of her work as a Banker Lady because it increased her profile in the community. She, like many others, shared that their members go beyond their community. Women who move to the United States or Canada remain in the Partner, making it transnational. It is thus not uncommon to hear that the membership includes the diaspora. Jamaica Partners work effectively because peer dynamics ensure members comply with payment rules, and the chief Banker Ladies will call for social sanctions when members do not respect the rules.

Banker Ladies conduct business in a serious manner because they know that the collective members depend on it. As Banker Ladies have told me in many focus group meetings and interviews, they do not put up with slackers, and people who do not follow the rules are banished from banking. As noted in Chapter 3, Alliance for Financial Inclusion (AFIs) try to connect with ordinary people because they see a lucrative business opportunity, as these women cooperators understand the fundamentals of group banking. They have been schooled informally about good banking habits. JN National Bank has a product line called the Partner Plan; and while people often joke that it is not the same Partner they know, lenders know the value of mimicking an African system of mutual aid to resonate with the masses.

A vibrant Susu culture in Grenada

Grenada, a small eastern island under British colonization until 1974, was the only English-speaking Caribbean country to experience a *coup d'état*. Led by Maurice Bishop, Bernard Coard, and the New Jewel Movement in 1979 (Sandford and Vigilante 1984; Gentle 1989; Meeks 2001), the People's Revolutionary Government (1979–83), run by educated middle-class Grenadians, was a left-wing experiment during the Cold War era. Grenada experienced a U.S. invasion and occupation in the 1980s under the Reagan administration (Meeks 2001).

The cooperative experience of Grenada developed under British colonization. In the 1930s, nutmeg and cocoa were important cash crops, and the colonial state created boards to manage these exports. In 1947, the Grenada Co-operative Nutmeg Association was formed to assist farmers to increase their incomes, allowing them to bypass the middleman. In 1951, the Colonial Welfare and Development fund provided the financing to organize the quality of production (Steele 2003). In 1954, the Banana Co-operative Society was set up to assist in trade with the Canadian Banana Company (Steele 2003, 338). Eric Gairy was the first head of state for Grenada (premier, 1967–74; prime minister, 1974–79), and the first political figure to come from a modest rural background (Sandford and Vigilante 1984). In the early years, Gairy was anti-imperialist and committed to increasing the incomes of rural farmers through cooperatives. However, Gairy's anti-local elite and white colonizer rhetoric was clouded by his own poor governance. By the mid-1970s, opposition grew against Gairy's undemocratic control and the violence of his secret police, the Mongoose Gang (Steele 2003).

Young educated Grenadians from middle-class backgrounds influenced by the U.S. Black power movement and the Cold War rallied dissenters against the Gairy regime. The 1979 bloodless *coup d'état* by the New Jewel Movement (NJM) installed the left-wing state, the People's Revolutionary Government (1979–83). Its leader, Maurice Bishop of the NJM, impressed by Tanzania's ujamaa (Swahili word for unity, collectivity, or oneness), adopted in the NJM's manifesto the idea of moving villagers to farm collectives, first put forward by President Julius Nyerere (in office, 1964–85).

Authoritarian politics left Grenadian people to cope on their own. The internal and U.S. interference meant that local people set up localized cooperatives, such as credit unions and Susu.

During the 1980s, the tumultuous political environment had more people turning to collectives and grassroot organizing. The 1983 U.S. invasion and occupation of Grenada, followed by the assassination of Maurice Bishop and members of the New Jewel Movement, made local life difficult. People were stressed and informal collectives are one way people cope in crises. It is not accidental that the country's largest cooperative bank, Grenville Credit Union, was created during this period of turmoil. American leaders were concerned about collective enterprises and viewed the group organizing of a colonized people as subversive, communist, and anti-American. Grenadian people have persevered in their use of cooperatives, and have a strong cooperative culture that can be attributed in part to the historical development of Susus on this island.

For Grenadians one cannot speak about cooperatives without mentioning the impact of Susus in people's lives. Grenada's Co-operative League (GCL) had ten credit unions and a membership of 42,000, or 40 percent of the population (interview, general manager, St. George, Grenada, June 4, 2013). According to Devon Charles, the general manager of Grenville Credit Union, "community banks are not concerned about blowing their trumpets but they are there to help people and cooperatives are not going away" (interview, St. George, Grenada, June 11, 2013). Ordinary Grenadians trust credit unions for their banking because of their roots in the community. "Jingle," the owner of a pizza and food shop at the bus terminal in town, was sceptical that commercial banks help small vendors:

> Government and dem [commercial banks] say dey would 'elp business in market and [bus] terminal. But they only talk, talk and give no help to us. They fear we can't pay. So I don't worry with [their] empty promises and I go to my Communal [refers to Communal credit union]. ("Jingle," interview, St. George, Grenada, June 16, 2013)

Susu in Grenada are similar to those found in Trinidad and Tobago, and they too are based on a rotating system. Grenadians participate in Susus, which also went by the name Maroons during the authoritarian regimes of Gairy (1967–74, 1974–9), New Jewel Movement takeover (1979–83), and the 1983 U.S. invasion (Sandford and Vigilante 1984, 32), as a way to cope and live. The Susu systems people use are based on daily or weekly plans, each cycle spanning from six to twelve weeks, where the "Banker Lady" manages the money collected from participants and usually charges a small flat fee (Besson 1996). People trust the Susu bankers. As "Mummy," an energetic elderly woman who has owned a mango-and-spice stall in the central market in St. George for more than thirty years, explained:

> Susu is di ting! [Susu is a good thing to have] You [can] get your money when you want it and nobody give you problem [referring to Susu banker]. You can say to the [Susu] banker, give me a hand [lump sum of cash] and she will because she know you and what you will do [with the money]. We bind (we come together) . . . no one can change this way. (Interview, "Mummy," Grenada, June 13, 2013)

Susu helps ordinary people who work in self-employment to access large lump sums of cash while among peers who know them and what they can do. This kind of access would never be possible at a commercial bank, especially for poor persons of African heritage. "Mummy" tried several times to get a loan at the commercialized microfinance bank called Microfin (now defunct), but it was a long, drawn-out process that was hard to follow—unlike the Susu banks. In interviews, members of the ROSCA were open about their difficulty in getting loans from banks, indicating that this was the reason the Susu banks were so important (Hossein 2014a, 2014c). My discussions with the Banker Ladies revealed it is a well-known fact that Susu helps people, and they were proud to speak about the many ways Susu has helped them get by.

The Haitian Sol: Pioneer cooperatives in the region

Haiti was one of the first slave colonies, and Haitians brought their collective money systems, known as Tontines, from the Dahomey (now Benin). French-speaking Benin and Togo, West African countries that Haitians claim as their ancestral lands, have always had strong traditions of Tontines. The Haitian Sols are born out of these old African cooperative systems. This makes the notion that cooperatives are new to the Haitian people or a project "introduced" to Haitians by local or foreign political elites most comical. While some colonizers interfered and introduced top-down control in their brand of cooperatives, resulting in limited development, it was not the only form of cooperatives in these very countries. Many Haitian people have vibrant cooperative economies today, and this is due to the ones they have been incubating for generations.

The first Haitian cooperative formalized in 1937 in Port-a-Piment du Nord, near Gonaïves soon after the U.S. occupation ended (Montasse 1983). More caisses populaires (credit unions) were formalized in La Valée (Jacmel) in 1946 and in Cavaillon (South) and Sainte Anne in Port-au-Prince in 1951, during a time of repressive politics (Colloque sur la Microfinance 2010). But these formal co-ops owe their development to Sol, the predecessor that continues on. Despite Haitians being banned from organizing Gwoupmans (Kreyol word for association) and cooperatives under the brutal reign of the Duvalier dictatorships that lasted from 1957 to 1986 (N'Zengou-Tayo, 1998), the people participated in Sols to meet their needs (Maguire 1997). Haitian cooperative scholar Emmanuel Montasse (1983) discovered a growth of credit unions in the period from 1951 to 1983 and he finds that it occurred because during these years people were deprived of basic services.

Not only does Haiti have a large formalized cooperative sector, but ROSCAs far outnumber formalized cooperatives. African ideas of Kombit (known as collectivity in Kreyol) come from the Beninese ancestors who brought banking concepts to the Americas as far back as the 1500s when slavery began. Oppressive country politics under leaders like Dessalines (1804–6) have adhered to *politiques du ventre* (politics of the belly) dictatorships, leaving the masses in complete suffering (Fatton 2002, 2007). Sols have assisted at least 80 percent of Haitians to meet their everyday financial needs. This collective approach to business is so well known that political elites have enshrined it in the preamble of the 1987 Haitian Constitution that Haiti is a cooperative republic, meaning that cooperatives are part and parcel of what it means to be Haitian. Political elites recognize the important role that self-help banking groups have played in the country's development, culture, and history.

Most Haitians I interviewed over the years (2008, 2011, and 2012) had a sentimental view about Sols and were proud of its African traditions. Haitian women have used Sol to grow their businesses. In December 2012, I met with numerous Haitian women who own coffee cooperatives in the north of the country near Cap Haitian. Sol has been an important financing device to assist in the growth of their businesses (Fig. 9.1).

Fig. 9.1 A cooperative business owner carrying out coffee production. Sol assisted this cooperative in developing their business

Local traditions of Kombit, Gwoupmans, and Sols have been the systems to reach excluded Haitians and to create civil society groups—and they are a testimony to the democratic spirit of the masses (Montasse 1983; Fatton 2007). A mainstream banker I interviewed attested to the importance of Sols in Haitian society:

> caisses belong to the Haiti people. The caisses are accessible, grassroots and embedded into people's hearts, because they focus on people's community, collectivity, and helping each other out which are very important traits for us [Haitians] especially those of us who are poor. (Interview with local businessman, Port-au-Prince, Haiti, October 2, 2010)

Sols are created by people in the community. Every month or week, members contribute a fixed amount, such as 100 gourdes (about US$2.5), for a cycle that can range from six to ten months, depending on the number of members. Members agree to contribute regular savings, and when their turn comes, they can use the money for a specified period, as managed by the banker, the "Mama Sol," who is usually uneducated. This system creates a place for the poor to save and borrow money. Sols may be completely free with no fixed fees, or may apply a small flat fee for the duration of the membership (Focus Groups 2010). Sols are trusted by their users because of their collective nature, and poor families have used these socially embedded banking systems for generations. ROSCAs mobilized from the grassroot level contribute to local organizing and give people who are normally ignored, the "*moun adeyo*," a way to feel a part of their community, which the state has failed to do (Focus Groups 2010).

So, it is not surprising that Sols have had a profound impact on the Haitian people. So much so that banks like Soge Bank, a commercial bank for the top 2 percent, has a *Mama Sol* product line to diversify their clientele and make ordinary Haitians want to bank with them. Mama Sol is the term for the chief Banker Lady in charge of the Sol, and it is a name that conventional bankers, as they look to expand their business base, hope will attract Madam Saras (traders) and *ti machanns* (market sellers) to bank with them. So the very bankers who have made lending near impossible to some of these women are now looking at ways to incorporate Mama Sol, to attract those women who compose the majority of business people in the country. And to do so is to draw on their cultural banking systems.

A tradition of collectivity

Across the Caribbean region, the Banker Ladies are revered. ROSCAs are a well-respected tradition of business in the Caribbean. What I learned from the hundreds of people I spoke to over a decade is that West Indians see ROSCAs as their own invention and credit only their African roots. The collective aspect among women who bond together to engage in self-help is admirable, and not in the sense that they are no longer society's bother. Instead, they are activating their own agency to show the world that business can be done humanely. It is the approach to cooperative business and the need to open up economies that make what they do original and important. And while Banker Ladies are free to share what they do, they remain on their own without any formal support for the work they are doing for society.

The Banker Ladies themselves speak with pride and with an authority about ROSCAs. They are free to discuss what they do in ROSCAs without shame or fear, and they know that people admire them for their contributions in cooperative building. All of the Caribbean women I interviewed told me that they use ROSCAs alongside conventional devices, because their ROSCA matters to them most. Partners or Susus are the preferred banking system in the region. And commercial bankers know this. This is why elite bankers bring the ROSCA system into their formal banks.

ROSCAs are cherished as an African tradition and one that has been molded for the diasporic experience. Women know that their ancestors conducted these money-pooling systems as a way of achieving their goals, and not to wait on others. Those who participate in ROSCAs, the direct users—and those watching the women do it—admire this long-held tradition. The Banker Ladies are inadvertently influencing the formal banking sector about humanizing finance. The emphasis on mutual aid and the collective brings more people into the fold of why ROSCAs are valued, and helps excluded people to realize their life projects.

9.7 Conclusion

Most Caribbean people know someone who belongs to a ROSCA. These systems do not necessarily change people's social standing or make anyone rich, but that is not their intention. It is about sharing goods and being there to help one another, as a society. ROSCAs assist excluded people to meet their social, financial, and political needs on their own terms and without external funding that may come with strings attached.

Whether or not the Caribbean women know it, their work has made a major contribution to the solidarity and cooperative economy. The very existence of the Caribbean Banker Ladies confronts unequal systemic oppression, and they show new ways of doing business in society. They have experienced exclusion daily. Yet, they move forward doing what they know in cooperative building and mutual aid. And formal lenders—others in their society—sit up and take notice of what they do to help people. Local elites in these lands feign ignorance as though they don't know these systems and their value. Banker Ladies rise up and are proud of what they do because they are in charge of money pools based on ancestral systems of collectivity that put people first.

The Banker Ladies are taking care of people because they are acutely aware of the dispossession that is taking place. And they are respected, loved, and valued for tackling inequities in business. The work they do is instinctive and cultural and they use money to do this. ROSCAs carve out a way for women in Jamaica, Guyana, Haiti, and Trinidad who are routinely denied access to finance and bring a sense of agency, local knowhow, and community. What these women do is development work. But they are not hired for this expertise. Experts will come into their communities, study these groups, and then access donor funds to create "social finance" projects.

The intertwining of capital and slavery haunts Black people throughout the Caribbean, and this relationship of money and enslaving people is the actual origin of commercial banks in the region (Hudson 2017). These structural inequalities are also the result of a plantation economy that has tiered the society class- and race-wise (Thomas 1988). These histories known to the Banker Ladies have solidified a place for ROSCAs in the Caribbean solidarity economy. No European invented Partner or Sol or Susu: the Caribbean people did and did this under duress. Acknowledging the ROSCAs held onto by African people for centuries disrupts the narrative that cooperative development is a colonial project. Pooling money and support makes the Caribbean Banker Ladies vested in what they do because they build trust and strengthen human connections in the world.

Works Cited

Ardener, S. and S. Burman (eds.) 1996. *Money-Go-Rounds: The Importance of Rotating Savings and Credit Associations for Women*. Oxford: Berg.

Austin, S. D. W. 2018. *The Caribbeanization of Black Politics: Race, Group Consciousness and Political Participation in America*. Albany, NY: State University Press of New York Press.

Banks, N. 2005. "Black Women and Racial Advancement: The Economics of Sadie Tanner Mossell Alexander." *Review of Black Political Economy*, 33(1): 9–24.

Banks, N. 2008. "The Black Worker, Economic Justice, and the Speeches of Sadie T. M. Alexander." *Review of Social Economy* 2: 139–61.

Banks, N. 2020. "Black Women in the United States and Unpaid Collective Work: Theorizing the Community as a Site of Production." *Review of Black Political Economy* 47(4): 343–62.

Banks, N. 2021. *Democracy, Race and Justice: The Speeches and Writing of Sadie T. M. Alexander*. New Haven, CT: Yale University Press.

Bekerie, A. No date. "Iquib and Idir: Socio-Economic Traditions of Ethiopians." *Tadias Online*. Accessed October 17, 2018.

Besson, J. 1996. "Women's Use of ROSCAs in the Caribbean: Reassessing the Literature." In Shirley Ardener and Sandra Burman (eds.), *Money-Go-Rounds: The Importance of Rotating Savings and Credit Associations for Women*, 263–89. Oxford: Berg.

Bhatt, E. 2007. *We Are Poor But So Many: The Story of Self-employed Women in India*. Oxford: Oxford University Press.

Bhattacharyya, G. 2018. *Rethinking Racial Capitalism: Questions of Reproduction and Survival*. London: Rowman & Littlefield.

Bohn, S. and P. Kreiger Grossi. 2018."The Quilombolas' Refuge in Brazil: The Social Economy, Communal Space and Shared Identity." In C. S. Hossein (ed.), *The Black Social Economy in the Americas: Exploring Diverse Community-Based Alternative Markets*, 161–86. New York: Palgrave Macmillan.

Bortei-Doku Aryeetey, E. and E. Aryeetey. 1996. "Mobilizing Cash for Business: Women in Rotating Susu Savings Clubs in Ghana." In Shirley Ardener and Sandra Burman (eds.), *Money-Go-Rounds: The Importance of Rotating Savings and Credit Associations for Women*, 77–94. Oxford: Berg.

Christabell, P. J. 2009. *Women Empowerment through Capacity Building: The Role of Microfinance*. New Delhi: Concept Publishing.

Colloque sur la Microfinance. (2010, September 28–9). Ministère de la Économie. Port-au-Prince, Haiti.

Devika, J. and B. V. Thampi. 2007. "Between 'Empowerment' and 'Liberation': The Kudumbashree Initiative in Kerala." *Indian Journal of Gender Studies* 14(1): 33–60.

Du Bois, W. E. B. 1907. *Economic Co-operation among Negro Americans*. Atlanta: Atlanta University Press.

Fatton, R. 2002. *Haiti's Predatory Republic: The Unending Transition to Democracy*. Boulder, CO: Lynne Rienner.

Fatton, R. 2007. *The Roots of Haitian Despotism*. Boulder, CO: Lynne Rienner.

Focus Groups. 2010. October 9. Bon Repos, Port-au-Prince, Haiti.

Gentle, E. 1989. *Before the Sunset*. Quebec: Marquis Book Printing.

Gibson-Graham, J. K., Jenny Cameron, and Stephen Healy. 2013. *Take Back the Economy: An Ethical Guide for Transforming our Communities*. Minneapolis: University of Minnesota Press.

Gordon Nembhard, J. 2014. *Collective Courage: A History of African American Co-operative Economic Thought and Practice*. University Park, PA: Penn State University Press.

Guinnane, T. 2001. "Co-operatives as Information Machines: German Rural Credit Co-operatives, 1883–1914." *Journal of Economic History* 61(2): 366–89.

Haitian Constitution. 1987. http://pdba.georgetown.edu/Constitutions/Haiti/constitution1987en.pdf. Accessed May 18, 2013.

Handa, S. and C. Kirton. 1999. "The Economies of Rotating Savings and Credit Associations: Evidence from the Jamaican 'Partner'." *Journal of Development Economics* 60: 173–94.

Harrison, F. V. 1988. "Women in Jamaica's Informal Economy: Insights from a Kingston Slum." *New West Indian Guide* No. 3(4): 103–28.

Harrison, F. V. 2008. *Outsider Within: Reworking Anthropology in the Global Age*. Urbana: University of Illinois Press.

Haynes, Jr., C. 2019. "From Philanthropic Black Capitalism to Socialism: Co-operativism in Du Bois' Economic Thought." *Socialism and Democracy* 32(3): 125–45.

Heinel, R. D. and N. Gordon Heinel. 2005. *Written in Blood: The Story of the Haitian People 1492–1995*. Expanded version by Michael Heinl. Laham, MD: University Press of America.

Herskovits, M. J. and F. S. Herskovits. 1947. *Trinidad Village*. New York: A. A. Knopf.

Hill Collins, P. 2000a. *Black Feminist Thought: Knowledge, Consciousness, and the Politics of Empowerment*, 2nd edn. New York: Routledge.

Hill Collins, P. 2000b. "Gender, Black Feminism and Black Political Economy." *Annals of the American Academy of Political and Social Science* 568(1): 41–53.

Hill, R. A. and B. Bair. 1987. *Marcus Garvey: Life and Lessons*. A Centennial Companion to the Marcus Garvey and the Universal Negro Improvement Association Papers. Berkeley: University of California Press.

hooks, b. 1981 [2015]. *aint i a woman: Black women and feminism*. New York: Routledge.

Hossein, C. S. 2014a. "The Exclusion of Afro-Guyanese in Micro-banking." *European Review of Latin America and Caribbean Studies* 96(1): 75–98.

Hossein, C. S. 2014b. "Haiti's *Caisses Populaires*: Home-Grown Solutions to Bring Economic Democracy." *International Journal of Social Economics* 41(1): 42–59.

Hossein, C. S. 2014c. "The Politics of Resistance: Informal Banks in the Caribbean." *Review of Black Political Economy* 41(1): 85–100.

Hossein, C. S. 2015. "'Big Man' Politics in the Social Economy: A Case Study of Microfinance in Kingston, Jamaica." *Review of Social Economy* 74(2): 148–71.

Hossein, C. S. 2016a. *Politicized Microfinance: Money, Power and Violence in the Black Americas*. Toronto: University of Toronto Press.

Hossein, C. S. 2016b. "Money Pools in the Americas: The African Diaspora's Legacy in the Social Economy." *Forum for Social Economics* 45(4): 309–28.

Hossein, C. S. 2017. "A Case Study of the Influence of Garveyism on the African Diaspora." *Social Economic Studies Journal* 66(3/4): 151–74.

Hossein, C. S. and K. Ceres. 2022. "Acknowledging Marxist Economist C. Y. Thomas's Legacy in Canada's Economic Development Sector." *Canadian Journal of Non-profit and Social Economy Research* 13(1): 27–43. Open access: https://anserj.ca/index.php/cjnser/article/download/384/333

Hossein, C. S. and P. J. Christabell. 2022. *Community Economies in the Global South: Case Studies about Rotating Savings and Credit Associations and Economic Co-operatives*. Oxford: Oxford University Press.

Hudson, P. J. 2017. *Bankers and Empire: How Wall Street Colonized the Caribbean*. Chicago: University of Chicago.

Hunter, H. 2000. *The Sociology of Oliver C. Cox: New Perspectives*. Bingley, UK: Emerald Publishing.

K'adamwe, K., A. Bernard, and E. Dixon. 2011. "Marcus Garvey the Entrepreneur? Insights for Stimulating Entrepreneurship in Developing Nations." *76 King Street: Journal of Liberty Hall* 2: 37–59.

Katzin, M. Fisher. 1959. "The Jamaican Country Higgler." *Social and Economic Studies* 8(4): 421–40.

Kelley, Robin D. G. 2002. *Freedom Dreams: The Black Radical Imagination.* Boston: Beacon Press.

Kinyanjui, M. N. 2019. *African Markets and the Utu-ubuntu Business Model: A Perspective on Economic Informality in Nairobi.* Cape Town, South Africa: African Minds Publishers.

Klak, T. H. and J. K. Hey. 1992. "Gender and State Bias in Jamaican Housing Programs." *World Development* 20(2): 213–27.

Lewis, R. 1987. *Marcus Garvey: Anti-Colonial Champion.* Kent, UK: Karia Press.

Maguire, R. 1997. "From Outsiders to Insiders: Grassroots Leadership and Political Change." In Robert Maguire (ed.), *Haiti Renewed: Political and Economic Prospects,* 154–66. Washington, D.C.: Brookings Institution.

Marable, M. 1983 [2015]. *How Capitalism Underdeveloped Black America: Problems in Race, Political Economy, and Society.* Chicago, IL: Haymarket Books.

Martin, T. 1983. *Marcus Garvey, Hero: A First Biography.* Dover, MA: The Majority.

Mayoukou, C. 1994. *Le systeme des Tontines en Afrique: Un systeme bancaire informel. Le case du Congo.* Paris, France: l'Harmattan.

Meeks, B. 2001. *Caribbean Revolutions and Revolutionary Theory: An Assessment of Cuba, Nicaragua, and Grenada.* Kingston, Jamaica: University of West Indies Press.

Mendell, M. 2009. "The Three Pillars of the Social Economy in Quebec." In Ash Amin (ed.), *The Social Economy: Alternative Ways of Thinking about Capitalism and Welfare,* 176–209. London: Zed Books.

Montasse, E. 1983. *La Gestion Strategique dans le Cadre du Développement d'Haiti au Moyen de la Co-opérative, Caisse d'Epargne et de Credit.* Port-au-Prince, Haiti: IAGHEI, UEH.

Mullings, B. 2021. "Caliban, Social Reproduction and our Future Yet to Come." *Geoforum* 118: 150–8.

Nussbaum, B. 2003. "Ubuntu: Reflections of a South African on Our Common Humanity." *Reflections, the Society for Organizational Learning and the Massachusetts Institute of Technology* 4(4): 21–6.

Nyerere, J. K. 1968. *Ujamaa: Essays on Socialism.* Oxford: Oxford University Press.

N'Zengou-Tayo, M-J. 1998. "*Fanm Se Poto Mitan*: Haitian Woman, the Pillar of Society." *Feminist Review: Rethinking Caribbean Difference* 59: 118–42.

Poto Mitan: Haitian Women, Pillars of the Global Economy. 2009. Film; 60 minutes. Prod. Tet Ansanm. http://www.potomitan.net/

Rapley, J. 2006. "The New Middle Ages." *Foreign Affairs* 85(3): 95–103.

Robinson, C. J. 1983. *Black Marxism: The Making of the Black Radical Tradition,* 2nd edn. London: Zed Press.

Rodney, W. 1982. *How Europe Underdeveloped Africa.* Washington, D.C.: Howard University Press.

Rutherford, S. 2000. *The Poor and their Money*. New Delhi, India: DFID/Oxford University Press.

Sandford, G. and R. Vigilante. 1984. *Grenada: The Untold Story*. New York: Madison Books.

Sen, Amartya. 2000. *Development as Freedom*. New York: Anchor Books.

Sethi, R. M. 1996. "Women's ROSCAs in Contemporary Indian Society." In Shirley Ardener and Sandra Burman (eds.), *Money-Go-Rounds: The Importance of Rotating Savings and Credit Associations for Women*, 163–79. Oxford: Berg.

Shragge, E. and J.-M. Fontan. 2000. *Social Economy: International Debates and Perspectives*. Montreal: Black Rose Books.

Sives, A. 2010. *Elections, Violence and the Democratic Process in Jamaica: 1994–2007*. Kingston, Jamaica: Ian Randle.

Smith, C.A. 2016. "Towards a Black Feminist Model of Black Atlantic Liberation: Remembering Beatriz Nascimento." *Meridians: Feminisms, Race and Transnationalism* 14(2): 71–87.

Steele, B. 2003. *Grenada: A History of its People*. London: Macmillan Caribbean.

St. Pierre, M. 1999. *Anatomy of Resistance: Anticolonialism in Guyana 1823–1966*. London: MacMillan Education.

Tafari-Ama, I. 2006. *Blood Bullets and Bodies: Sexual Politics below Jamaica's Poverty Line*. USA: Multi-Media Communications.

Thomas, C. Y. 1974. *Dependency and Transformation: The Economics of the Transition to Socialism*. New York: Monthly Review Press.

Thomas, C. Y. 1988. *The Poor and the Powerless: Economic Policy and Change in the Caribbean*. New York: New York University Press.

Tirfe, M. 1999. *The Paradox of Africa's Poverty: The Role of Indigenous Knowledge, Traditional Practices and Local Institutions*. Lawrenceville, NJ: The Red Sea Press.

Ulysse, G. A. 2007. *Downtown Ladies: Informal Commercial Importers, A Haitian Anthropologist, and Self-making in Jamaica*. Chicago: Chicago University Press.

Wallerstein, I. 2000. "Oliver C. Cox as World Systems Analyst." In Herbert Hunter (ed.), *The Sociology of Oliver C. Cox: New Perspectives*. Bingley, UK: Emerald Publishing.

Willoughby-Herard, T. 2015. *Waste of a White Skin: The Carnegie Corporation and the Racial Logic of White Vulnerability*. Oakland, CA: University of California.

Witter, M. 1989. "Higglering/Sidewalk Vending Informal Commercial Trading in Jamaican Economy." Department of Economics occasional paper series No. 4 (June).

Wong, D. 1996. "A Theory of Petty Trading: The Jamaican Higgler." *Economic Journal* 106 (Mar.): 507–18.

10
The Black Social and Solidarity Economy as a Site of Politicized Action

Sharon D. Wright Austin

10.1 Introduction

Each chapter in *Beyond Racial Capitalism: Cooperatives in the African Diaspora* explains the manner in which local residents work collaboratively to empower themselves and their neighbors. Yet, their efforts are about more than self-sufficiency. They are also members of historically marginalized groups sending strong political messages against exploitation. As we have explained, they pursue their goals via a Black solidarity economy. Our co-editor Caroline Shenaz Hossein (2013) coined the term "Black social economy" to characterize the collective economic solidarity of marginalized individuals. It requires them to build a sense of trust with each other and also is evidence of the political stand they have taken to prioritize the needs of Black women in particular. In *The Black Social Economy* (2018), Hossein and a group of scholars and activists explore community-driven collective businesses across the Americas and how African-descended people from Haiti to Canada to Argentina are able to organize cooperatives. Her contributions allow us to take an internationalist lens to this canon of emerging research of which this edited book builds upon. The Black radical tradition is the "continuing development of a collective consciousness informed by the historical struggles for liberation and motivated by the shared sense of obligation to preserve the collective being" (Robinson 1983). Combined together, the Black social economy and the Black radical tradition make up a solidarity economy that I will discuss in this chapter.

African diasporic residents have had to cooperate in informal business ventures because of the burdens they carry. Members of the larger public are often unaware of these collective and community-driven institutions. These endeavors forge many paths towards freedom by drawing on the wisdom of the ancestors and inspiring new generations of freedom fighters. In contemporary times, people of color have continued to practice the strategies they received from their ancestors in response to the hatred they continue to endure. The stories in this volume detail the many ways in which Black and racialized people continue to use cooperativism as a problem-solving method and in direct confrontation to the racial capitalism model. In this final chapter, I address the questions raised in Chapter 1 about the activities and

Sharon D. Wright Austin, *The Black Social and Solidarity Economy as a Site of Politicized Action.* In: *Beyond Racial Capitalism.* Edited by Caroline Shenaz Hossein, Sharon D. Wright Austin, and Kevin Edmonds, Oxford University Press.
 DOI: 10.1093/oso/9780192868336.003.0011

experiences of participants in Black solidarity economic efforts in protest against racial capitalism. This research contributes to the small body of literature that examines the relationship between racial capitalism and the Black solidarity economy.

10.2 Cooperativism, Collectivism, and Rebellion against Capitalism

Capitalism is often defined as an economic system in which individuals own and control resources to serve their interests. It primarily emphasizes individual competition for the purpose of securing a profit and minimal government intervention (Patomäki 2017). According to the theory of racial capitalism, racism has been a vital component used to maintain capitalist systems. Capitalism and racism feed off each other so that some individuals prosper, but others are placed in a position of inferiority.

Racial capitalism has thrived during the eras of slavery, Jim Crow, and in the modern era. Guyanese scholar activist Walter Rodney argued in the 1972 book *How Europe Underdeveloped Africa* that every person of African descent should not only understand capitalism, but also work for its overthrow. Its emphasis is "racial," not because of some conspiracy to divide workers or justify slavery and legalized segregation, but because racism had already permeated Western feudal society when these institutions began. Gargi Bhattacharyya (2018) reminds us in her reading of Robinson's work that capitalism has not existed to homogenize the way we do things but to differentiate between people. The capitalist economic system continued to benefit white wealthy individuals after the expansion of slavery. In contemporary society, the legacy of capitalism remains apparent because of the continued economic discrimination and marginalization experienced by people of color. Because of this unfair treatment, people of color have participated in the initiatives mentioned in the chapters for their personal and economic uplift.

Each chapter mentions empowerment efforts that are as precious as they are potent. They further the resonance that slavery, economic exploitation, and exclusion does "not [wholly] define the Black condition because we were Africans first, with world views and philosophical notions about life, death, possession, community and so forth that are rooted in that African heritage" (Robinson 1983, xix). The values of cooperativism, mutual aid, land stewardship, and economic democracy are part and parcel of the cultural possessions that enslaved Africans brought with them to the New World, "significantly distinct from the foundation of Western ideas . . . and powerful enough to survive slavery to become the basis of an opposition to it" (Robinson 1983, 5). In recounting and centering the preceding stories, the respective authors turn again to the practices of cooperativism and collectivism to unearth the continued resistance to the modern global racial capitalist order.

In Chapter 1, Caroline Hossein points out that Ethiopians have said that they developed some of the earliest financial systems, called Equub. Cooperative banks and credit unions provided access to money, but also instilled pride in their members. During the 1920s, allies of Marcus Garvey's United Negro Improvement Association opened the Toronto United Negro Credit Union. Others followed in Toronto, including one founded by Canada's first Black Union, the Order of Sleeping Car Porters (Chapter 1). These groups founded these unions during the post-World War I, Great Migration, and pre-Great Depression years (Kornweibel 1976, 307–8). As James Weldon Johnson (1930, 161) pointed out, white middle class and affluent citizens reveled during the "roaring twenties" before the stock market crash of 1929. This environment of celebration began in the United States and spread into Canada (Pearson Canada 2010, 61). For Black Americans, however, the 1920s was a decade of continued struggle as many remained mired in either urban or rural poverty. Not only were Black workers the "last hired and first fired," they were also confined to lower paying, unskilled, or semi-skilled positions (Spero and Harris 1931, 168).

These problems pale in comparison to the terror many endured for even thinking of pursuing economic parity with whites, especially in the rural South. There American sharecroppers carried out long and arduous labor, but were locked in an inescapable status of debt in a virtual police state (Austin 2006). The situation was not much better in Canada as workers participated in numerous strikes after their demands for higher wages, better working conditions, and the right to join unions were rebuffed (Pearson Canada 2010, 62). Wealth-building was unimaginable for most people of African descent in America, Canada, or anywhere else in the world. That is why these cooperative banks and credit unions served such a vital role in the economic empowerment, racial solidarity, and overall sense of pride for Black citizens in a number of places.

As Hossein also mentions in Chapter 1, the earliest founders of co-op banks influenced other Black Caribbeans to establish credit unions in later years. In 1969, residents of the Black Canadian town Africville, Nova Scotia, established the Seaview Credit Union. Decades later in 1993, the Caribbean African Canadian Credit Union opened in Toronto in 1993. Although neither of these are still in operation, they can teach us important lessons about the attempts of Jamaican Canadians to pursue cooperative development strategies for their communities' fiscal benefit.

Even before the era of slavery, Black people engaged in various forms of solidarity economics. Marronage refers to the process of escaping slavery and developing independent communities (Quan 2017). Its formal definition refers to it as "a flight from the negative, subhuman realm of necessity, bondage, and unfreedom toward the sphere of positive activity and human freedom" (Dilts 2017). In Chapters 6 and 7, Kevin Edmonds and Silvane Silva, respectively, argue that escaped slaves assisted each other so that they would not be forced back into bondage and also developed an economic support system. These and other marronage tactics allowed people of African descent to gain independence and thus rebel against the horrific practices in their countries of residence.

Obviously, any effort made by Blacks to gain economic parity with whites was violently squashed during colonial times. However, these efforts have become more sophisticated in recent decades. A contemporary form of marronage involves the achievement of economic independence as a method of rebellion against societal oppression. Individuals in the communities we have discussed may not still be enslaved in a legal sense, but encountered other barriers to their personal and financial well-being. For example, the Cooperation Jackson group (see Chapter 5), the self-help groups in St. Vincent and St. Lucia by Rastas (see Chapter 6), and the Quilombolas in Brazil (see Chapter 7) are alternative business models that have enabled people to pursue economic liberation for a very long time. In Jackson, Mississippi, solidarity cooperatives were the goal to empower workers in a predominantly Black city with a 32 percent Black poverty rate that is triple the national race (Welfare Info 2021). In St. Vincent and St. Lucia, glaring economic disparities exist among Blacks and white/ned minorities (Chapter 6; *Encyclopedia of the Nations* 2021). Finally, Afro-Brazilian women and men have been driven out of the rural countryside and experience blatant employment discrimination in urban cities and their quilombo systems are under attack (Chapter 7).

10.3 Knowing the Black Social Economy

While the verbiage of Black social economy is relatively new, the practices of Black economic solidarity throughout the diaspora are steeped in a rich history of praxis. Jessica Gordon Nembhard's (2014) work on African American cooperativism (2014) and Monica White's (2018) work on collective Black agricultural resistance were both seminal works in establishing and analyzing the history of cooperativism as a Black economic tradition and means of resistance. Gordon Nembhard (2014) and White (2018) both highlight tenets of collective agency, community resilience, and autonomy as common to Black cooperativism.

When placing these texts and histories within the Black radical tradition, we must focus on the transformative possibilities of this praxis. In building on the body of work known as the Black radical tradition, Kehinde Andrews' (2018) *Back to Black: Retelling Black Radicalism for the 21st Century*, urges Black radicals to stop considering Black radicalism as a tradition and to reclaim it as its own political ideology. Andrews (2018, 5) posits that Black radicalism is only truly "radical" if it seeks to topple the systems of Black dehumanization. Indeed, for Andrews, *Blackness* itself is a commitment to a liberatory politic that transcends borders shaped by the struggle of those facing racial oppression (2018, 176). In engaging Andrews' contributions, it begs the following questions: First, what does a Black social economy look like that seeks to topple the systems (capitalism, patriarchy, imperialism, ableism, heteronormativity, and other systems of caste and oppression) of Black dehumanization? Second, what kind of political economy supports the full humanization of Black people around the world?

In reference to the first question, Chapter 7 provides one example of a Black solidarity economy that does more than seek economic parity. Silvane Silva explains the many cruel efforts powerful actors have engaged in to deny land rights to Brazilians, drive them away from rural areas, and deny them of equal employment opportunities in urban areas. Black women have been at the forefront of resistance efforts to ensure equity in land ownership. Rural Black communities have been denied land rights because of systemic racism that continues to be practiced by contemporary Brazilian governmental officials and private developers (Bowen 2021). Because of their desire to own land and to protect it from environmental abuses, quilombolas have engaged in activities like the 2015 March of Black Women in Brazil, women's meetings, and the creation of a collective garden.

Concerning the second question mentioned, the Black solidarity economy is one way to conceptualize an economy that supports and empowers the full humanization of Black people around the world. It is that slice of the Black social economy that is explicitly anti-capitalist and anti-imperialist. More than a form of resistance or economic survival, it is a counter to what we know about the standard social economy. When the term Black social economy came into being, it was to animate the social economy with thinking about citizens who are discriminated against, and who then co-opt goods to create their own social economies.

The Black social economy is defined as a politicized space in which people of African descent consciously collectively organize self-help to financially support Black-led and focused development. In Chapter 2, Salewa Olawoye-Mann explains the role of Nigerian female immigrants in the evolution of the Ajo cooperative banking system. In its current form, it assists Nigerian immigrants who recently arrived in the United States and Canada with their finances and to adapt to the ways of their new countries. As Olawoye-Mann mentions in her chapter, the tradition of Ajo and money pooling has existed in Nigeria and has been utilized in America since the post slavery era. Subsequent generations of Nigerians have used Ajo for financial empowerment. In this system, participants pool their resources, especially their cash, with others that they trust in a mutual aid system.

Nigerians continued to utilize informal cooperative banks, such as the predominantly female Ajo system, even after the creation of formal banking systems. This is in direct rebellion against racial capitalism because Nigerian immigrants in Canada and the United States trust the Ajo system, but distrust white-owned banks and financial institutions. Because banks classify immigrants as "high risk applicants," American immigrants are much less likely to open savings and checking accounts, apply for loans, or hold home mortgages (Paulson and Singer 2004). Also, many have lower incomes, limited English language proficiency, a lack of collateral, and/or a lack of familiarity with banking and financial practices (Paulson and Singer 2004).

Ajo provides the kind of assistance that banks usually fail to. Rather than deal with the humiliation of applying for and being rejected by white-owned institutions, many Nigerian women turn to the support provided by the Ajo. Women of various ages and occupations rely on "the old and trusted credit system they grew up with, Ajo, to pay off their loans, fix their credit ratings, and work toward to more secure financial future" (see Chapter 2). But it is about more than just finances. These Nigerian women are participating in an "Ajo community" that allows them to freely interact with other Nigerian women. Thus, this mutual aid activity enhances their finances, personal sense of well-being, and feelings of solidarity with others from their native homeland.

The same can be said of Nigerian women in Dublin, Ireland, a predominantly white Catholic society with a growing Nigerian immigrant population. In Chapter 8, Ebun Joseph and Kesiena Mercy Ebenade discuss the contribution of Nigerian women in assisting with immigrant assimilation there. Like women in the other countries mentioned in this book, these Black Irish women establish ROSCAs that allow Dublin residents to save money and accumulate funds. These Adashe, Ajo, and Esusu savings schemes have existed for many years on the African continent (see Chapter 8). African Irish women in Dublin adhere to the African philosophy of ubuntu, which rejects individualism and embraces cooperation among persons in a community.

The ubuntu philosophy is very important for these women because of the severity of Irish racism. Nigerian women must support each other because of the unwelcoming, and often hostile, environment they encounter in Ireland. The racism directed against Black immigrants has been described as "a very active thing in Ireland—it's just hidden" (Corr 2020). In September 2021, Pamela Uba received hate mail after becoming the first Black woman to win the Miss Ireland pageant (Murphy 2021). This is only one example of the racist abuses Irish people of Nigerian descent encounter, but racism is also all across Europe. Indeed, Cedric Robinson suggested that European racism and a racial hierarchy have been ongoing (Kelley 2017).

The Black solidarity economy is also about bearing witness to racial exclusion and figuring out how to live, work, and play as Black people. It is rooted in mutual aid and transforms business as we know it. In Chapters 3 and 9, African American women use the Susu and Caribbean women transform business practices through the usage of ROSCAs. These female cooperators not only emphasize business inclusion, but also focus on the collective well-being of women who have endured various forms of trauma. Black women are much more likely to be victimized by intimate partner violence, rape, and homicide in countries around the world (Barlow 2020; Summers 2020; Duhaney 2021). ROSCAs and other solidarity economic efforts provide fiscal resources for traumatized women and, more importantly, give them hope for their futures.

As Tatiana Benjamin and I explain in Chapter 3, women in the District of Columbia have established more sophisticated ROSCAs in the form of start-ups that are geared to women from all socioeconomic backgrounds. Both in Washington, D.C., and in Brooklyn, New York, women have received financial independence and stability from ROSCA communities that assist female immigrants with poor or limited credit to receive funding. Yet, we know less about the way that ROSCAs benefit women from higher socioeconomic classes. The Sou Sou Group of Washington, D.C., provides a sum of money to individuals after a designated period of time (Chapter 3). Yet, it is more than that. This Susu start-up is similar to a cooperative bank, has assisted more than 100 American entrepreneurs in one year, has contracts with twenty-four financial institutions, and earned over $15,000 in revenue in 2018 (Chapter 3).

In Brooklyn and the District of Columbia, Marie Lumen Clersaint and Fonta Gilliam have continued the legacy of cooperation passed from generation to generation in their own particular form of Black solidarity economy. These two case studies provide examples of Black women's resistance to a misogynoir culture that promotes demeaning, anti-Black, and misogynistic images of them (Bailey 2021). Racial capitalism is designed to exclude Black women and men, but women in the District of Columbia and Brooklyn have used mutual aid strategies to help those who have been left out (see Chapter 3).

The case of Indigenous Mexicans (see Chapter 4) also shows that Tandas and cooperatives fight racial capitalism to benefit newcomers to the United States. That Black, Indigenous, and racialized women, who are often left in the margins, are the ones taking on extra work to make finance inclusive is a major contribution; however, it is one that is usually ignored (Banks 2020, 2021). Tandas and cooperativas create a sense of community and belonging that makes it easier for undocumented migrants to adjust to unwelcoming Staten Island, NY, and Perth Amboy, NJ communities. Before the 1965 Immigration and Naturalization (Hart-Cellar) Act, discriminatory quotas limited the entrance of Latin American immigrants and other immigrants of color into the United States (U.S. House of Representatives 2021). In later years, these undocumented workers provided a cheap source of labor, but suffered from unequal treatment. Tandas and the worker-owned cooperative provide economic resources, autonomy, and dignity for non-citizens. Patricia Campos Medina, Erika Nava, and Sol Aramendi show that Mexican immigrants are rebelling against racial capitalism by developing Tandas (a non-interest savings and loan saving system) and a worker-owned cooperative home-cleaning venture. Black and racialized women continue to play a large role in the advancement of cooperativism and solidarity economies.

10.4 Turning to Black Feminist Political Economy

The Black solidarity economy is not cited and drawn upon in the cooperative and solidarity literature, but Black feminist scholars are informing others about its promotion of Black resistance and cooperation (Ferreira 2021; Hooker 2009; Kinyanjui 2019; Mullings 2021). Societies can learn valuable lessons from this research about Black solidarity economies in marginalized communities. The concept of the Black social economy is also being taken up in organizing spaces such as the Ujima Co-operative, Collective Diaspora, Grassroot Economic Organizing, New Economy

Coalition, Cllctivly mutual aid group, and the Black Solidarity Economy Fund. A growing cadre of organizers and scholar-activists are exploring, theorizing, and experimenting around the Black social and solidarity economy. Missing still is the proper acknowledgment of Black feminist solidarity economic scholars-activists. In essence, the Black solidarity economy is a politicized and pragmatic response to counter racial capitalism as Black people draw on ancestral systems of collectivity that can actually help all people.

This book illuminates the voices of Black and racialized women who are practicing the Black radical tradition via solidarity economics. Scholars (Davies 2016; Harris 2021) have noted the absence of radical Black women intellectuals, such as Beatriz Nascimiento, Angela Davis, and others from the Black radical tradition literature. Some of these women have lost their lives because of their work in this tradition. In Brazil, Beatriz Nascimento was shot and killed on January 28, 1995 by Antônio Jorge Amorim Viana, known as Danone, who believed that she had advised his wife to leave their violent relationship. Some believe that her murder was politically motivated because of her active involvement in civil, human, and women's rights efforts. Nascimento, an outspoken feminist, protested the invisibility of Black women in academic writings and challenged feminist scholars to acknowledge the experience of women in the African diaspora (Smith et al. 2021).

Moreover, Black women have explained the contribution of economic cooperatives to the Black freedom struggle. Mary Njeri Kinyanjui's (2019) work on Kenya's Chamas has explained that a cooperative economy is not only a coping device; it is also an ethical business system that aligns with the ways in which some women choose to live. For women who experienced economic discrimination based on intersectionality (oppressive treatment because of their race and gender), the cooperative model has been very useful (Hill Collins 2019). Black women receive the lowest pay when compared to other workers and are more likely to live in poverty (Oxfam 2021). Black feminist scholars are writing about the role of Black female leaders of economic and political resistance efforts (Austin 2006; Gordon Nembhard 2014; Hossein 2018). For example, economist Nina Banks (2021) has carried out extensive archival work uncovering the life story of Sadie T. M. Alexander, a PhD economist who could not find work as an economist because she was Black and a woman.

Black feminist scholars like Nina Banks are not alone in being ignored (Nelson 2021). Black women cooperators are also sidelined. This is changing with foundational work by Barbara Ransby (2005), Jessica Gordon Nembhard (2014), and Keisha N. Blain (2021) who show the contributions of women cooperators such as Fannie Lou Hamer, Amy Jacques Garvey, Ella Baker, and Halena Wilson. There is room to insert Black feminist economics not only into mainstream economics but also into the masculinist Black radical tradition. Nina Banks (2021) argues that Black diaspora women have been excluded from formal economic arenas, but this erasure should not be interpreted that they are not working on changing unjust economic systems.

Black women are leading cooperative organizations that continue the Black solidarity economy movement. Esther Enyolu of the Women's Multicultural

Resource Centre has worked with seven start-up worker cooperatives in the region of Durham, an hour outside of Toronto. In Atlanta, a successful co-op is Sevananda Natural Foods Market and its General Manager for the past couple of years has been Ahzjah Netjer Simons. Nia Evans, the Executive Director of Ujima in Boston, has created Black on Black investing and a community economy controlled by local working-class residents of color. Others like Dara Cooper, the National Organizer at the National Black Food and Justice Alliance, are supporting and convening Black farmers and land stewards towards Black food sovereignty and self-determination. Noni Session, the Executive Director of the East Bay Permanent Real Estate Co-operative, is organizing to take land off the speculative market to provide much needed housing in one of the most expensive areas in the country. These are but a few examples of stories of Black cooperativism that are still to be written. For many years, the labor of Black women has been excluded from discussion about the Black radical tradition. Over the years, minority women have spearheaded these efforts and thus exemplified the kind of radicalism mentioned by W. E. B. Du Bois (1907, 1933, 1935, 1940), Curtis Haynes Jr. (1993, 1994), Lloyd Hogan (1984), Jessica Gordon Nembhard (2014), and others.

As these scholars, and the authors of the chapters in this book, have explained, cooperativism continues to be a key part of struggle toward Black liberation. Black female activists have exhibited bravery when pursuing life-threatening work and ideas about Black empowerment that many consider to be radical. This places them in the same category as scholar activists like Claudia Jones who fought for Black empowerment despite numerous attacks. An elected member of the National Committee of the Communist Party USA, Jones was deported from the United States for her Black feminist, nationalist, and Communist activities. She dedicated her life to the upliftment of Black women in the employment and political sectors. In 1948, she was imprisoned for the first of four stints during her lifetime. In 1951 at the age of 36, she suffered her first heart attack while imprisoned and was convicted of "un-American activities" for publishing an article entitled, "Women in the Struggle for Peace and Security" in a political magazine. She was refused entry to her native Trinidad and Tobago and instead continued to work in the Community Party of Great Britain while residing there until she died on Christmas Eve 1964 at the age of 49 (Boyce Davies 2007).

Black women in countries such as Brazil, Mexico, Nigeria, and the United States have lost both their livelihoods and their lives because of their fight for Black liberation. The economic efforts mentioned in these chapters provide evidence of this. Because of the dangerous climate for female activists, women who in any way seek to empower their communities are taking great risks. On March 14, 2018, 38-year-old Marielle Franco, a Black lesbian human rights activist from the Maré favela, was assassinated in her car after leaving a Black women's empowerment event that she had organized and after winning a seat on the Rio de Janeiro city council (Alberti 2019; Freelon 2018).

10.5 Carry it Forward

As Cedric Robinson's (1983) work in *Black Marxism* makes clear, confronting racial capitalism and other forms of oppression is intergenerational work. While some might turn to this book for an antidote to racial capitalism, this book and the stories contained within are an offering. An invitation to learn more about the contemporary co-op institutions that Black and racialized people throughout the diaspora are building to address their collective problems and co-create new worlds of care and abundance. While there is much to be learned from the case studies, these are only some of the recent contributions to liberatory struggle. Much like the Black radical tradition, the Black social and solidarity economy is iterative and evolving. Black solidarity economy practitioners benefit from the struggle and contributions of our ancestors and contemporaries. In turn, we attempt to apply that knowledge in our own praxis. As we seek to build our ranks towards a better world, we hope that the stories offered in this book might inspire new generations of solidarity economy practitioners and organizers.

Works Cited

Alberti, M. 2019. "'Marielle Lives!' Brazil Remembers Slain Activist." Aljazeera. March 15. Accessed December 3, 2021. https://www.aljazeera.com/news/2019/3/15/marielle-lives-brazil-remembers-slain-activist

Andrews, K. 2018. *Black Is Back: Retelling Black Radicalism for the 21st Century*. London: Zed Books Ltd.

Austin, S. D. W. 2006. *The Transformation of Plantation Politics: Black Politics, Concentrated Poverty, and Social Capital in the Mississippi Delta*. Albany: State University of New York Press.

Bailey, M. 2021. *Misogynoir Transformed: Black Women's Digital Resistance*. New York: New York University Press.

Banks, N. 2020. "Black Women in the United States and Unpaid Collective Work: Theorizing the Community as a Site of Production". *Review of Black Political Economy* 47(4): 343–62.

Banks, N. 2021. *Democracy, Race and Justice: The Speeches and Writing of Sadie T. M. Alexander*. New Haven, CT: Yale University Press.

Barlow, J. N. 2020. "Black Women, The Forgotten Survivors of Sexual Assault." American Psychological Association. https://www.apa.org/pi/about/newsletter/2020/02/Black-women-sexual-assault. Accessed on November 20, 2021.

Bhattacharyya, Gargi. 2018. *Rethinking Racial Capitalism: Questions of Reproduction and Survival*. London: Rowman & Littlefield.

Blain, K. N. 2021. *Until I Am Free: Fannie Lou Hamer's Enduring Message to America*. Boston: Beacon Press.

Bowen, M. L. 2021. *For Land and Liberty: Black Struggles in Rural Brazil*. New York: Cambridge University Press.

Boyce Davies, C. 2007. *Left of Karl Marx: The Political Life of Black Communist Claudia Jones*. Durham: Duke University.

Boyce Davies, C. 2016. "A Black Left Feminist View on Cedric Robinson's Black Marxism". *Black Perspectives*, available at: https://www.aaihs.org/a-Black-left-feminist-view-on-cedric-robinsons-Black-marxism/

Corr, J. 2020. "Racism is a very Active Thing in Ireland—Just Hidden". *The Sunday Times*, June 14. https://www.thetimes.co.uk/article/racism-is-a-very-active-thing-in-ireland-its-just-hidden-mv2hzvsct. Accessed on November 21, 2021.

Dilts, A. 2017. "Project MUSE—Social Death/Life, Fanon's Phenomenology, and Prison Riots: Three Questions for Neil Roberts' Freedom as Marronage". Johns Hopkins University Press. January 1. muse.jhu.edu/article/646856. Accessed on November 18, 2021.

Du Bois, W. E. B. 1907. *Economic Co-operation Among Negro Americans*. Atlanta: Atlanta University Press.

Du Bois, W. E. B. 1933. "Where do we go from here?" (A lecture on Negroes' economic plight). An address delivered at the Rosenwald Economic Conference, Washington, DC. (First published in The Baltimore Afro-American, May 20, 1933. Reprinted in Andrew G. Paschal, Ed., 1971, *A W. E. B. Du Bois Reader*, pp. 146–63. New York: Collier Books)

Du Bois, W. E. B. 1935. "The Present Economic Problem of the American Negro." Reprinted in Andrew F. Paschal, Ed., 1971, *A W. E. B. DuBois Reader*, pp. 163–179. New York: Collier Books.

Du Bois, W. E. B. 1940. "Dusk of Dawn: An Essay Toward an Autobiography of a Race Concept." *W. E. B. Du Bois: Writings*, 549–801. New York: Harcourt, Brace.

Duhaney, P. 2021. "Criminalized Black Women's Experiences of Intimate Partner Violence in Canada." *Violence Against Women*, September 21. https://doi.org/10.1177/10778012211035791. Accessed on November 20, 2021.

Encyclopedia of the Nations. 2021. "St. Vincent and the Grenadines: Poverty and Wealth." Nations Encyclopedia. https://www.nationsencyclopedia.com/economies/Americas/St-Vincent-and-the-Grenadines-POVERTY-AND-WEALTH.html. Accessed on November 21, 2021.

Ferreira, P. 2021. "Racial Capitalism and Epistemic Injustice: Blindspots in Theory and Practice of Solidarity Economy in Brazil." *Geoforum* 132: 229–37.

Freelon, K. 2018. "Say Her Name: The Assassination of a Black Human Rights Activist in Brazil Has Created a Global Icon." *Quartz*. March 18. https://qz.com/1231910/brazils-marielle-franco-murder-has-made-her-a-global-human-rights-icon/. Accessed on November 20, 2021.

Gordon Nembhard, J. 2014. *Collective Courage: A History of African American Co-operative Economic Thought and Practice*. University Park: Pennsylvania State University Press.

Harris, A. 2021. "Forward: Racial Capitalism and the Law." In Destin Jenkins and Justin Leroy (eds.), *Histories of Racial Capitalism*. New York: Columbia University Press.

Haynes, C. 1993. *An Essay in the Art of Economic Cooperation: Cooperative Enterprise and Economic Development in Black America.* PhD diss., University of Massachusetts Amherst.

Haynes, C. 1994. "A Democratic Cooperative Enterprise System: A Response to Urban Economic Decay." *Ceteris Paribus* 4(2): 19–30.

Hill Collins, P. 2019. *Intersectionality as Critical Social Theory*. Durham: Duke University Press.

Hogan, L. 1984. *Principles of Black Political Economy*. Bloomington: Trafford Publishing.

Hooker, J. 2009. *Race and the Politics of Solidarity*. New York: Oxford University Press.

Hossein, C. S. 2013. "The Black Social Economy: Perseverance of Banker Ladies in the Slums." *Annals of Public and Co-operative Economics* 84(4): 423–42.

Hossein, C. S. 2018. *The Black Social Economy in the Americas: Exploring Diverse Community-Based Markets*. New York: Palgrave Macmillan.

Hossein, C. S. 2019. "A Black Epistemology for the Social Solidarity Economy: The Black Social Economy." *The Review of Black Political Economy* 46(3): 209–29.

Johnson, J. W. 1930. *Black Manhattan*. New York: Atheneum.

Kelley, R. D. G. 2017. "What Did Cedric Robinson Mean by Racial Capitalism?" *Boston Review*. January 12. https://bostonreview.net/race/robin-d-g-kelley-what-did-cedric-robinson-mean-racial-capitalism. Accessed on November 20, 2021.

Kinyanjui, M. N. 2019. *African Markets and the Utu-Ubuntu Business Model: A Perspective on Economic Informality in Nairobi*. Cape Town, South Africa: African Minds.

Kornweibel, T. 1976. "An Economic Profile of Black Life in the Twenties." *Journal of Black Studies* 6(4): 307–20.

Mullings, B. 2021. "Caliban, Social Reproduction and Our Future Yet To Come." *Geoforum* 118: 150–8.

Murphy, S. 2021. "Pamela Uba: First Black Miss Ireland Reveals She's Suffered Racism and Bullying Since Win." Sky News. September 9. https://news.sky.com/story/pamela-uba-first-Black-miss-ireland-reveals-shes-suffered-racism-and-bullying-since-win-12403312. Accessed on November 21, 2021.

Nelson, E. 2021. "The Economist Placing Value on Black Women's Overlooked Work." *New York Times*, February 5. https://www.nytimes.com/2021/02/05/business/black-women-economists-nina-banks.html. Accessed November 15, 2021.

Oxfam International. 2021. "Why The Majority of the World's Poor Are Women." https://www.oxfam.org/en/why-majority-worlds-poor-are-women. Accessed n November 20, 2021.

Patomäki, H. 2017. "Capitalism: Competition, Conflict, Crisis." *Journal of Critical Realism* 16(5) (June 1): 537–43.

Paulson, A. and A. Singer. 2004. October 1. "Financial Access for Immigrants: Learning from Diverse Perspectives." Brookings. https://www.brookings.edu/research/financial-access-for-immigrants-learning-from-diverse-perspectives/. Accessed on November 20, 2021.

Pearson Canada. 2010. *Counterpoints: Exploring Canadian Issues*, 2nd edn. British Columbia: Pearson Canada. Accessed on November 18, 2021.

Quan, H. L. T. 2017. "'It's Hard to Stop Rebels That Time Travel': Democratic Living and the Radical Reimagining of Old Worlds." In G. T. Johnson and A. Lubin (eds.), *Futures of Black Radicalism*, 173–93. Brooklyn: Verso.

Ransby, B. 2005. *Ella Baker and the Black Freedom Movement: A Radical Democratic Vision*. Chapel Hill, NC: North Carolina University Press.

Robinson, Cedric. 1983. *Black Marxism: The Making of the Black Radical Tradition*. Chapel Hill: University of North Carolina Press.

Rodney, W. 1972. *How Europe Underdeveloped Africa*. London: Bogle-L'Ouverture.

Smith, C., A. Davies, and B. Gomes. 2021. "'In Front of the World': Translating Beatriz Nascimento." *Antipode: A Radical Journal of Geography* 53 (1): 279–316.

Spero, Sterling D. and A. L. Harris. 1931. *The Black Worker: The Negro and the Labor Movement*. New York: Atheneum.

Summers, H. 2020. "Ngozi Fulani: 'Black Women Don't Want to Risk Their Abusers Being Murdered'." *The Guardian*, September 22. https://www.theguardian.com/society/2020/sep/22/ngozi-fulani-black-women-domestic-violence-police. Accessed on November 20, 2021.

U.S. House of Representatives. 2021. "Immigration and Nationality Act of 1965." *History, Art, and Archives* https://history.house.gov/Historical-Highlights/1951-2000/Immigration-and-Nationality-Act-of-1965/. Accessed on November 20, 2021.

Welfare Info. 2021. "Poverty in Jackson, Mississippi." https://www.welfareinfo.org/poverty-rate/mississippi/jackson. Accessed on November 21, 2021.

White, M. 2018. *Freedom Farmers: Agricultural Resistance and the Black Freedom Movement*. Chapel Hill: University of North Carolina Press.

Afterword

Esteban Kelly

For years, we have needed a body of scholarly work that could lay the groundwork for how we consider the Black diasporic cooperative and solidarity economy practice as a political-economic strategy for dismantling racial capitalism. *Beyond Racial Capitalism* brings together evidence of cooperatives taking place, often in locations prioritizing the capitalist firm. This collection's intervention of noting the cooperativist work by the African diaspora is a necessary one. That is particularly true when one considers the insidious discourse from the nonprofit industrial complex that would have us believe that Black people have simply been left behind and that subsidies can help excluded peoples. Across the Black diaspora from Haïti, Jamaica, Guyana, St. Vincent, St. Lucia, Brazil, Ireland, Canada, to the United States, this narrative ignores the expropriation of Black and Indigenous labor and lands to create wealth for Western economies, perpetuating the myth that the African diaspora depends on aid. When one learns of the cooperative institutions organized by Black and racialized people, this begins to reveal the prospects for justice and abolition in a multiracial, democratic, decolonized expansion of cooperative and circular economies.

The scholars engaged with the concept of racial capitalism as a world system that organizes Black and racialized people in ways to contain our quest for equity and justice. The late Professor Cedric Robinson catapulted us forward in his foundational work on *Black Marxism*, and so many of his students, such as H. L. T Quan, Tiffany Willoughby-Herard, and Robin D. G. Kelly, continue the tradition of amplifying people-focused political and economic development. In *Histories of Racial Capitalism*, historians Jenkins and Leroy (2021) made clear in their book that racial capitalism "does not stand alongside merchant, industrial and financial as a permutation, phase, or stage in the history of capitalism writ large. Rather, from the beginnings of the Atlantic slave trade and the colonization of the Americas onward, all capitalism, in material profitability and ideological coherence, is a constituent of racial capitalism. In other words, we reversed the basic assumption that racial subjugation is a particular manifestation of a more universal capitalist system."

Similarly, in eulogizing Robinson (1983) and his towering oeuvre of political theory, Professor Robin D. G. Kelley (2002) distinguishes that "Capitalism and racism . . . did not break from the old order but rather evolved from it to produce a modern world system of 'racial capitalism' dependent on slavery, violence, imperialism, and genocide." This has absolutely everything to do with the varying conditions under which Black communities throughout the diaspora navigated the contradictions between our exploitation and our survival through forms of economic solidarity, whether these institutions are quilombos, ROSCAs, or cooperatives. While neoliberal capitalism dispossessed Black and other racialized people in a centuries-long process of hoarding wealth for a ruling elite (coded as white), the dispossessed leaned on various cooperative forms to live another day. These are the stories that the authors in this book gather in illustrating the Black social economy, casting light on cooperative economic practice. At scale, that economic solidarity may be the key to further evolving our fraught, unsustainable world system to a just, regenerative, and mutualistic economy.

Cooperatives, both those which are formally and those informally organized, put agency back in the hands of members and set into motion dynamics that are democratic, equitable, and autonomous, though intentionally affiliated with other cooperatives and in service of their communities. One such example is worker co-ops where workers decide, directly or through accountable representative elected leaders, on how to share equity, dividends, and management issues of the firm. What's more, cooperative businesses put capital, and the means of production in the hands of workers. In the most banal of circumstances, those assets can be leveraged to resource workers under economic duress. But the revolutionary potential is that, at scale, such capital becomes an instrument for shaping the laws and structures that govern our society. To be sure, confronting racial capitalism is a decades-long, massive political project; however, within that, movements themselves will require solidarity and cooperative business tools and resources woven throughout diasporic communities.

When presenting the cooperative solution to social movements, there are challenges. Cooperatives are businesses too, albeit organized under a different set of structures and principles than conventional corporations. The question to ask is: What is anti-capitalist about co-ops? It's clear that cooperatives are not a direct confrontation with the state and racial capitalism. Are co-ops just a tool for a more comfortable coexistence with the dominant capitalist system, or can cooperatives build a basis for a broader culture of mutuality and perhaps some infrastructure for an anticapitalist political economy? For white-led co-ops, especially those that sprout from professional, managerial class founders, there may not be much incentive for comfort, change, or confrontation with the current world system. But when Black and other racialized cooperators lead democratized workplaces, they are certainly faced with these questions.

The Black radical tradition compels us to dismantle racial capitalism by building new worlds. To be sure, our current co-op movements would be hard pressed to truly comprehend the political project of pursuing Black liberation through cooperative economic practice. Without a structural and historical analysis, case studies of Black cooperatives and social economies come across as niche alternatives—boutique one-off experiments. But if we coordinate and act strategically, our work sows the seeds for an emancipatory project that would transform our political economy, advancing the Black radical tradition and fundamental values outlined in this volume of buen vivir and ubuntu.

How then are solidarity economic practices a contestation of racial capitalism? Without considering political strategy, the Black social economy on its own risks its own continued marginalization, perhaps allowing for some Black folks to thrive but not actually functioning to change our conditions. Quilombos, as described in Chapter 7, are powerful zones of self-preservation and elevated Black consciousness, but more so in their inspiration for the MST and the millions of families (multiracial to be sure, but heavily Afro-descendent), which the Landless Workers' Movement has settled into land-occupying cooperative structures. As many writers in this book articulated, whether from the KKK in the USA, or Jair Bolsonaro in Brazil, such explicit political-economic work comes with a risk, one which many Black practitioners are wary of. But there's strength in numbers.

A massive collective project at scale—some might call it socialism—also marshals a groundswell of allies and institutions, including elements of the state. That would require a cultural and strategic shift away from the 1990s-style anarchism, which birthed many of today's Black-led worker co-ops in North America, toward an explicitly socialist endeavor, more akin to the MST's organizing from the 1980s to today. By themselves, the case studies on the Black social economy presented here in this book might not be quite enough, but when these cases are woven together across countries, we can see a movement—an antidote to the commercial model. The power herein attracts not only the eye of hostile racist and capitalist enemies, but engages those in the anti-racist majority that extends even beyond the diaspora. That is why organizing is so critical and why I have dedicated my own efforts to building structures and institutions that help to scale this work so that it is no longer marginal.

It is easier to do this organizing when we have got some momentum and clarity of vision, which needs to be substantive, visible, and compelling. Visionary, multiracial worker ownership is young enough that I still remember being a part of the ground level building. Noteworthy is the international worker co-op association, the International Organization of Industrial, Artisanal, and Service Co-operatives (CICOPA). Fifteen years before I joined their board, I was inspired by their positioning, because it indicated the potential of a global social-solidarity movement to contest the dominant world system. Because of that, back in 2004, I participated in the inaugural deliberations that launched the USFWC at the Minneapolis Summit. Once there, it was the democratic and expertly facilitated process to establish a grass-root worker-led cooperative institution that would endure for decades. Even embedded within the politics of that era, those foundational USFWC deliberations disproportionately amplified the voices of the Black participants at the summit including scholars, activists, and organizers such as Dr. Jessica Gordon Nembhard, Dr. Ajamu Nangwaya, Ajowa Nzinga Ifateyo, and Omar Freilla. This experience of cooperative institution-building embodies the very principles of the Black social economy of the world we are trying to build.

We are still quite far behind where we need to be. As of this writing, I am the only Black director on the board of CICOPA, and outside of Brazil and a few hot spots in the United States, France, and Cuba, there remains a paucity of worker-ownership throughout the African diaspora. The very tools of economic democracy, like most gems cut from the global economy, are heaped in Northern, Western, wealthy countries, within which Black ownership and leadership are exasperatingly rare given all we would stand to gain. Reclaiming our history, sharing stories of Black economic solidarity—from Marielle Franco to Fannie Lou Hamer—and digging into organizing does change the picture.

The horizon of this work presents many options. Raizes do Campo is a sustainable agricultural cooperative that links MST farmers with Brazilian and international sustainable consumption markets around the world. Agricultural, producer co-ops are robust throughout the African continent and countries like Colombia and Cuba with their substantial Afro-Latino workforces. In the case of Cuba's agricultural co-ops, they are responsible for a significant base of Black food security on the island and in partnership with the Communist government. That government only recently opened a pilot program to experiment with worker-owned cooperatives, primarily in artisan, services, and certain light industrial sectors, a move supported through a cross-border solidarity initiative that brought technical assistance and training from throughout the Black diaspora, including delegations I participated in from the United States, to support Cuban worker co-ops.

This models what we are capable of through a Black-led, diasporic approach—but we can do more. For example, embedded in the USFWC is a Racial and Economic Justice Council, which became the vehicle for endorsing the Movement for Black Lives Alternatives Pod and Policy Platform. The USFWC also organizes members into "peer networks" of workers who share affinity by virtue of being in the same industry (e.g., a build-and-design peer network, a worker co-op farms network, a tech workers' group, or a space for converted co-ops that until recently were run by a conventional owner or family). The potential of these spaces is tantalizing. Here, I am referencing the possibility of one day having the stature for our workers to set the industry standard for the best treatment of workers in a given field and establish state and federal policy for their conditions, acting like a supercharged union, as the worker co-ops do in Uruguay and Argentina. Without the need to negotiate with profit-seeking owners, a care-worker peer network could take the fight directly to the state where policies affecting "pink collar" jobs in nursing and childcare are set. Industry peer networks of co-ops could insist on a new standard of wages and subsidies for home healthcare and childcare workers, a super majority of whom are Black and brown women within our cooperatives.

Similarly, as our movements talk about the hazards of Black communities on the frontlines of climate disaster and the need for a global, decolonized, Red, Black, and Green New Deal (itself, a framework of reparations), multiracial, internationalist coalitions can help organize formal and informal co-ops in a range of industries from solar to construction, landscaping, sustainable waste management, food systems, and transportation. By building more of these kinds of institutions, our movements can wield a new mode of power, similar to the robust worker co-op concentrations in Argentina, Brazil, Italy, France, Spain, and Quebec. We have the capacity to fortify unions and then to complement the jobs that are not public sector or unionized as we retrofit a world economy with green jobs for immigrants, formerly incarcerated workers, and Black and brown workers who, after all, ought to be the ones building wealth during this historic investment in a global, worker-led, Black and Indigenous-led, green transition.

Just as with anti-racist organizing, the goal is for those interested and fired up about this work to get off the sidelines and join us as agents of change. Indeed, as the contributing authors to this book have emphasized, truly confronting structural racism will require the establishment of a robust social and solidarity economy. This means that our networks must not only reach co-ops that are formal and established, but also somehow connect with ones that are hidden, especially insofar as many informal co-ops are led by Black and other racialized people throughout the diaspora.

There are many ways to advance this collective work. CICOPA is active in over thirty countries around the world, and is one place to start for those seeking to connect with cooperative organizing campaigns, or even with militant labor organizing, such as the Congress of South African Trade Unions (COSATU). Organizers can find those networks to share ideas and to build. They can invite Black and brown cooperative leaders to community organizations that expand the impact of cooperative solutions.

The more that movements concerned with justice hear from co-op leaders, the more the cooperative sector can provide a substantive way for rethinking narratives and questions on identity. Every cooperative and association, whether they are formal or not, is a site of practice—a space where everyday people are coming together to share power and to rebuild the commons. Shining a light towards a greater understanding of cooperative economies is fundamental if we are to build a new world, one that is fair, just, and equitable.

US Federation of Worker Co-ops
Philadelphia, PA, USA, December 1, 2022

Works Cited

Jenkins, D. and L. Justin. 2021. *Histories of Racial Capitalism*. New York City: Columbia University Press.

Kelley, R. D. G. 2002. *Freedom Dreams: The Black Radical Imagination*. Boston: Beacon Press.

Robinson, C. J. 1983. *Black Marxism: The Making of the Black Radical Tradition*, 2nd edn. London: Zed Press.

Robinson, C. J. 2019. *Cedric Robinson: On Racial Capitalism, Black Internationalism, and Cultures of Resistance*. Edited by H. L. T Quan. London: Pluto Books.

Index